The Other Side of the Couch

The Other Side of the Couch

WHAT THERAPISTS BELIEVE

Edited by
E. Mark Stern

The Pilgrim Press
New York

Library of Congress Cataloging in Publication Data
Main entry under title:

The Other side of the couch.

1. Psychotherapists—Psychology. 2. Psychotherapists —Religious life. 3. Psychology and religion.
I. Stern, E. Mark, 1929–
RC480.5.O86 616.89'14'001 81-12017
ISBN 0-8298-0462-5 AACR2

The Pilgrim Press, 132 West 31 Street, New York, N. Y. 10001

To my wife, Virginia Fraser Stern
whose personal and professional partnership
with me continually annoints my faith in life

And to our daughters,
Sarah Rebecca Stern and Cailean Fraser Stern
who remain the miracles of this faith

ACKNOWLEDGMENTS

I wish to express my sincere gratitude to the contributors of this volume. Some of their essays appeared in abbreviated form in *Voices: The Art and Science of Psychotherapy* which is the Journal of the American Academy of Psychotherapists. I am convinced that their words and thoughts will continue to make significant contributions to the seminal relationships of personal belief systems and the practice of psychotherapy.

I remain deeply indebted to Russell Claussen for his encouragement and personal assistance during the course of editing this book.

Esther Cohen, my editor at The Pilgrim Press, has steadfastly stood by me throughout this project. Without her faith, this book could never have come about.

Finally, I wish to thank Genevieve Izinicki, M.S.W. for her help as my trustworthy Administrative Associate.

CONTENTS

The Other Side of the Couch

INTRODUCTION

SPIRITUAL BELIEF TRANSCENDS and informs a person's work. Some people admit they are influenced by it; others swear by its irrelevance. Both are seen in this book. All of the contributors, however, live by some degree of faith, recognized or unrecognized. Faith, like the newly fertilized mustard seed or the precarious widow's mite, has no standard form, no trademark. Clergy, journalists or green grocers have no exclusive rights to the citadel of the spirit.

Why, then, do we single out one vocational group to demonstrate the foundations of inspiration? Psychotherapists who are trained and empowered to disarm tensions and ease the pain of emotional conflicts, after all, do not stand apart from the confusions of our times. However, like few other professional groups, they seek to heal by being made whole themselves. No secret that the psychiatrist, psychologist, clinical social worker and pastoral counselor clarify their own minds as much as those of their patients; they watch the baton of emotional processes and pick up the beat of meaning for themselves as well as for others.

Contemporary therapists follow in the footprints of patients whose upbeat moods lead down paths of inspiration, even as the downbeat paces profane life's best intentions. The obsessed and confused are drawn to psychotherapists because they seek renewed vision. Baring the crazed soul exposes the gravity of the immediate concerns to which the therapist gives a special form of genius tolerant of the world of unconscious mystery. In that process, we, too, gain new personal insight.

In some ways their mediating role parallels that of a priest. As mediator between someone and that person's experience, the psychotherapist is mandated to be open to what ultimately may be possible between people. Here, the therapist becomes the channel of redemption and restoration. As the ancient philosopher Origen wrote, "If it be one who will be weak with the weak, who will weep with the sorrowful, and who understands the discipline of condolence and fellow-feeling, so that when his skill shall be known and his pity felt, you may follow what he shall advise." This, in part, characterizes the therapist's role.

Yet our work is different from that of the priest because the psychotherapist must lay stress upon the emotions. In that sense, we are free to ask for a type of trust which is open to discovering the patient's truth apart from our own personal opinions or beliefs. Certainly, psychotherapists are not value-free agents operating within a scientific vacuum. We, too, struggle with conflicting emotional impulses. And through these conflicts we work towards our own personal syntheses. But the therapist is willing to advocate for self-determination so that the patient can regard past experience with reverence and respect and move ahead despite the obstacles which will intrude in everyday living.

This book exposes the therapist as a person attempting to grasp the fates of another's despair victoriously. The collection can be seen as confessional statements in their own right, but it never loses sight of how those beliefs attempt to bestow life on others. Whether theist, deist, gnostic, agnostic or atheist—Jewish, Christian or Buddhist, each entry demonstrates the commitment of one person to be at the healing service of another to discover hope and meaning together.

OUT OF CHAOS: BEGINNINGS

E. Mark Stern

I'VE JUST FINISHED giving a spirited lecture in my "Specialized Problems in Counseling" course. Carelessly, I'd misplaced my notes, but somehow came out ahead. A dream fragment I was able to get hold of provided enough content for my presentation. Ferreting out the plain facts from the symbolic language of dreams forces me to look frankly at myself. Dreams are pathways to the vast varieties of emotional and spiritual rebirth.

Driving back to New York City from the class, I chide myself: "Hey, Mark, you can't make a habit of forgetting lecture notes. Deliverance through dreams has to have its limits. Life makes some heavy demands. It has a right to. You'd better throw away those magical wands of inspiration."

Continuing along the East River Drive, it occurs to me that my distraction is caused by more immediate stuff. A transit strike is impending. A previous strike a decade ago resulted in the death of Michael Quill, the head of the transit union, who had been my neighbor and friend. Always zealous, Mike's end came while being held hostage of that strike in a New York City jail. Presently, despite my reassurances to patients—"Oh, it can be fun. Everyone learns to love

---

E. Mark Stern, Ed.D is a Diplomate in Clinical Psychology of the American Board of Professional Psychology and Professor in the Graduate Division of Pastoral Counseling at Iona College. Dr. Stern is Editor of *Voices: The Art and Science of Psychotherapy,* the journal of the American Academy of Psychotherapists. He is Editor Emeritus of *The Journal of Pastoral Counseling* and President of Psychologists Interested in Religious Issues, a division of the American Psychological Association. Dr. Stern maintains a private practice in New York City.

everyone in a crisis"—I am not at all comfortable about the fallout from what might once again turn out to be mass chaos. This time around the thought of urban anarchy is menacing. Links to the survival of my immediate world seem askew. I feel log-jammed and fragile. The sight and sound of angry union officials and self-righteous government mandarins seems like another sign of the dismembering of Western civilization.

Barely scratching the surface of the threatening menace, I ask myself, "Where are those redeeming inner forces I so rely on in moments of trouble?" Suspiciously, the anxiety I now experience has reverberations from the distant past. And yet, haven't I learned from the past that crumbling structures have always presented me with other options?

I've just hurdled the initiation rites of scouting. Billy Benson, my companion on the hiking trails at the Ten Mile River Boy Scout Camp, announces that we are lost. The desperation of our thirst surprises us both. Not a drop remains in either of our khaki canteens. Terrified and thirsty, our 12-year-old backs bend down as we drink like ravening dogs from a slowly modulating green swamp.

Retrieving our ebbing strength, we ultimately meet the road and hail a car which wings us back to camp. I wake up in the infirmary. Blessed peace. Days later I find myself walking past the outdoor Catholic chapel, Our Lady of the Lake. Memories of Mary, my first governess, secretly taking me to weekday masses in a church hidden somewhere on the west side of New York.

I kneel before the outdoor altar self-consciously. The lake reflects my weary body. I am aware of earlier periods of fatigue. Sipping polluted swamp waters accentuates childhood brushes with death. Memories return of being an anorexic four-year-old, of hearing at age seven a pronouncement (supposedly beyond my comprehension) that the surgery about to be performed on my seriously infected mastoid bone could be unsuccessful due to my emaciated condition. Later, being alive against all odds, I sense an accompanying Presence.

The priest, not at all sullen in his cassock, strolling near the waterside reading from what I later learn is his breviary, casts a friendly eye. I feel enmeshed in an unfamiliar arena and flee back to the infirmary where I stay for one more day of observation.

I'm now 14 years old and a pupil in Sunday School. My teacher, Mr. Goll, is approachable. And while he sometimes seems riveted to the dogmatic formulas of Christian Science, I feel good about turning to him in this time of adolescent turbulence. It's the year my father divorces his second wife and my mother marries her third husband. Autumn is in splendor and classmates have that fresh look of a new school term. But my mind is further confused by the unusually high academic demands of the Horace Mann School for Boys. In contrast, Sunday School offers me a combination of peace and challenge. George Goll becomes one of my adolescent idols. His faith is fully with me; consequently, Christian Science Sunday School becomes a source of redemption with its emphasis on emotional freedom and spiritual restoration. Intimate connections to lurking inspirations are made. Out of this growing sensitivity, I begin to recognize a growing personal faith.

Two years later, George Goll and his wife visit my father's home. In the course of conversation, I hear about Christian Science Class Instruction. Beyond being a training ground for Christian Science practitioners, Mr. Goll explains it as a deeper means of recognizing and appreciating the Presence which Mary Baker Eddy, the founder of the religion, referred to as Love, God, Truth, Life, Omnipresence, the All-in-All. All too abstract to this sixteen-year-old.

I am the youngest student in this two-week Class Instruction. The Golls' teacher, and now mine, is a man who had once been a civil engineer. We meet at the Barclay Hotel in a class limited to thirty members. The spiritual discipline is steady. I sit in the front row and faintly grasp at the Presence. But I find the teacher's words difficult to comprehend. I recall him saying, "Evil is to good as darkness is to light." In adulthood, I recognize the similiarity of his statement to the Catholic doctrine of *privatio boni,* the declaration that evil is merely the absence of good. Evil has no other basis.

College years: I read Thomas Merton's *The Seven Storey Mountain,* an autobiographical testament through which the writer charts his journey from the secular world to a contemplative monastery. As I read of his sacred expedition, I wonder whether home for me ought not to be within a cloister.

I weigh my options.

One Sunday morning I go to the Cowley Fathers monastic community right on the Charles River near Harvard University. A possible sense of direction is becoming clearer. The Cowley monastery feels like an ark built for the impending storm, but is actually for an Episcopal order of vowed priests. I learn the kinds of work they do: missions, teaching, preaching. I am initially tempted, but I need to draw the lines. Nevertheless, my horizon expands. I drink deep of the contemplative life—the laying on of hands—the splendor of the universal Church—a sense of the holy—the pull of an everlasting unity that transcends time and circumstance. Imbued with Merton's saga, I long for his undiluted unity of prayer and communion.

Soon I make arrangements for a quiet retreat at a Trappist monastery. I find myself in the company of a parochial high school class making its obligatory senior class retreat. Two monks who are in charge of hospitality exchange jests with the young men. The sparse diet I expect turns out to be ham and eggs and rare roast beef. In the lush retreat house I am separated from the monastic chambers of Trappist silence. The first evening, everyone kneels at the toll of the Angelus bell. At once I feel the presence of my fellow retreatants and their sense of sacred obligation. I am at the center of the earth.

On my way to matins at 4:00 A.M. Sunday, I remain in a world of my own. Ensconced in a small, screened-in niche hidden from the monastic choir proper, I steal a glance at the hooded men in white robes. Slow wavelengths of Gregorian chant are intoned in measured Latin. I desire to enter the flow, to penetrate the mystery of the swamp waters now deep and tranquil. Drinking from a swamp, toxic as it had been at the Ten Mile River Camp, had touched me with a sense of rapport with the humming and buzzing vividness of God's creation. Now I experience being a constituent of my Creator's fullness.

While in a heightened state of spiritual fervor, I am granted a conference with Father Raphael Simon, a psychiatrist who became a monk. He is mild-mannered and direct. He knows that I am experiencing a sense of transformation, but advises me to go slowly in deciding how best to make use of my life. He particularly urges me to continue my analysis with Dr. Andras Angyal.

Angyal comes into my life when I need him most. Like so many others, I approach psychotherapy needing to discover the outposts of my personal struggles. Angyal is the angel with whom I wrestle. He is the friend beyond friends.

My presentation of complaints is half-hearted since what I really expect is total personal acceptance. I recognize that my early life had been a jumble of friendlessness, incessant depression and recurrent disharmony with my parents. In the aftermath I alternately blossom and sink. Through it all, I indefatigably pursue my goal of being a full human being.

Angyal states that the effects of psychotherapy would not really surface for some time; probably only after treatment ceases. Like so many other analytic patients, I am to have a good deal of amnesia about what he said to me during therapy. But as the years progress, tones begin to sharpen. I now recall Angyal's willingness to meet my insatiable wish to know something of his youth.

In the course of my applying to graduate school, he tells me how he decided to take a temporary leave from his medical studies in favor of an immediate Ph.D. in psychology. It seems that he was on a train returning to medical school after his summer vacation. Across from him sat a man who soon proved to be a nuisance. Fighting boredom and annoyance, the young Andras began to fill the man's ears with fanciful psychological theories. He did this in order to ward off the man's incessant banter. Nevertheless, by the time Angyal arrived at his destination, it dawned on him that he had unleashed seminal ideas that would change his own life and become the cornerstones for his ultimate work in psychology and psychiatry.

His struggles are easy to identify with. He, too, has a sense of the Presence. I learn that his obvious penchant for caring transcends my hours of pleas, confused silences and self-wrath. His voice expresses discretion and respect for me.

Our work takes many turns. My experiences bring me to the Friends Meeting House in Cambridge, to an Episcopal Church in the Back Bay of Boston, and to a reading of psychiatrist Karl Stern's autobiography which tells of his journey from Judaism to Catholicism. Angyal takes pain not to tip my wobbly search in any particular direction. It is I who get the impression that my direction remains adrift. But once I seem to respect my own track, he unexpectedly invites me to a lecture he is to give on the convergence of psychotherapy and religion. I discover the spiritual journey he is on.

Angyal is right. It is to take years of living in order to appreciate the effects of my struggles on my life. The later years have a way of healing the breaches. Angyal helps me prepare for a reconciliation with myself and my yearnings. He always will remain my essential therapist and mentor.

I leave my therapy with him with a mixture of excitement and regret. I know that as much as I feel attracted to a life of contemplation, I must attend to other priorities. Had I spent my youth on borrowed time—been somewhere else, lived in another era—I might have joined the desert sages and intoned the *Tu autem Domine, miserere nobis* with my monastic brethren. But for now . . .

Throughout the years of graduate study, I remain attracted to the spirit of a calling. Then as a young psychologist in the midst of self-destructive digressions and diminutions, I begin regular visits to Mount Saviour Monastery in upstate New York. For several years, I return to spend major moments in their retreat house and later in a small hermitage. Brother Peter becomes a regular correspondent. Together we open doors to the moorings of St. Benedict whose rule makes room for devotion to the twin energies of prayer and work.

I decide on a more formal association with the monastic community and take the promises of a Benedictine Oblate—a lay person who maintains minimal monastic practices in his secular setting. My visits and letters are now bolstered by a clear sense of belonging. In time, however, quiet visits to the Monastery are interrupted by the Prior who asks me to serve as psychological consultant to several troubled monks. I seem to do well in this capacity. I'm now convinced that I'm called to continue my profession as a clinical psychologist in New York City. I experience a growing contentment that my own sense of spiritual devotion frees me to revere the life patterns of my patients and confirm my conviction that each person has a spiritual essence which expresses itself in a unique life journey.

Equally ingrained is a deep appreciation of what of me I see and seek in the other person. Whatever mutual identity I am able to appreciate flows from the mystery of two separate autonomies communicating in a spirit of love and expansiveness. Like Angyal, I welcome this spirit as the Superindividual, an Incarnational Presence and unity expressed in the form of a universal, transpersonal language. Isn't this what Boris Pasternak meant in his book, *Doctor Zhivago:* "Communion between mortals is immortal"?

I consciously work at understanding the Incarnation as the manifestation of the working Presence in my day-to-day life as a psychotherapist. Little known to my friends and colleagues in psychology is my spiritual pilgrimage; that is, except for George Hagmaier, dead since 1971 but a confidant through fifteen years of my professional practice. He was one of the first to be a Roman Catholic priest, psychologist, and psychotherapist. Happily, I enjoyed sharing a common language with George, who eventually brought me into the fold of his Church, witnessed my marriage and my older daughter's baptism.

With George I meet Jacques Lacan, the French rebel psychoanalyst. Lacan, certainly no obvious religious figure, fosters constructs of unconscious "transindividual" language. I often had intuited that the writers and commentators of the Hebrew Talmud and kabbala used numerology and alphabet analysis as a means of reaching an unconscious transindividual language. Lacan makes me sensitive to the fact that underneath a patient's "murmurs" rests an accessible language. Language must assume the reality of the Other. When there is a gap between me and the Other, I am in a state Lacan sees as *desire.* I may not be able to satisfy this desire, but its presence forms the earliest basis for worship. Human beings have a need to pray to another person. Psychotherapy often becomes this kind of worship. My insatiable desire to know the other and his or her desire to know me may be no more satisfied than my longing to penetrate the mystery of the Presence. Yet, they intertwine. Our mortal communication is immortal.

As I deal each day with my commitment to the language of unconscious longing, I realize the unconscious is the presence of universality. But it is a presence which only can be known in part. I learn, yet know already, that the constant intimations of unconscious through all its channels (dreams, personal rhythms, extra-sensory phenomena, empathy, coincidence-synergy, *déjà vu,* love) provide a humbling awareness of the increasing superindividual constructs of life. Alpha and Omega, beginning and end, are one.

I strive to see how the differences between my patient and me make us one. We are one in our strivings. I think of Tony, who tells me that growing up means accepting the fact that he can never drink alcohol again. What must I give up? Or Anna, who washes her hands up to 50 times a day in order to keep herself from infecting the world. What do I feel I must do to protect the earth? Or Clem, who simply has never been able to trust. How do I regularly conceal my fear of others? And Ruth, whose depressions keep her from appreciating the tiniest morsel of pleasure. How do I back away from life's potentials because of my sadness and agitation?

I feel a oneness with my patients. Within this sacred covenant, I know that what looks like an impossible situation will ultimately work itself out as patient and I wait for the Incarnational Presence. This need not be done in any prescribed manner, nor in a language or set of beliefs similar to mine. We are one in the moment we share together. Our presence to each other heals. It builds the foundation for the appearance of "what we shall be" as we are transformed by our experiences together.

Psychological and spiritual maturity happen as we heal our memories. While we all need to protect ourselves from the hurts of the past, we can revalue it in order to see the merit of each tottering step. I have learned that as I ratify the unbroken unity of my life, I begin to grasp the spiritual essence of atonement, Being at-one with my own life helps me see my patient as a copemate in striving to comprehend the value of pain, suffering and joy. As problems are redressed, so are we each made more whole. I learn through my personal strivings that wholeness results from surrendering my autonomy for the sake of an enlarged sense of the flow of life. In losing my life, I literally find it. In surrendering my need to always have the "answer," I become a more effective mate, parent and therapist.

As I continue to drive along the roadway which skirts Manhattan's East River, I begin to realize that my uneasiness in the face of a disrupted New York has kaleidoscopic appropriateness. Disruption can bring exciting, though possibly fearful, new unities. I am reminded of that uneasiness which my patients graphically feel when they claim to be anxious before, during and after a psychotherapy session.

That there is a unity of all life is my central faith. Passive and active striving towards it is my lifelong pilgrimage. This also occurs in my teaching at Iona College. My graduate students include parish priests, contemplative nuns, Hassidic rabbis, Black evangelical bishops, mainline Protestant ministers and successful businessmen and women who are making career changes from corporations to lay ministries. Over the years I have taught a wide variety of courses focusing on therapeutic intervention. But more important, I feel a fellow traveller with my students in their respective journeys. Many things converge during class discussions: Old and New Testament talk, crisis counseling, dogmatic and moral theology, family therapy, the Talmud, recent developments in psychoanalytic theory, counseling the dying, the Rule of St. Benedict, anxiety reactions, ministering to the lonely, psychological mechanisms of defense, prayer and meditation. The brogues, pieties, idioms, insights and babble give way to the universality of Pentecost and atonement. I doubt if I would be interested in teaching elsewhere. My tenure at Iona is the culmination of my work with all of my mentors.

But one of them is especially important to my pilgrimage, my dear late friend Robert Pollock. I studied philosophy with him several years after finishing my doctorate in psychology. His life reminds me that the frontier of the future is as close as I am, that my participation in everything I take hold of has Immanence for me. I continue to learn from his vision of a reality which points beyond itself, an essential awareness that takes place in the surreal corridors in which all persons and places emerge as one.

Robert Pollock's remarkable explorations spark new impressions. I grow to appreciate the greater interplay of all experiences as the intimation of an eternal unity. I learn that the true theologians and philosophers of our time, in fact, are the psychologists and physicists. It is they who are in an advantageous position to describe the sur-real world, the world beyond linear reason. Nevertheless, it is the world of perception beyond perception, encounter beyond encounter. Pollock made me aware that my patients may express universal revelation as they plummet the mysteries of their souls. In my vision of the future, new levels of inspiration and revelation have yet to emerge.

My personal quest for spiritual maturity is best exemplified in revering the sense of the infinite in each of life's moments. The future reveals the presence of God in the potential of the community. This is what makes working with therapeutic groups so vital and exciting. People find faith in their lost potentials as members of a second-chance family. Healthier group members redeem those who still have a long road to travel.

Emotional health is never final. My patients, like me, are in the process of becoming. I doubt if any of us actually reach our respective goals. To do so would be to assume a knowledge of perfection. Yet we seek the Perfect. We seek a unity with this Perfection. That quest results in an expanding identity.

I chide my patients to welcome unconscious revelation. I recall the confused adolescent who learned that she could temper her ravenous appetite by letting herself be "fed" with her own poetic inspirations. And the besieged lawyer, who found that he could better serve his clients and himself by restoring a sense of trust based on the clients' needs rather than on his father's unrealistic expectations of him. Unconscious truths may well approach perfection. They are not logical, but from them we receive inspiration. The Presence of the unseen is available through a new sense of communion with unconscious sources mediated by the psychotherapist.

I turn off the East River Drive and soon arrive home. The strike begins the following Tuesday. The city is uncoordinated, but rather than chaos it reaches a new crescendo. On the second evening of the strike, two patients arrive at the same appointment time; both were delayed by snarled traffic. The two strangers agree to share the time. Frank is temporarily shy, but Rachel sparks the conversation. They both speak about their troubles in getting to my office. Strangers to begin with, they gradually relax. All goes well. It has taken a work stoppage to switch our priorities. We have become a trinity of mutual support. A sense of creative community has emerged. I discover what may become a shift in my own work style.

Out of chaos—external and internal—beginnings . . .

DIRGE ON A LOVE

Rosalind Inslicht Edelstein

LITTLE HAS BEEN WRITTEN about the impact on the therapeutic process at a time of the most intimate loss—the death of a spouse. What happens in the flow, the connections when the anchor is loosened, the pain is raw—a bleeding gap cutting through the searing flesh? The symbiotic tie is loose, left waving in the wind, unanchored. And there is no new tie, no road to take. No lover to enjoy, no husband to share sighs or laughter, about the tribulations or successes of offspring.

I was suspended in time—those first few months—freshly ripped and bleeding. . . . The cut went deep, and when it was intolerable I totally denied it with numbness, until a tune, a word, a place, a bird, cut into me sharply and cruelly, evoking a memory, a connection. . . .

Time had stopped for me and numbness and raw pain enveloped me while my sister and friends distracted me for periods of time from the real truth—that I would never hear his warm, earthy, throaty laugh. It came from the belly—his laugh—and would shake the room with his earthiness, his Czech accent, or the special way he curled a word when he told his stories.

There are moments in living when the impact of the full truth is impossible to bear in one complete dose. But this holds true for the living experience and the therapeutic process as well.

And so very soon I returned to my clients. I could not stay home,

---

Rosalind Inslicht Edelstein, M.S.W. is associated with a family counseling center. As a clinical social worker, she is in the private practice of psychotherapy in Atlanta, Georgia.

stay with the rawness that was too raw nor accept the full truth for too long an expanse of time. The first day was my survival test. I found I could connect for some of the session. My office, my clients were the world that Otto had not inhabited. Or so I thought. I found him there that first day. He had hung my bookshelves. His hands had measured the wall, had touched those shelves. He was no more and yet he was everywhere. How could he not be with me as I struggled so many times with the entangled web of the marriages that unfolded in that room—ours and theirs—the lovingness, circularity and the stubbornness.

I knew I could not, would not, overlay the pain I really had. But would I ever be able to care again about people and their pain? Would I care what happened to them or to me? Would I ever be able to be with anyone again?

I could only start with those I thought I could be me with, who would be least frightened by my pain. The first day back I walked through one session. I was surprised I could connect at parts of the session. Always the underlying refrain, "He is no more. He is so very dead." No, just one more moment—one hour, five minutes, to say good-bye. I bargained.

The second day my sessions were a haven from the horror of the nightmare, a welcome relief. I dreaded the end of the session when the demons of reality would destroy my fantasy, that it was only a bad dream, that his voice would boom through the house, "Rosaleend, I am home!"

It touched those who had a significant connection with me from the moment they learned. "What are you thinking? What are you feeling? How can you listen to me? to us?" A couple obsessing with each other, in their circular dance of accusations and confrontations, were resisting my interventions. They maneuvered their arena to complaints they had flung at each other many times. Suddenly the woman cried out, "My God, how petty all this must be for you with all the pain you are carrying." The man faltered, and picking up on my intervention a few minutes back used it to try some new approaches . . . allowing himself to express a caring that was so out of his usual style. And the woman then too responded in a different way. That day we tried some new steps, tested a new way that sputtered and started. But it did start. My unspeakable pain ran deep, and the shadow of the ultimate, in effect, stopped them short and dented the circular anger and blame that went nowhere.

Marian was referred to me two years previously, when her husband demanded a divorce after 10 years of marriage and four children. She had attempted suicide twice and came for help in "getting back" her husband as she could not bear the terror of the abandonment. When I could not give her back her husband she experimented with other therapists, returning to me finally to deal with the pain and to sort out her own identity. Then she finally began to work at the implications of the loss, adjustment to the single parent role and redefining herself as she redefined her relationship with me.

That day she must have checked the obituary column at dawn. This woman who spent nights plotting how she would outwit her ex-husband's niggardliness, sent a lush plant overflowing with foliage. At the next session of the divorced women's group I co-led, she announced simply, "Now you are one of us." And so she, who had checked out a number of therapists, who had bargained and complained as she struggled for equilibrium, offered her supreme gift—her lovingness. "You helped me during my nightmare. I want you to call me whenever you need to talk to someone. I know how it is. I have a boyfriend now, but when you are up to it, let me take you to the right bar. I know the right places," reassuring and planful and practical as her style was.

There were frightened responses. Pat and Norman epitomized the successful fulfillment of the American dream, and its emptiness. Norm, in his early 50s, had achieved everything he once dreamed about. His beautiful wife carried out her role with aplomb. Pat was dazzling in a dramatic style. Her hair was jet black and coiffed in a semblance of carelessness that hinted at the time it took to create. Her clothes bespoke taste and an ambiance of luxury and comfort.

Their oldest of four children eloped with an offbeat young man and was now expecting Pat and Norman's first grandchild. Norm could share his aversion to becoming a grandfather and the empty feeling of having no more worlds to conquer. He referred to the emptiness of their relationship, and Pat referred to his dependence on her. To light up the fire of the emptiness of the relationship, Norm proceeded to have an affair with the married woman next door who was close to his daughter's age. This relationship lasted for over a year. Pat supposedly suspected nothing.

At the point that they came to me Norm had been cast out of the house. I saw them briefly, at which point they rekindled some of their lost flame in his apartment—a flame which Norm protested they never had had—certainly never equalled the fire of the affair. I had sensed the shakiness of the tie, to me and to each other. When I made my first phone call to them as I returned to pick up my practice, I learned that Norm had moved back home. He thought they did not need any further help. Pat knew they did but was apathetic about pushing him. Her first confrontation to me was, "I was shocked to see in the papers how old your husband was. You were much younger than your husband, weren't you?"

The terror of death had stared at them and they closed ranks.

But "quoth the raven, 'Nevermore!'"

Nevermore the tenderness when he held me when I was disconsolate, when he patted the children when they were frightened. . . .

Nevermore the brilliant sweep of history he encompassed—the generous imparting of knowledge to anyone who was thirsty—the intellectual curiosity that radiated to all who knew him. All that knowledge and gentleness and passion buried.

Time had stopped for me. For some of my clients it had frozen their family crises and sobered others to break through a congealed impasse. For I and they were shocked that there is so little time.

Lena and Louis, struggling with their symbiotic tie to each other and to their respective families, had been married four years when they first came to me. They were expecting a third child. The boundaries of each were thoroughly enmeshed with each of their families of origin. And so the struggle in differentiating from their families and facing the realities of babies, finances and job management, was tackled in the arena of their relationship. Struggles with one set of parents were projected and acted out with the parents of the other. What better way to vent one's anger at Jewish in-laws for real or projected grievances than to deprive them of seeing their grandchildren?

During the weeks of numbness for me, life was remarkably calm and quiet for Lena and Louis. It was as if the heat of their conflict had stopped for reflection, for pausing. They were gentle with each other in ways they had not been since they courted. Lena allowed Louis to take the children over to visit his parents. She informed me of this over the phone when I called to make our first appointment. She described it as a gift to me. When I questioned my investment in this, she responded by saying that my tragedy had sobered her to evaluate her actions. She realized there was so little time, that the games she had played with her in-laws had so little point.

Could I share with them? Could anyone ever know the emptiness? . . .

The tugging, searing memories: the resort where we met, where he came because he'd heard the girls were "liberal." Times Square, the streets of New York where we courted, 57th Street, the Third Avenue El, Macdougal Street. We laughed at the people, at ourselves —his deep, throaty laugh about my craziness and his stubbornness— my stubbornness and his obstinacy, my obsessiveness and his compulsiveness. The loving—the quarrels, the passion, the intense passion. And the clouds—my childhood and his flight from the Nazis. The panorama covered the globe. And the way Karen kicked up her legs in her crib when she heard his booming voice, "I am home!" Or his wonder as he looked at her beautiful face. And his beaming face when he leaned over me and said, "So now we have a son."

And the reunion in Vienna with his brothers, Paul and Hanza, and their wives Gerta and Dita. And Prague and the ferry ride on the Vltava, and Tirezin and his mother's name etched on the synagogue wall as testimony to Auschwitz, and Francie, his sister, always Francie, cut off in her youth. And Pzibram, where he was born, with the bedroom looking out at the sacred mountain as the spring breeze blew gently, blew the white curtains. And I stood in that room and later I climbed that mountain to the monastery. I still hear his father chuckling proudly as he looked at his son and at our dark-eyed, pensive daughter, at our son, articulate and striving. . . .

Months later, a member of my therapy group in her anguish about her dying marriage and fears of leaving a psychotic husband, cried out to me in a session, "Roz, do you cry a lot? Are you lonely?" No friend, no therapist, had ever hit me so directly. "Yes, Ellen, I cry a lot. And I am lonely."

Vulnerable as I was, I could only be real. She had extracted from me the simple statement of pain as she plumbed the depths of her own despair. The following week she left her husband.

And where did it all go? The knowledge, the span of history, the Romans, the Greek philosophers, the facts spiked with raciness; the languages he spoke so well, and the Polish and Russian he got by with . . . the fluency, the wit, the outrageous humor. All that knowledge turned to ashes in that grey vault!

Are those strong, lusty arms really reduced to cinders? And those thick, peasant hands I held in Caracas, when we heard Tchaikovsky and Beethoven; and Toscanini in Atlanta when he played Dixie; or

Paul Robeson at the Lewisohn Stadium; will they smolder too? Once he was mine, and now he belongs to the ages. Was he ever mine? He was so private to himself, he, whom no one could ever own.

How luxurious it was to be with him and his booming, laughing voice, his twinkling blue eyes; and the sturdy, robust gait before a worn body took over!

The women's therapy group was to have ended the day Otto died. In working out the many terminations the group was faced with that night, members of the group pressed my co-leader for a picture of what my husband had been like.

Jane, a member of the group, whose mellowed pain had taught her to zoom in on essences and identify the hurts, remembered my expression of pain about my empty nest. What would I do now?

Some of them wrote that day. Others waited until after my numbness. Each in her own way found a way to touch me. Weeks later as I made my way back to living, each arranged individual sessions with me. Each came with an agenda. How did I deal with this? What was it like for me? I was as real as I could ever be. How could I be otherwise?

Carrie sought me out when her individual therapist was on vacation, as she and her therapist had planned. During previous leaves she thought she could wait until her therapist returned. But this time she was to have closure with me. She questioned me very carefully and in detail. What had it been like for me? And I shared with her the hope that I would feel some anger at him, to ease my enormous pain. In the group, Carrie would express the practical solutions, the simplistic responses. Now, for the first time, she poured forth her anger and her pain on the loss of her fiancé two years previously. The buried pain and shame were extracted from the vault inside her, and the despair and anguish and memory of the lover who had jilted her surfaced. These were the first references Carrie had made to the relationship or to the loss. She, who had maintained an unflappable flat exterior in the group and in her individual therapy up to now, wept openly and deeply. Once she had tapped those feelings and that experience, and the permission for anger (even at the sanctified moment of death) she could continue her individual therapy in a very different way. What had been frozen, my own suffering could melt. No shared revelation of past losses in the group had evoked this.

Another member, Nita, 38, had nurtured an almost lifetime impasse with her dying father. She was withholding from him and had closed him off. She could begin in her closure meeting with me to remember his tenderness and the limitations he had in protecting her. In that meeting she began to discover ways to engage in another way with this dying man; memories of what he had given her came back. She could then not be ashamed of her anger at his destructiveness to her. The dam had opened up and she gave him her anger and with it her tenderness. She activated her brother and sister to visit him and was no longer afraid of an encounter with them.

In a number of long painful weeks her father, dying of terminal cancer, returned home. His remission continued for a year, while Nita shuttled back and forth between her therapist and her family and their hopelessness, trying new ways with them. His death stalled a year, only after a network of support had been built up between the siblings.

I am as empty as I could ever be and more powerful. How powerful it is to be devoid of hope. I do not have the investment in life I once had. No passion for tomorrow.

How can I take in the void? How get in touch with that which was Otto? The lusty arms that held me firm—the warm, sturdy hands I loved to hold, as I listened to his special way of telling stories! There were so many. I loved to watch his face, his chuckle, his twinkling eyes as he told them.

And the intensity would be broken by his cynicism or my depression, expressing itself in anger and anxiety as we risked in the world outside. I thought he would always take care of me. I had told him I could not go it alone. I never had enough of him, his quiet strength, his gentleness. . . .

I weep and grieve for his sadness, his sense of loss. Our room is suffused with him, his walk, his chuckle, his strong body. Surely he will blow the horn and come through the door . . .

So many dreams never fulfilled—the trip to Greece, to the little town of Ladino, where the people came down to the ship with food and candy to help them escape when the world had closed their borders, to Brno where he studied, to Budapest, his special playground, and to Brisbane where his brother fled. . . .

And past the searing pain, the loss, I was here. And my patients knew it.

"I can take in only a little today, so let's deal with you. How fortunate that you come to me now." Never was I so authentic, so direct, so firm, so real, so gentle, or so rich with wisdom and with reality, and with feeling. I was authentic as I could never be again, with its ultimate vulnerability.

I had chosen to be. And they—my patients—had helped me to choose.

THE INTUITIVE IN AN ABSURD WORLD

Donald Broughton

I AM STRUGGLING with a person who, after an initial five minutes of silence, declares each week his worry that the therapy isn't getting anywhere. And I wait. Then he says that he doesn't think that our personalities are compatible. And I wait. Then he declares that he can't stand the fact that I used to be a professional philosopher and, worse yet, an ethicist. And I wait. Then he says, "You don't have the answers, do you?" So I tell him that I am really warmed by the focus of his attention on me. He then tells me that I'm crazy, and the hour is in motion. My faith has paid off again.

My faith is rooted in my experience of trying to live intentionally and putting together my cherished values and my understanding of human development. This struggle generates paradoxes from which comes a balance that allows me to affirm living in spite of considerable experience that the breeze that cools my face is blowing off the garbage dump. With my fellow struggler, the test is whether the fear of separation and alienation is stronger than the bond of acceptance.

When I think about my faith as a psychotherapist I am struck by how readily the language of theology forms the structure for me. Even though I formally rejected my theological commitments fifteen years ago, there is no escape. So, when I talk about faith, it is going to be mediated by my personal religious experience first. Of course it is true that, fundamentally, what I say I think about faith is an

---

Donald Broughton, Ph.D. earned his first doctoral degree in philosophy and his second in clinical psychology. He is a Diplomate in Clinical Psychology of the American Board of Professional Psychology and practices in Atlanta, Georgia.

expression of my personality as it developed in my past and informs my present. Also, since psychotherapy is an interpersonal event, my thinking is informed by my social understanding which is grounded in an early acceptance of the social theories of Karl Marx, even though I am not a Marxist.

As a psychotherapist, I identify with the proletariat, even though I abhor most proletarian values, because I see psychotherapy as very hard work. The fundamentally antihumanist attitudes that sentimentalize misery and regard the therapeutic struggle as some sort of adventure are seductive but miss the more general truth. On the other hand, when I address myself most concretely to the question of the faith of the psychotherapist I am individualistic and decidedly unimpressed with the notion that impersonal forces of society define a person's nature and destiny. The choices people make shape their destiny even though the alternatives often seem equally hopeless or are not even apparent.

When a person who has struggled for several years to find a way to appreciate living says to me, "The whole thing boils down to the fact that I'm neurotic, doesn't it, Don?" my initial reaction is to crawl under a chair. So far, I haven't done that. Sometimes I sing a song and sometimes I laugh, but if I am in good shape that day I tell him that he's one of the most lovable neurotics that I know and that if he needs to stay that way, I'll stick with him. Being a therapist is hard work.

I understand psychotherapy to be a new way for a person who is suffering in his life predicament to struggle. The struggle seems to pull him or her deeper into the mire than more out of it. My stance as a therapist depends on the nature of the struggle, its history and its current state. A therapist can deal only with the latter aspect of the struggle and try to ease the suffering. On the other hand, we can choose to deal with both aspects and, consequently, involve ourselves intimately and with commitment in the total life of the struggler. As a struggling person, I am a part of the work and create value by mixing my person and knowledge with that of the struggler who has come for help.

A main difference between the therapist and the person who comes for help is that the therapist's moral stance structures and disciplines his or her involvement in the struggle. By a moral stance I mean that we take full responsibility for ourselves in the risk of experiencing personal openness with another. Occasionally, this may mean experiencing the confluence of terror and joy at the moment of a hard-won breakthrough in the struggle. Most often it means persistent and patient "being there" while a person tacks first to one oblique and then the other as he runs his course. Many hours can be excruciatingly boring but those hours are an important part of the process. Thinking about that aspect of therapy brings me closer to the mysteries of faith.

What I do with my boredom can be a crucial contribution to the life of a patient who feels he is not in charge of his life. To be honest about it, the more boring the hour is, the crazier I become. But that is my life's pattern of experiencing separation or alienation as negation of my value as a person. Consequently, I feel ungrounded, frightened, and desperate. In some cases my craziness is expressed in withdrawal, so that I am drowsy, inattentive or conversational. In other cases, I voice my unconscious process which, to the patient, is usually bizarre or incredibly intimate (for example, I will comment on how he or she smells). When this happens I know that I am connecting in whatever way I can in spite of my experience of alienation and separation. I am operating out of my faith because if I stick to my Marxism I will overthrow the oppressive yoke of alienation and if I stick to my rational self I will begin carefully and critically to analyze, theorize and ultimately dehumanize. In brief, I'll get enraged or I'll run.

Coming to this point as a person young in being a psychotherapist though not so young in being a person, has been a struggle as much of the spirit as of the mind. In order to write about my faith, I must give due consideration to the high values of rational and scientific structures which order my profession but must acknowledge and claim the equally high values of my more personal, spiritual and interpersonal experience.

For some, a statement of religious faith means dogmatic religious belief, and, in my case, would therefore have to do with received truths about being a psychotherapist or the process of becoming one. While I am not accepting this assumption, it is a legitimate concern. To start with, many people, who might otherwise have seen a therapist, have solved their problems through the help of some religious institution, person or service. In another context, the notion of the faith of a psychotherapist would be dealing with how having religious faith (beliefs, convictions, connections) makes one a better, more legitimate, or maybe worse psychotherapist. While I do not know how to answer these questions or presuppositions, I am convinced that failure to include one's religious experience in the consideration of the making of a therapist is either arrogant or naive.

My faith has to do with who I am as a person. When on a pastoral counselling internship at a Boston psychiatric hospital, I was removed from a case when the psychiatric resident protested that bringing God into a patient's life was an intrusion into medical authority. I remember this as an example of how frightened persons who are insecure can become when vested with power and responsibility over another's life. Nevertheless, it could be held that therapists are agents of God in the healing process. From the standpoint of theology, psychotherapy could be another way through which God works out the destinies of persons.

In a rather delightful way, the implications of that theological assumption can get worked out into a concern with the demonic as the antithesis of God and consequently an assertion that God is on the side of mental health. Suppose that one believed that therapists have a perfect ear to God and that their definition of health has divine sanction? If that were so, psychotherapy would rightfully be a subcategory of theology and, from the administrative and institutional standpoint should be under the governance of ecclesiastical authority. Further, the demonic, being so powerful, must have its supernatural ally and hence we must deal with Satan and his or her followers.

While all this is playful, it points out the practical difficulties in mixing the language and structures of psychotherapy with those of religion. In my early experience with structured religion, I was always bothered by the general indifference of contemporary culture to the "truth" that theology presented. Upon reflection, it is clear that in the face of this threat of separation, I withdrew from personal contact to a place of studying the world or righteously attacking its values. I'm aware of how impoverished I made my life at that point.

One delight was in Bertrand Russell's treatment of epistemology and, in particular, his teachings on the differences between matters of fact and matters of belief. Twenty-five years later, I still hold to those teachings as I understand them and they have helped me accept my limitations as a psychotherapist. We cannot change historical facts since they are past events. We can change beliefs about facts by riding them back to their source and reordering the set of beliefs built on the first experience of the facts.

Once a patient learns that this can be done and is persuaded that value judgements can be suspended for that exploration, it really can be done alone. Then an important function of the therapist is to maintain the support that provides safety. When persons give permission for therapists to keep the pressure on with confrontation, explanation, and directed structural reexperiencing of past trauma or poor learning, the process often is accelerated.

But what audacity allows the therapist to take this position? How dumbfounded I am when an orthopedic surgeon comes to me out of the distress of his marriage and asks what my procedure is and what is my "hit rate?"! Mending a relationship is like mending a bone? I should be scientific and explain to this sufferer how dysfunctional behaviors, when reinforced under appropriate circumstances, will build a personality which, as a whole, will not work very well. I could explain that scientific psychotherapy is a procedure for reversing this process. That will not help him, although it might ease my own anxiety.

When I think about my faith, I'm involved in matters of belief. When I acknowledge this, the lines of certitude become blurred and arguments become murky. Beliefs are built out of experience and each person's experience mixes his past conclusions about reality with an incoming flood of information which has to be processed. Since feelings precede thoughts, my major task is to find ways to bring order and system to the intertwining of the information of a person's life with the complex of feelings accompanying it.

For me, the most powerful non-interpersonal expression of disciplined feeling is in music. When I am ill at ease or lonely or confused I know that, aside from the presence of a loved person, music will help me to reorder myself. Pre-twentieth century music energizes and complements the complexities of my own rhythms and the intertwining of my various themes.

Again, I am driven to the theme of faith as I move to autonomy. Spiritual discipline and the intuitive position are so difficult because there are no rules and no enforcers save the inside experience of integration vs. confusion at best; or, at worst, of craziness, guilt and conflict. I yearn for the clarity and sparkle of logical, scientific, rational language and the parched experience that goes with it. Living with the spiritual and the intuitive can be living with the Abyss, the awesome experience of constant change and timelessness. Apart from being a recluse or a monk, it is living with being dependent. To live comfortably in the world, the intuitive person must be willing to live creatively and comfortably with his dependency, counting on the rational structures of society to protect him in his allegiance to the non-rational. This is not a very popular position, especially with those upon whom the intuitive person is dependent because they mark proper behavior in terms of fairness, justice and equity.

Fairness, justice and equity are alien phenomena to the intuitive person. It is not that they are rejected concepts, it is simply that they do not seem to have primitive grounding. We form rational institutions to protect ourselves from the potentially horrible consequences for a society of intuitive dominance and subjectivism.

There is a current vogue of dealing with psychotherapy and so-called "spiritual" matters by referring to phenomena such as unusual experiences under altered states of consciousness induced by meditation, drugs, special diet or strong suggestibility such as the Cabalistic intricacies of astrology and other forms of strange wisdom. This is different from the more common use of the term "spiritual," which refers to the "vital principle or animating force within human beings." When dealing with terms such as the latter, the category of "faith" becomes more obviously connected to the category of psychotherapy since faith, or confident belief, is an attitude built on connotative procedures. But, what is admissible as components of this "confident belief"? On the one hand, if I accept a strict and traditional understanding of the spiritual, I end up becoming subservient to the structures of theology. On the other hand, if the spiritual is bounded by irrationality and utter subjectivity, then I'm into nihilism in all its meanings. A vehicle for the resolution of this dilemma is religious mysticism which is disciplined subjectivity.

Thomas Merton, in his wisdom, wrote that the mystical experience of God is such that it cannot be communicated from father to son. I suspect that that holds true in general for intimate relationships and about intimate experiences. It remains for the language of myth and metaphor to carry my need to bring my inner self into contact with others. Because of this fact, I know that there is a gap between the ground of my understanding of faith (which is my personal experience) and my effectiveness in explanation.

An essential component in the discipline of mysticism is a willingness to listen to exceptional variations on one's usual perception or interpretation of experience. This may come in a moment of ecstasy or in a voiceless sense of being grasped, often a body sensation. Genuine mysticism claims authority about the experience inherent in the experience itself. It neither requires nor includes references to external circumstances. My understanding of this position provides for me the bridge between my understanding of reality as a user of scientific methods (upon which my comfort as a psychologist rests) and my broader experience of reality (upon which my effective functioning as a therapist rests). I am convinced that the depth of human experience is beyond scientific methodology. I am driven, therefore, to the category of faith and from heteronomy to autonomy.

The key element of faith for me is that there are explanations. Things don't just happen. Since all knowledge is of a piece, what my reasoning self does not know, my intuitive self might. Consequently, if I persist and keep tracking, an answer will emerge.

I must acknowledge, however, that what often turns a slow, painful collaboration with pathology into an exciting meeting with a person is when I stop tracking my patient and attend more to tracking me. Frequently I will hear some music or remember vividly some event from my own life that I can tell my fellow struggler. When I persist in responding to his groaning over the misery of life with countless intrusions, absurdity suddenly becomes a working tool. It is not that his experience is wrong. It is his experience and it is so. The goal is not to "solve the problem," it is to be intimate with me about and with it. It is to feel his pain as human experience and not alien intrusion. It is to claim the pain and grow in it. The explanation is in his rejection of being a person and the terror of knowing the quality of absurdness which is in all life.

When I move to relating at the intuitive level I am at great risk. The niceties of history and logic are paper airplanes in the swirling currents of the intuitive struggle. When I tell a fantasy I often do not know what it means to me, let alone to my patient. The answer may be that I'm faced with someone stronger than I. His need to keep the gates of his soul shut or to keep the smoke machine going or to go down with the ship or whatever is greater than his desire to commune with me or to risk the awesome look into the Abyss.

I am sad when I experience my helplessness and sometimes enraged. It is helplessness because I am convinced (have faith?) that there is a part of that person who really wants to take the risk. But he may not be victorious this time, and that may be because I do not have the skills to draw him out, or he just may need to struggle more. This position is true to my own experience.

Years ago, when I was a pastor of a small Methodist church in upper New York State and a junior in college, a woman loaned me a copy of the Book of Common Prayer. From it I found the form of liturgical worship which has remained for me the only legitimate religious bridge between experiencing myself in the world and some notion of a transcendent reality.

The bridge is aesthetic and close to mysticism, along with a sense of corporateness that is more a statement about the mix of being a person than about the sameness of persons. This is the way I understand music in my life. Because of this gift from a beloved parishioner, I could learn the forms of religious faith while still a stranger to the substance. However, churchly religion still does not present for me an acceptable mode for the substance of religion.

My attempt to accept the churchly mode formed the battle that symbolizes the development of my faith. To declare and profess to others a theology of love and forgiveness, of ultimate trust and comfort in the means of grace, while at the same time tenaciously holding on to a conviction of personal shame and rage at the injustice of an uncaring and impersonal world which demanded that I be infinitely perfect was an impossible bind. So, resigning from the cognitive hope of God, I let myself be carried by an unfathomable experience until the fathomable aspect of living could make sense. Without a doubt, it was my reading of Paul Tillich's book *The Courage to Be* that gave some words to this process.

A dominant theme of Tillich's book states that the task of the person is to proceed in spite of all the evidence indicating that to proceed is futile and dangerous or will provoke anxiety. And so to proceed in faith is, at base, to be willing to live even while doing battle with those parts of myself which hurt me and contribute to my estrangement from other persons. For years, I tried to find a reasoned pattern for living and a comfortable way to avoid the price of responsibility. Now, it is easier to see that persons, not books, continuously provided the material for my personal change if I had been available to make the intimate connection.

Years after I had cut myself off from a loving teacher and good man, denying the value of my association with him, I dreamed a number of dreams in which he was looking out the window of a high tower and I was sulking about in alleys below smoking cigarettes. These dreams symbolized for me the persistence of self-destructive behaviors or feelings while simultaneously distancing myself from the possibilities of life and love. That dream characterizes the struggle of many persons who come for therapy. It was necessary for me to reject many men who otherwise would have enriched my life and been enriched by me, before I could at last let go of my shame and rage with my own father.

I believe it is so for many people who come to therapy and find it a terrible struggle. I believe it is also true of persons who feel estranged from God and out of touch with any awareness of the ground of their being. In literature, there is no greater illustration of this than Job, who maintained his essential connection with God, as opposed to the persons of his tormenting friends who urged upon him a common sense interpretation of his misery.

A dramatic demonstration of this fact is in severe cases of somatization of deep psychological pain. In these cases, people frequently exhaust their bodies, their funds and their friends in the hopeless pursuit of a medical cure for a dysfunction rooted in self-alienation. And the occasional symptomatic relief afforded by medicines simply strengthens the dilemma. The resolution of the problem often happens only when the patient courageously faces inward (autonomy) instead of outward (heteronomy) for a solution.

It isn't surprising that persons are reluctant to let go of the familiar way that they have lived, even if a lot of pain was part of the familiarity. The pain is part of the definition of themselves. They are in the predicament of the person who is drowning. The drowning person struggles for air and so causes himself to sink. If he would relax and trust the water to support him, he would find that he could discover the means to breathe. In therapy, a person must come to the point of abandoning his drowning mode of struggling and move to a struggle that uses the strength of relationship. He must be willing to let go of a part of him that he has cherished; namely the myth of his own sufficiency.

At this juncture with a person, the therapist must be willing to ride with his or her own authority, and at that point, is declaring his or her faith. Powerful moments of therapeutic movement come out of the fusion of personal authenticity. The language of mysticism or even of subjectivism often seem to be the only instruments to transmit the meaning of that event.

In the room where I am face-to-face or side-by-side with a person who is struggling to find courage to change, I know there is no way that I can fit this person into some system. It is her struggle, and if I am to support the unleashing of all those latent powers she shuns, I must be willing to find common ground in our persons on which to stand. Frequently I don't want to do this because it forces me once again to confront myself where I would prefer to be secret. It is embarrassing when I finally have to confront the sneaky dependency in my own self which is so like that of my patient. But then we are more free, and in the intimacy of shared humanity we can shed the shielding of our former beliefs for the anxious vulnerability of simple facts.

The world in which people live has large elements of terror. One aspect of the terror is that our knowledge is belief mistaken for fact. Consequently, there is a whole network of contradictions and confusions. It is an era when international amorality is taken as a given and persons no longer depend upon their community or nation to protect them or be the servant of their interests. I wonder whether to distrust the government and often feel caught in the currents generated by an anonymous and self-serving system of interlocking cartels.

I live with persons who entertain fantasies of or actually make plans for personal survival in the event of economic and/or political disaster. Bags of gold pieces, boxes of dried nutrients, and caches of arms are the common responses to distrust of the nation. It is, of course, no less terrifying to the person who sits with me in my office. I am inviting him or her to risk personal change at least partially as an act of faith. Psychotherapy requires, among other things, that some fantasies, cherished angers, dependent hopes, favorite ways of pulling the rug out from under one's self, be given up. In the trusting surrender, psychotherapy intersects with the language of faith.

I remember with particular warmth the day a brilliant but driven graduate student, trudging persistently through the hours of therapy, ripped her fourth draft of a paper into shreds and resolved to take a year's leave from school to be free for her therapy. The test of faith was in commitment to self in uncharted territory.

The logical, rational, empirical, ordinary language of the defined world is clear and clean and seductive. The discipline of the world grounded in the spirit is so difficult because there are no rules and no enforcers save the inside experience of integration vs. confusion. My faith is an "in spite of" orientation. Such faith states an internal demand to persist in intuitive relationships moving toward intimacy even though that task is relatively uncharted and the end unknown.

I think that it is complex and difficult to stay alive in this world. Human existence is a constant paradox and my commitment to tracking the tortured paths of wanderers and struggling for deliberate directions is often painful. I believe that it's worth it. It is better in the long run to understand myself, to be realistic about my place in the world, to be appropriately open to other people and to choose reality over sentiment, prejudice or tradition. By so choosing I will often be living in close awareness of my intuitive, subjective experience and will experience anxiety in the paradox of these data as matched against the convictions of much of the world around me. I will often be wrong, frequently nasty, and sometimes impossible to be with. It's all right. I have chosen it, and in living this way I am as content with my choice as an absurd world could allow.

FAITH IN THE RHYTHM OF GROWTH

Orlo Strunk, Jr.

WHY NOT ADMIT IT? I no longer get a bang out of reading term papers. I wonder if this is what academic administrators mean when they talk about faculty members "dying on the vine"? I often wonder whether administrators ever die on the vine? I know they do. But how can you tell?

Anyway, it was a term paper that drove me to my writing desk a few moments ago. The paper was on the topic of the human soul. The student who wrote it struggled with the age-old notion of the soul. Her fingers and her intellect had shuffled through the literature diligently: Soul. Psyche. Pneuma. Nous. Ka. Self. Ego. Proprium. At first I felt saddened by her plight. The *déjà vu* of the whole thing made me feel old, very old. And I thought, "So this is what it's like to die on the vine . . ."

And then an insight came. I no longer become enthusiastic over the many arguments on whether or not there is a soul, because it is one of those queries I have answered. I know for sure. Indeed, I am a soul. I am certain of it!

The dogmatic quality of this assertion sounds strange coming from me. I am not, after all, a dogmatic person. Indeed, students frequently moan over my propensity for tentativeness. My toleration for ambiguity irritates some of my colleagues, most of my students and supervisees, and all of my family members. "Can't you give a

---

Orlo Strunk, Jr., Ph.D. is past President of Psychologists Interested in Religious Issues, a division of the American Psychological Association. He is Professor of Pastoral Psychology and Supervisor at the Danielsen Center of Pastoral Counseling, Boston University School of Theology.

simple 'yes' or 'no'?" "Must you always answer a question with a question?" "Aren't you certain of anything?" "Why must you qualify every truth?" "You drive me crazy with your 'yes-but' attitude!" "If you use that phrase 'all-other-things-being-equal' once more, I'll scream!" "Please, please, tell me what to do!" "I know you know; why won't you tell me?" These recordings and their relatives are scratched into my brain. I've heard them, and variations of them, thousands of times. They help to define me. They sometimes coagulate into a label, like liberal or mutable or agnostic or open-minded or wishy-washy or dimwitted.

But when it comes to the notion of a soul, I indeed do know. It is a truth. And it is the sort of truth arrived at after many years of questioning, denial, affirmation, dismissal. It is one of those rare and precious bits of knowledge arrived at through a sometimes-tortuous, sometimes-joyous process or movement. It is what I call a rhythmic truth.

That's why a term paper on the human soul is dull. I'm not dead on the vine after all! I may be out of rhythm with this student—but I'm not dead on the vine. In fact, I'm alive with a truth I really own at last. To start over from square one is what's deadening.

Rhythmic truth is the kind of truth that I own through a process of movement—back and forth, in and out, up and down. It's not necessarily developmental. It's dynamic. And it's the kind of truth that can be arrived at through psychotherapy, although there are other ways to be sure. But in certain kinds of psychotherapy, one can monitor the rhythmic movements—perhaps even come to delight in them.

Two Images: a pot-bellied stove and the ocean's tides.

I like images. For me an image frequently takes a million threads, loose ends and all, and wraps them in a ball that I can handle and play with. And it's lovely when the image is beautiful, pristine, pleasant, poetic.

My first image of rhythmic truth wasn't attractive. It was a memory flung at me from the past. Its central object was a pot-bellied stove, pink with heat, sitting in the center of a quonset hut. I knew immediately where the image came from. It was an experience of an eighteen-year-old boy in the midst of a great war. There was that stove, banked with soft coal, radiating heat in all directions. And there I was, chilled and frightened, searching for warmth.

Also with the image came the frustrating process of trying to find just the right degree of warmth by moving towards or away from that stove. I'm in the midlands of England in late December and it is cold. Raw cold. When I'm too far away from the pot-bellied stove, I'm cold. When too close, hot. Outside elements—temperature changes, wind, rain, snow—complicate matters. And, too, there's the condition of the stove itself, crimson with heat at one time, just barely warm at another. So the image is dynamic, as I remember moving toward, back, toward again—until, thank God, I find the right stance for that particular time and under those particular circumstances.

The second image is more recent, more attractive. It is a New England coastline with its crashing waves and its persistent tides. In recent years I have lived close to the sea, and I have come to love it and to respect it. It too is a dynamic image, always churning, flowing, moving, changing. One day the waves seem cruel and angry; the next, they are gentle and soothing. At times the waters appear gray, foreboding; at other times, blue and inviting.

But what captures my imagination is the dependability of the tides. No matter how viciously the breakers pound the rocks or how gently they caress the beach, the tide goes through its changes; it comes in and it goes out. Even as the tide varies from high to low, there is in it a dependable process I can observe and, with patience, monitor and delight in.

The tides, too, are like rhythmic truths.

These simple images are signs of the faith I have gained in working with others and in working with myself. In one sense, it is a radically empirical kind of faith, based on experience. However, there are times when it is severely tested and I wonder about its validity.

Like working with Dan, for instance. I had been seeing Dan for nearly five months. He had come to me originally in a deep state of depression. At first, he spoke of suicide as a viable option. He had lost a very close friend and the loss had driven him into a deep, dreadful depression. Frightened by his suicidal thoughts, he reached out.

Having had many bouts with depression myself, I felt, truly felt, what Dan was feeling. I knew something about his despair. It is bleak, cruel, and desperate. And it is real—far more real than those who urge you to "pull yourself together" ever seem to realize.

For weeks we met. I was searching for a single spark that might be fanned into a flame, Dan seemingly stuck at a dark and cold place removed from the warmth of hope. There were sessions when I sensed Dan's voice shift in tone, a slight melody of hope; but just as quickly it would fade and we were left with a flat silence filled with emptiness. And so it went.

There were times when even I found myself moving away from the warm glow of hope. After such sessions, I would ruminate on the theories of depression which I had studied. It helped, just a little. But underneath it all was the conviction that somehow, in some fashion, Dan's condition could be changed and that my being present to him made a difference. It was this conviction, this faith, which kept me from joining Dan in his depression, at the same time keeping him company.

Time and time again, I listened to Dan's self-reproaches, his negative ruminations, his agonizing arguments against himself and his world. Despite his words and his mood, I knew I was spending my time with an attractive, intelligent, engaging young man even though these qualities were not recognized by Dan. "A dung heap," he said one day in summing up his self-portrait. "A dung heap."

But then there was the session when he told me that a young woman accidently touched his hand when he gave her change at the checkout counter of the supermarket where he was working. "I felt the warmth of her finger charge up my arm. And when I looked at her, she half-smiled. It was the best thing that happened to me all day."

I encouraged Dan to try to recapture that moment, to feel again the life force rushing from his hand to his chest. As he did so he began reflecting on similar experiences in his past. And then for the first time in our conversations, he began to talk in detail about his mother. Previously, he had spoken of her nonchalantly as a "true saint," a "perfect, loving person." Now he began to express some ambivalences. Yes, she was a good person—warm and accepting. No, not always; sometimes she drifted away. . . . Absent. As Dan's eyes began to mist, he caught his breath. And then he was back talking about the loss of his friend, and that whole story began to be told again.

Dan had begun to feel the heat of that potbellied stove, but it was getting too hot for him. So he retreated. He would do that again and again in the weeks that followed. It was part of the process, part of the rhythmic qualities of growth. It took Dan a long time to find just the right "spot."

Resistance can be positive and necessary.

When I first learned about counseling and psychotherapy and during those early days of supervision, I was taught that resistance is The Enemy. After all, it is out to sabotage the therapeutic process, to disrupt, to delay, to harm. Not only that, but it is pervasive; its expression is legion. Resistance may take the form of suppression and repression, self-devaluation, intellectualization, surface conversation, lateness for appointments, acting-out, and so forth. All of these maneuvers were seen as negative ways of bringing the therapeutic process to a halt. It has taken me some years to come to recognize resistance as simply one of the signs of the rhythmic qualities of growth, an integral part of the rhythmic process. It is not only part of the way we grow, it is a necessary way of keeping from being burned by the pink-glowing pot-bellied stove.

What makes me treat resistance as basically a positive force is based as much on my personal journey as it is on theory. I find it impossible to see my own development in terms of "phases" or "stages." Instead, I sense at a much deeper level a movement toward, a retreat, another advance, a step backwards. Kierkegaard's notion of the "double movement of infinity" seems closer to my experience than do most contemporary theories of development: out of the world→into oneself→out of oneself→into God→back into the world. . . . That's the way I have come to experience my life and to have faith in the psychotherapeutic/growth processes, including that part we call resistance.

What is it that requires resistance? What is at stake that directs me to be cautious in my journey? Why a rhythmic way instead of a direct and straight movement? Why not simply run up to that red-hot, pot-bellied stove and have done with it? Why back away from the truth about myself and avoid acting decisively?

I do not know the answers to these questions. Nor do I believe that I will ever know for sure. But life so far has offered me some inklings, some glimpses which have fashioned themselves into what I call a heuristic faith:

First, my faith is that there is in you and in me a centerpoint, a quiet place that truly identifies you as you and me as me. I think of this as the true Self. Not only that, but this centerpoint is secret, perhaps unknowable.

My faith is that this centerpoint, this secret Self, is in essence good. It can be trusted and intends to actualize itself in the world. I've no scientific proof of this. The strongest evidence I have is empirical: that is, my own inner journey and my involvement with others who have willingly shared their journeys with me.

I think, for example, of Joanne, a religious sister who came to me with "problems in interpersonal relationships." At the time, her anger was so intense that after our early sessions together, I myself suffered from intense headaches, a rare experience for me. Her anger seemed overpowering; it flooded the room. Yet I could sense that Sister Joanne had another potential. Just when it seemed that the anger was beginning to subside, she discovered that she had cancer. Our conversations were interrupted during the period of a series of operations and some early cobalt treatments. But when Sr. Joanne returned, she seemed a different person. The interpersonal conflicts could still be talked about and were, but now there was a different perspective present. A touch of humor frequently surfaced, a philosophical and religious aura began conditioning even her sharpest words. In the last months of our meetings, I began to feel that I was coming to know the authentic Sr. Joanne. In our last session, I half-facetiously said, "Now, will the real Sr. Joanne please stand up."

I did nothing to Sister Joanne. Nor did I do anything for her except to be present and to listen to her early anger and her later hope. Several weeks after her death, I received in the mail a copy of Thomas Kane's *The Healing Touch of Affirmation.* Inside, a note read: "To Dr. Strunk, from Sr. Joanne, with deep appreciation." Joanne had chosen a book with a word in its title far more appropriate than any of my technical ones: *affirmation.* Its power, I suspect, was instrumental in helping Joanne to recover her center, to once again recognize it as having priority over the conflicts and turmoil of the outer world.

Holding to this notion that the secret Self is good, can be trusted, and intends to be actualized in the world is an article of faith which makes a difference. But I doubt that it is a stance which can be arrived at through argument, logical propositions, formal theoretical constructs, or violence. It comes, I suspect, only through a rhythmic process of discovery.

I also believe that drawing closer to the secret Self and beginning to recognize its essential goodness, its trustworthiness, and its intention for growth may be facilitated by the psychotherapeutic process. I do not mean to suggest that psychotherapy is the only or even the best way of discovering rhythmic truths about ourselves and the world. It is one way, however.

But I must note that my faith in psychotherapy is guarded and it is conditional. I do not think of modern psychotherapy as total salvation in any ultimate sense. My faith is that psychotherapy can play an immensely important and, for some, an absolutely essential role in drawing closer to the real Self—the "heart," to use Thomas Merton's apt term for the deepest psychological ground of one's personality.

Although my personal faith in the reality of the Self, its essential goodness, its trusting qualities, its actualizing tendencies, and the potential value of psychotherapy in the discovery of such rhythmic truths are vital realities for me, they nevertheless remain essentially mysterious. I find the task of naming that mystery both threatening and sad.

Often I have wondered and have been perplexed over why it is that others so often demand a name for faith. There have been times when I thought this to be a kind of artifact of the sub-cultures in which I spend a goodly portion of my life. After all, Christian theology is an explanation of the Word; and religion itself is frequently seen as a project of naming what is often nameless. Even the world of psychology is heavy on names which give the appearance of capturing what merely are stances and assumptions. And in psychotherapy we seem to rely heavily on what we call "talk therapy" where, we obviously presume, words have power to change. Thus it is that naming takes on considerable importance, and it is easy to see why there are heavy demands to do it.

But I have come to believe that the expectation and the mandate go much deeper than the peculiarities of theology, religion, psychology, or psychotherapy. In fact, I think the expectation stems from our bodies, especially the brain. If we can only name the mysterious or the ambiguous, we feel we have come to control them, brought them into an acceptable framework, given them a structure to help maintain our need for security and our wish to be in control. Despite the deeply-rooted nature of such a process, I am always saddened by the demand to name my faith for two reasons: the naming expectation rests heavily on language, and naming implies closure, completeness.

The truth is that faith cuts across all language. This means that when someone says to me, "Name your faith," I am endangered. The demand usually implies a particular language, and it is not possible for me to do this. My faith not only cuts across ordinary, psychological or theological languages, it transcends them as well.

Still, the demand for naming is a constant. An example.

Several months ago while having lunch with a young man who was looking for a graduate program suited to his needs and expectations, I found myself being forced to the naming wall. The potential candidate, George, had bombarded me with questions about the intellectual climate of my university, about the "theoretical orientation" of our academic and clinical settings, about the theological "thrust" of the school and the graduate division. We chatted nearly an hour about such things. I tried as best I could to articulate some generalizations and to identify major themes which might help him make a decision about whether or not to work with us on an advanced degree. But it was not enough. He wanted me to name my faith. When I told him much of what I have written above, he became even more persistent. At this point our conversation went like this:

George: It's important for me to know your faith.
Orlo: I sense you're looking for a word—maybe a label?
George: Well, yes. I'm an evangelical Christian, for instance. Are you?
Orlo: Gosh, I don't know. If I am, I'm pretty sure it's only part of what I am. But I don't think I am.
George: (Impatiently): Let's say someone's holding a gun to your head. He says, "Tell me what you are or I'll blow off your head." What would you say?
Orlo: Are you holding a gun to my head?
George: (Laughs): Let's just pretend for a minute. What would you say?
Orlo: I guess I'd say, "I'm a theistic-humanist." Yes, that's what I'd say.
George: (Shaking his head): That's a contradiction in terms, isn't it? How can you be a humanist and a theist at the same time?
Orlo: Is the gun still at my head?
George: (Laughs)
Orlo: Okay. I'm a humanist because I think persons are what's important. Persons are important—more important than ideas, or ideologies, or institutions, or religions. And I'm a theist because I believe that beyond the manifest is a much greater reality, the unmanifest. And in some fashion—I don't know how—I am at times in harmony with the unmanifest. . . .
George: What about Christ? You call yourself a Christian, don't you? You haven't mentioned Christ.
Orlo: Well, my conviction is that the best clue I have so far of what the unmanifest might be like is through the life of Jesus as I understand it through scripture, per-

sonal experience, and the traditions of the Christian community. I guess that makes me a Christian. . . .

George: (Relief showing): That's really interesting. . . .

We chatted a bit more, shook hands, and went our separate ways.

As I was walking back to my office, I realized that I felt very pained and more than a bit sad. I wondered why. After all, I had not lied. Indeed, I had tried very hard to be honest. And then I recalled a conversation I had had years before with a rape victim. She had struggled to explain to me what it had been like to have someone make a demand on her body—a demand she could not accept because, as she put it, "Sex is so very much more than that gross physical penetration." Now I'm sure that being urged to label my faith was far less intense than that young woman's traumatic experience, but I suspect the feelings I was having were similar to hers. Even as I write this, I wonder if George might be saying, "Orlo Strunk is a theistic-humanist," and if he understands how incomplete that linguistic trickery really is.

Yet, as I reflect on this event and feel, once again, how dangerous and crestfallen such an exercise can be for me, I recall the expression of relief on George's face when I spoke of Jesus. He so badly needed to hear that. I am glad that I could say what I said authentically. In that sense, I suppose, forced confessions of faith can have an altruistic quality to them. They do help the needful person to control perceptions.

Perhaps we all like to hear names and labels because we assume that in some way they carry with them a set of specific behaviors, attitudes, and values. Did George feel that by knowing I was a Christian theistic-humanist, he could count on me in some concrete ways? He could close his eyes in my presence. He could trust me.

But it's not that simple. Yes, my faith is partially responsible for what I do in therapy. At the same time, simply knowing or naming my faith cannot predict what I will do in therapy or how I will do it. I feel confident, for instance, that my faith in the rhythmic process may at times help me to be patient with the slowness of the process, to wait with greater hope than I might if I did not have such a faith. And I am pretty sure that my faith in the goodness, trustworthiness, and actualizing possibilities of the Self often informs me in what I am about as I am present to another person and when I struggle with myself. Equally sure am I that a certain kind of relationship between client and therapist facilitates growth and discovery, allowing the movement to continue, come to a halt, continue again. I am even convinced that being person-centered and believing in the reality of the unmanifest contribute in specific ways to what I do and who I am in the therapeutic setting.

Still, I insist that my faith does not begin to exhaust who I am. Faith is not enough to account for the unfolding and the discovery of the secret Self. Nor is technique. Nor is skill. Nor is training. Nor is credentialing. Nor is naming. When the appeal of a whole person is answered by the presence of a whole person, we have an authentic encounter, only slightly short of a miracle. It can happen in psychotherapy. When it does, faith undoubtedly has played its part.

HUMAN DECENCY

Martin Grotjahn

I DO NOT BELIEVE in a personal God; nor even in a Divine principle. I used to say, "God does not show Himself in person. Nor does He show Himself in words. He shows Himself in deeds: that the sun shines is His gift to us today—that it may be raining tomorrow will also be His gift. God shows himself in life, in love, in goodness and in truth."

I do not say it quite this way anymore, although it sounds good and poetic. But it uses the word "God" as a symbol, an analogy or as a metaphor. It is not God who shows Himself. It is life itself towards which I feel reverence.

The Judeo-Christian tradition teaches that there is only one God. For me that means there is only one life—and that is sacred: in me, in you, in that ugly banana slug on the ground, and in that dreadful shark in the ocean.

My reverence for life has a religious quality because I believe death follows life; then eternity has replaced change. What is dead is dead in eternity. Do people know what that means? To have only this one chance? Would they louse it up so easily if they would know it?

I do believe in man; in his quintessential goodness—or at least in his wish to be good. In this sense I believe in myself. If I would not do so I could not work with people. I try to restore their belief in their fellow men—and in themselves. Not even Jesus told us to love our "next one" more than ourselves; equally much would do very nicely.

Martin Grotjahn, M.D. is Professor Emeritus at the University of Southern California and is also Training Analyst Emeritus at the Southern California Institute for Psychoanalysis.

I refuse to learn by experience. There is a German saying which says, "Those are truly noble people who do not learn by bad experience."

This is what I have learned to believe in 75 years of living and in fifty years of working as a therapist.

The roots of my belief in people—and myself—go back into my childhood. When I was three, my mother delivered my brother into this world, which I considered my world. As far as I was concerned his presence was totally unnecessary. It then happened that this baby got mortally sick, and both parents turned to him in love and concern. They saved his life but I felt left alone and abandoned.

I turned to my kinderfrau, an old and loving woman who accepted me in my despair, rage, and guilt. I found a new mother and a good one. I learned that there always is a good mother; one must only find her. Through all my life I found such mothers: in my marriage, in my coming to America, and in my profession.

There is a second root which leads to my faith: when my mother was pregnant with me, my father studied Martin Luther's works. When I was born, his brain child, a collection of writings and sayings of Martin Luther, also was born and I was baptized "Martin." Through all my childhood Martin Luther was a living presence in our house. I always believed that Luther was a member of our family and I identified with him.

Many years later, when Erik Erikson published his book *Young Man Luther,* I deepened my understanding of him and it advanced my own analysis. I read his book at a time when I studied the works of Albert Schweitzer.

I recognize my indebtedness to Martin Luther, who influenced my moral growth; to Sigmund Freud, who guided my moral action in my profession; and to Albert Schweitzer, who became a symbol of a moral person for me. Martin Luther showed the way from medieval dogmatism to Protestant ethic, which I understand to be an insistence on the individual's right, duty, and ability to decide, and to act for himself as a moral person. Sigmund Freud continued where Martin Luther left off by showing a new dimension of moral consciousness. He made man responsible for his unconscious too. He never stated this in his works because, for him, "das moralische versteht sich von selbst" (morality is self understood). Albert Schweitzer gave the search of the Protestant man a new direction. Psychoanalysis charted the way we came. Albert Schweitzer showed us the road to take, and called it "Reverence for Life." He did not offer an anchorage in our age of doubt; but he showed a new direction to orient us in the search for identity, which is the most torturing question of our time.

Luther postulated being honest to one's self. Freud included the unconscious in this postulation, and Albert Schweitzer showed the use of it in life. The psychological man was joined by the moral man. The integration of both will lead to the free man of the future, whose freedom is the expression of his belief in a reverence for life as something sacred.

Man's fight for his soul is to understand the meaning of his life, and is still the most important task he has to accomplish. Freud called it the conquest of the unconscious. Modern psychology calls it the search for ego identity, a decisive step toward final integrity. Martin Luther spoke to his God directly, without an intermediary. He was seeking an intimate and personal relationship to his God. Luther exposed man's right, duty, and ability to feel, to think, and to determine his relation to his God.

In his struggle, Martin Luther joined the monastery, just as a lost man of our time may retreat to a psychiatrist. The monastery became for Luther a spiritual hospital. He prepared himself to give all of his obedience to God. With passionate sincerity, he saved himself from the danger of regression into a psychotic depression.

He found temporary identity through ideology. This relationship between ideology and ego-identity is a major point in understanding Martin Luther. Psychoanalysis has emphasized and systematized the search for an even deeper honesty, which includes the unconscious. Psychoanalysis has neglected to chart the extent to which parents, family, and society define, and should define, ideas and ideologies to the growing adolescent. Man is not only driven by his instincts, but also drawn by his ideals.

The historical development of the last 500 years leads from Martin Luther's protest against hypocrisy to a demand for individual conscience, to Sigmund Freud's new dimension of conscience. Psychoanalysis is essentially a fight against self-deception. Finally it leads to Albert Schweitzer's formulation of reverence for life.

The three men: Martin Luther, Sigmund Freud, and Albert Schweitzer believed and trusted in human decency. So do I.

It is not easy to describe how my faith influences my daily work. However, I do know with certainty that without it I could not work the way I do.

Indifference does not work at all, even if it looks strong like the Rock of Gibraltar.

Tolerance is benevolent arrogance and is resented. Love in the true sense of the word leads to trouble in our work. Love alone does not help in therapy. Affection seems to be a better word, but belief and faith is the right term and the right idea, as I see it.

I often ask myself, "Are there impossible people?" There are certainly people with whom work is impossible for me. There are good and not so good patients, boring and exciting ones. But are there impossible people?

A person is boring when he or she disregards my existence and does not give me a place in the therapeutic process. A good patient is one who builds a working alliance with me. This may include hostility, doubt, suspicion and other negative feelings at times.

I suppose a person becomes therapeutically, and perhaps also educationally, impossible when he consistently and determinedly denies my good faith in him or at least in a part of his personality. He may doubt it and he even may test me, and may do so repeatedly and skillfully, but when I cannot at all convince him of my faith in his and my essential decency, then I have lost.

Surely I have been disappointed in people. That is not the right word; it sounds too patriarchal. I have seen truly bad people, people whose main aim in life was to hate, to hurt and to destroy. Sometimes they do it out of inner need but more often out of self-preservation as they see it. And still, I believe, they are not voluntarily bad. They have felt in their own experience that to destroy is their only way out. Many of them cannot be helped by me but the attempt to help them is always justified, because of the hope that somebody may still reach out for the hand extended to them.

To be a good therapist is to be human. In order to be human I must believe that my brothers and sisters are human too. To be human, however, is not enough. And therein lies the therapist's dilemma: We must be well trained, we must know ourselves, we must have learned what there is to be learned in our profession; we must learn technique and develop our own style. To have learned everything that there is to learn is not enough. With all our professional knowledge we must remain human, free, spontaneous, communicative and, at all times, honest.

DRAMA, HUMAN AND DIVINE

Charles Ansell

Young soul:	Whence cometh our faith?
Older soul:	Faith does not come; it awaits us.
Young soul:	How then do we summon it?
Older soul:	It is with us at our first breath.

A CHILDHOOD MEMORY. It is the Sabbath Day and I am in the synagogue. Ahead of me on the rise of the altar stand the Cantor and the Rabbi. Two men have been called up from their seats to ascend to the *bima,* there to stand at the sides of the Ark of the Covenant where the Torah scrolls are closeted. The entire congregation rises and sings as the men swing open the doors of the Ark and gently remove the scrolls.

They are draped, one with a red velvet mantle, the other, silken white. Along the rounded breasts of their velvet mantles are letters threaded in gold. The men hoist the scrolls over their shoulders and lead a procession down the center aisle. The worshippers swarm toward the aisle to press either their prayer books or their *tallit* (prayer shawls) to the Torah, then kiss their books or their *tallit.*

When the procession reaches the foot of the long aisle they turn around and walk back up the aisle to return to the altar area. Here one of the Torah scrolls is placed gently on the reader's desk, its red mantle lovingly removed and folded. The Rabbi approaches the desk

---

Charles Ansell, Ed.D., J.D. was trained in both law and psychology. Dr. Ansell has been President of the California State Psychological Association and other professional societies. He was formerly on the faculty of the California School of Professional Psychology and is presently practicing in Encino, California.

and unrolls the parchment scroll to the text of the week. Other men are called up to recite the blessing, but before they begin they press the fringes of their *tallit* to the sacred text, then kiss it before they begin to chant the prescribed chapter of the week. Later that afternoon the Rabbi sits with a group of men and expounds on the text.

The Torah is more than text for study, more than occasions for prayer. It is, in the language of the psychoanalyst, a libidinal object, clung to as fiercely as the lover cleaves to his beloved. To the kabbalist the Torah is the *Shekhina,* God's sacred presence. It is in and through the Torah that the Jew attains a measure of divinity.

The Torah service in the synagogue is magic, it is theater; it is sometimes spectacular. There is no audience, there are only participants in this drama. Every Jew in his lifetime has embraced the Torah and held it fast to his body. He has marched with it, read from it, and danced with it. The Torah has a gender. It is female. It is eternally fertile. It is draped like a queen, and is always escorted regally. It is open to the eyes of the beloved to behold its message. It bakes into memory from childhood; it grows alongside the Jew throughout his life, matching wit and wisdom until his hoary old age.

Therapy too is theater. When some errand takes me to my office on a week-end, it feels as barren and as cold as a deserted stage. But on the mornings when I await my first patient, my office becomes theater. It is the synagogue on the Sabbath before the Torah service. The Ark of the Covenant, soon to be opened, is the unoccupied chair where my patient will sit.

When my patient arrives and takes a seat, it is as if the Torah scroll were opened to the text for the day's study. My office becomes a sanctuary. It seems to glow with a light different from the grey light of a chance visit there on a week-end morning. It is drama in which all are actors.

Another childhood memory. I am returning home from the synagogue with my father. I walk at his side past the commonplaces of my boyhood life on the streets of my neighborhood. We walk past an unbroken series of sights and sounds mindlessly familiar from my errands to and fro. Here the small grocery store, beyond is a junk yard faintly smelling of rusting iron and decaying oil; now we pass a dimly lit notions store. When at last we reach the doorstep of our house, my father raises his hand to the *mezuzah* nailed to the side of the door and slowly kisses the fingers that touched the sacred symbol. I ape him in a chill at performing an awesome act. Then we open the door to our home and enter a place made sacred by the ritual of greeting the *mezuzah.* I am suddenly away from the commonplaces of the street. I feel centered in an orientation to the world. Without this orientation I would feel profoundly isolated from the world, I would be in a great hollow void.

I recall how, from the isolated primitive tribes in Africa to the great centers of western life, all human societies reveal a universal pattern in designating certain places as sacred: a clearing in the compound of a tribal village, the interior of a cathedral, the Ark of the Covenant. All these are held sacred because we will them to be sacred. Even a time is designated as sacred: the Sabbath, a holy week; certain measures of time marked off from the rest of the calendar as a time to feel sacred.

We gain an orientation, not alone in a need to separate the sacred from the profane, but more because of the special character of our lives as sentient beings. For the secular to say that the stone of worship is like all other stones in the world, or that the tree of worship is like all other trees is so to homogenize the cosmos that our senses are condemned to live through a monotony of existence in which there can be no distinction between the ordinary and the extraordinary.

This mode of living in an undifferentiated continuum can only drain the world of all meaning. The meaning we choose to give to this time, to that place gives our lives a critical orientation to existence. The endless sameness of time and place can only reduce us to despair and nothingness.

How has this theater of faith led me to a definition of existence? How has it evolved into those meanings which endow my life with direction? My answers are in part intuitive, in part historical. Though devotion to Torah as text and as an agenda for communal life may seem at the surface to be a group faith and, hence, leave little opportunity for individual guidance, the outcome is quite the contrary. It is precisely the genius of the Torah that compels each of us to face it in a profoundly personal dialogue.

There are ministries that require aspiring clergy to give testimony to a Call if they would serve God. The image of the Call to qualify for service to the Lord is intriguing; it is also a doubtful psychological experience. We know that religious experiences come in a variety of ways. For some, religious experiences attain peaks of ecstasies that transcend normal bounds of perception. In any case, ecstasy remains the domain of the mystic. Alas, I can claim neither a Call nor a state of ecstasy to explain my career choice.

Certain experiences undoubtedly predisposed me to my career choice. From earliest times, the practice and teaching of my faith seemed informed by the central theme of enlightenment. As a child I recall a late Yom Kippur afternoon service at which men discussed the Jonah legend. They were working men who earned their living peddling fruit and vegetables from open, horse-drawn wagons in summer and winter. They were also garment workers and tinsmiths and shoemakers and butchers, but they debated Jonah's strange behavior with a drivenness I found in my clinical seminars years later. They argued and reasoned, searching for motive and intention. They hypothesized premises and advanced strange metaphors to understand Jonah's flight from the Lord's command to redeem the fallen city of Nineveh.

From early on I equated the practice of my faith with uncovering motive and meaning in human behavior. I recall my fascination with the story of the brothers Jacob and Esau and their mother Rebecca who conspired to deceive her husband Isaac in winning his blessing away from Esau, the elder son, because she favored Jacob. I remember my chagrin at her vehement offer to bear the sin of the deception. I was to be mystified later in the story when Jacob, now a man successful and rich with flocks and wives and servants, returned to the home that he had fled years earlier to meet his brother Esau, in battle if need be, but more in peace that he had prayed he would find in their reunion. On the eve of his reunion with Esau he ordered his retinue of wives, children, servants and flocks to leave him to sleep alone in a cave where he would spend the night. He wrestled there with a stranger and at dawn returned to his family, limping and sore with pain from his bout in the cave. Once with his family, he announced that henceforth his name was no longer Jacob but Israel, one who contended with God.

The enigmas posed by the Biblical legends of the patriarchs excited my curiosity because of their dramatic symbols that conveyed messages not immediately acceptable to the literalist.

It was not entirely the intellectual challenges my faith thrust at me, there was also history. Here I found a story of a people exiled in strange lands, forced to live in enclaves, apart from the mainstreams of their host societies, where they reflected on existence as seen from the margin of history. Even in this isolation, deprived of the normal civilities accorded to the native inhabitants, they were far from creating a literature of lamentations. Instead, they created ways of life devoted principally to understanding and serving humankind. They wrote of *Tzedaka*, a word which connotes a special form of philanthropy, one that can be experienced in the act of giving as a deeply felt religious experience. The word also connotes social justice. It also suggests saintliness in its declension to *Tzadik*. There is a Jewish penchant for human service.

Long before the Holocaust, the Jewish mind reflected on man's inhumanity to man. They seemed driven by a surpassing restlessness to search after the unknowable. Throughout its two millennia history in Europe, the academies in the Jewish ghettos produced an abundance of scholars whose works are still revered for their illumination of sacred text. Theirs was not a literature of suffering; it was a literature of divining man's way with God and God's way with man.

The scriptures speak of the God of Abraham, the God of Isaac, and the God of Jacob. It seemed important to emphasize that each of the patriarchs understood the Deity uniquely. In later rabbinic commentaries, this mode of assigning a separate understanding to each of the patriarchs permitted others to do the same. Given this wide permission, the Deity was available to those whose studies demanded wider and wider dimensions in divining purpose and expressions. It was perhaps this restlessness in later scholarship that led three secularized Jews to break new ground in their separate spheres of interest.

I think here of Karl Marx, Sigmund Freud and Albert Einstein. All three followed ways of thought known to the Talmudists from earliest times. Like their Talmudic predecessors, each saw beyond appearances and reached for a new version of reality. Mainly, however, Marx, Freud and Einstein were of a piece with the intellectual heritage of the Jewish penchant for search.

When I consider how my faith accounts for my career choice I call upon memories of Talmudic discourse and their ways of probing beyond appearances, beyond the givens. I call up memories of my parents' zeal to follow after the precepts of their faith in aiding the needy, tending the sick and consoling the bereaved. I recall my mother sitting beside my father as he worked over a massive presser's buck board, reading aloud to him.

My parents were immigrant Jews, but the life they followed in the new land was little different from the life they had followed in their small community in Lithuania. Despite our own low economic condition, education held a high priority. I had barely finished one year of high school when my father fell ill and died. The family income was virtually at an end. Along with my brothers and sister I was compelled to leave school at fifteen and work at a variety of unskilled jobs, pooling my small salary with my brothers and sister to maintain ourselves. In time I discovered the downtown YMCA evening high school where I enrolled and spent six years until I finished its high school and evening college.

Career choices fifty years ago were severely limited, even more limited for evening students. I chose to study law. Three years later I was a lawyer, licensed and qualified to take on clients. The nation was locked in a severe economic depression. Unemployment was high, banks were closed and homes were lost to mortgage holders. I applied for a position on the legal staff of the Home Owners Loan Corporation and was taken on as court attorney to stand at the side of home owners in their legal struggles against large banks and insurance companies who pressed for payment of inflated mortgages issued in the lusher years of the previous decade.

This work took me to working-class audiences throughout the city where I soon lectured on other opportunities available under the broadening umbrella of Franklin Roosevelt's New Deal. A settlement house soon asked me to join its staff as director of adult education. I accepted quickly. Though I did well as a law student, the prospects of life as a lawyer in the 1930s were far different from the opportunities available today to socially-minded lawyers. Consumerism, poverty law, environmental law, class action suits on behalf of beleaguered groups, and other public service opportunities were unheard of. The prospects were limited to commercial law matters concerned mainly with property rights.

Leaving the law for settlement house work was an easy decision. I yearned to enter the world of social and human services. I was now free to return to school, this time in day classes, a luxury denied me since I had left high school. I entered graduate studies at Northwestern University and earned a Master's Degree in a field of study totally foreign to me: the psychology of adult learning.

Following World War II, I moved to New York City to become the director of various settlement houses and once again returned to school, this time to Teachers College, Columbia University, where I earned the doctorate in counseling psychology. Shortly after I began my studies at Columbia, I knew I had arrived at some destiny in career choice for I quickly learned that I had come full circle. I was now one of the synagogue discussants pondering the mysteries of human behavior, perhaps not as exalted as divining Jonah's flight from the Lord, but concerned with the behavior of a hundred mirror images of myself in the clients I counseled.

The complexity of human behavior has never failed to interest me. I am drawn to the ways we conceal our motives, leading us to express ourselves in ways seemingly unrelated to motives we express at the surface of our behavior. I remain moved by the drama of anger and tears that sometimes betray us in our search after meaning, for it is only in the meanings we uncover in our behavior that our lives gain a measure of divinity.

A parable: An apocryphal legend tells of the tests God placed before the people at Mount Sinai before they received His covenant. The legend holds that when Moses first descended from Mount Sinai with the tablets, the people waited at the base of the mountain and called out their eagerness to accept the covenant. But God was not pleased with such quick acceptance. When Moses returned a second time, the people repeated their willing acceptance, but added their promise to obey its commandments. Still God withheld His covenant. When Moses descended a third time the people grew silent and reflective. Finally, they turned to Moses and spoke slowly and carefully. They would accept the sacred covenant, they would obey its commandments, but more than these, they vowed to understand it. Understanding thereafter became each individual's responsibility if he would know the meaning of the covenant.

Elaborate systems have developed since the nineteenth century which attempt to answer questions about human behavior. Yet however elaborate these systems became, only recently have they come under serious scrutiny for their deliberate avoidance of the psychologist's role and responsibility in experiencing the client in ways that had been sharply derided.

Early in the history of psychoanalysis, Freud observed how the fears and fantasies which his patients gathered in their childhood were projected on to the analyst. Freud referred to this unconscious phenomenon as transference. Later Freud warned that the analyst might recognize these same fears and fantasies within himself, find himself unconsciously reflecting the patient's feelings and, thereby, lose a necessary neutrality in attitude. The analyst must be clear of those countertransference feelings that reflect the patient's problems, Freud argued. Sixty years later, psychoanalysis has developed away from Freud's early warnings against breaching the principle of neutrality. Yet, the experience of empathizing is a necessary effort for the therapist.

Martin Buber chose the image of the I-Thou dialogue to suggest the profoundly personal nature of understanding another. Understanding grows out of a form of participation, indeed as a form of internalization of the other, in Buber's dialogic spirit of engagement.

The psychological term to bridge the I and the Thou in therapy is found in the developing meaning of empathy. Empathy is more than a recognition of what another is feeling; it is the effort to probe one's own psyche for feelings that parallel the other. The empathy that is limited only to a recognition of the other's distress may create distance that could lead to detachment from the patient's feelings. But the empathy that directs the therapist to locate a genuinely parallel feeling within himself not only opens him to his own humanism, but deepens his understanding of the patient.

Therapy is a theater of creativity because it is active within the relationship between client and therapist, and because it occurs within the experience both feel. The therapist in relation to a client is not simply an actor reading a script written by another, but is genuinely acting in a living psychodrama. The clinical situation he faces hourly is not contrived to serve as instructional media, but rises out of the client's genuine difficulty with life's experiences. He may claim to be inadequate to meet the demands others place on him, or may inveigh against others for their unfair uses of him, but throughout the drama the client plays out the role of the victim. Victim is here defined to mean one who feels compelled to follow the will of others and is hence denied the experience of selfhood. He frets under the illusion that he lives to fulfill the wishes of others and is, therefore, compelled to exist without meaning for himself, compelled to feel himself as barren as the day before Creation.

Therapy, in intention and more in hope, would deliver the victim from a state of selflessness to selfhood, from a barren and void cosmos to a world where he is free to discover Will, free to fashion meanings out of experiences. But throughout the encounter, the therapist, by words, manner, animated exchanges with the client can finally lift the enterprise beyond the simple analysis of external experience.

At this juncture the therapist's faith enters the experience and gives it direction. Without empathy, without the often painful effort to experience another's distress, therapy may be reduced to lifeless scientism. The faith of the therapist proceeds from his belief that he shares a common divinity with his client.

For example, a rabbi came to me several years ago in an agitated depression. He was physically ungainly, an inch or two above five feet and seriously overweight. He had a precarious medical history, open heart surgery, diabetes and certain orthopedic problems. He spoke in a rasping voice that often broke into falsetto tones which were disagreeable to the ear, particularly when he grew excited and raced his words. He often surprised me by bringing his wife to our sessions, for her to hear from me how disabled he was, and how he needed her love and understanding. With his wife present he debased himself all the more as if at the lowest depth of his ritual of self-deprecation I would rise from my chair and work a miracle that would elevate him to a dignified state and cause his wife to rush to his side and hug him.

At one of these histrionic sessions with his wife I stopped him suddenly and asked, "Are you really that powerless?" He became quiet and turned to his wife silently as if to study her eyes for answer. Then he turned back to me in a voice querulous and frightened. "Is that what I'm saying?" I nodded my head in slow agreement. "That's exactly what you're saying." "But they robbed me of my dignity, they threw me out like garbage." He returned once more to his obsessive re-telling of his experience with his last congregation, a group of young suburbanites who with his help built a handsome edifice, but thereafter decided (according to my client) that the roly-poly rabbi with the squeaky voice did not fit the grand design of the temple. It had been a devastating humiliation, made even more painful because of his own image. When he finished his tearful account of his ouster I found myself in a momentary conflict.

Clinically I knew that his physical grossness was in some part a neurotic actualization of a far earlier self-image. At some remote past, he had fastened onto an image of himself as a lost child, unloved, uncared for. His later life as an ingratiating rabbi was a manic defense against the darker fear of loss and abandonment. His young suburbanites had stripped him of his defense and he was dropped back into the lost, unloved child. My conflict lay in the hesitation I felt at helping him to unravel the serious character disorder he had become because of his toxic self-image and the manic defense he developed, a task that would mean months of intensive peeling away of the defense leading to a recognition of the destructive nature of his abandoned-child image. My conflict lay in the intent of his pleading

—that I had the power to rise like a Jehovah figure that could deliver him then and there into some exalted state of instant dignity.

"Yitzchak," I addressed him by his Biblical name, "I am not God. You make me feel like I can perform miracles. I can't perform miracles." He smiled quickly and rushed to assure me that he had no such illusions. "Doctor, of course not! Of course not!" He repeated it emphatically.

I rose to face him and placed my hands on his shoulders. "Yitzchak," I paused, "I am a man; like you, a man. We are the two of us men." "Of course," he cried again, but it was an empty agreement.

"I don't think you hear what I'm saying," I went on. He was silenced. I continued to hold him at the shoulders, but pressed my fingers into his soft flesh. "As I am with God, you are too. We are both His creation. I try to carry His gift with joy. How do you carry His gift?"

He turned away from me again to look at his wife. It was a silent appeal. I turned his shoulders around to face me directly. "Esther is not your mother. She is a woman, a human being like you, like me. You have turned her into a mother." We stood facing each other silently until I felt something stirring in me, a rising wave of feeling I could not turn from. I drew the rabbi close to me and embraced him. "You're a mensch," I whispered.

It was no miracle. Clinically, it was a moment of weakness, a foolish capitulation to transfer feelings of my own remembered identity with his present stage. But I had no choice. I felt driven to acknowledge our mutual divinity, almost as a reassuring statement that I needed at the moment. The embrace was a statement of my faith. For his part the rabbi sat sobered for the remainder of the session. Our work continued for several more months, but it grew subdued, less obsessional, less agitated.

A pulpit opened for him in a distant city, which he accepted. We parted in a curious ceremony of mutual gratitude. He has been at the same pulpit since our last visit, now five years ago.

Engagement, encounter, internalization are not attained free of one's own painful memories. Yet, apart from my own direct confrontations with sorrows and losses, there is additionally for me the poignant reminder of the Holocaust, the slaughter of six million innocent Jewish mothers, fathers and children. The reminder often throbs in my pulse like a raging fever. It cries out for meaning, for response, but no response came to me out of that dark night in history until my faith led me to a life-sustaining resolution. I felt led to take on an Eleventh Commandment, to order my life in a renewed affirmation of the faith I shared with the six million. It finally remains for the living to fix meaning to their lost lives lest their deaths pass into an oblivion of meaninglessness.

The Holocaust victim was a phenomenon of history. He did not choose his destiny. He was simply felled by his history as a Jew. I have found "holocaust behavior" in my clinical practice, a behavior whose predominating illusion is the obsessive feeling of helplessness. These "victims" move through life as helpless prey to forces beyond their control.

Catherine Bingham, born in Wisconsin of Protestant stock, was one such "victim." Her blank expression of staring into the space behind me, her frightened and confused recoil at even the most casual remark I made strongly suggested a pervasive fear of being struck down. Though her husband adored her and her only child, a fine young man of fifteen, was unfailingly kind to her, she nonetheless felt that both her husband and son were "short-changed" by having her in their life.

Her life had no meaning. It was without purpose. Each day was a torment of guilt at her failures. She inhabited a psychological concentration camp where she performed her tasks under some imaginary compulsion, where she was held captive to serve an indeterminate sentence.

I perceived her as a responsibility given me under the compact of the Eleventh Commandment. I would "free" her of her self-imposed internment. We are still at work, Catherine and I, but in place of blank stares we have at last reached a hidden sorrow that now yields to tears; we are focused on feelings that have come into awareness slowly. We have entered a new land where meaning and purpose are coming into view and will one day offer her direction. No miracles, only the patient program of peeling away layers of feeling states. But a commitment has been formed and in the end will sustain us.

Her captivity and that of the lost millions is different, however. In the dark moments of my private encounter with those who perished at Auschwitz, I envision myself standing at the side of those grey, emaciated faces who wait their turn to die in the crematoria. I feel myself standing with them on a cold wintry dawn and sense their dread. I must memorialize them, not in the vacant memorials reserved for ceremonious occasions, but more in a daily life that comes alive in my being at work with clients, at home with intimates.

I read my prose here and observe that its flow and style is uncharacteristically lyrical. Psychological writing carries its own unspoken instruction that the data advanced are empirically based, that the argument is reasoned and takes its authority from the data, that the case material be described in the bare-boned language of the clinician, and that even though reader and writer alike know that the matter under discussion is a human being in torment, the torment is concealed under a convention of styles in scientific writing that put aside all feelings.

Does a religiously-based faith compromise a therapist's work? For some, the mention of faith hints at the presence of rigid doctrinal views, a charge sufficiently grave to question one's competence. My faith does not constrict me with doctrinal orders in my daily life, nor was it necessary for me to suspend my beliefs during those long years of training to become a psychoanalyst. For those for whom a religiously-based faith stands in antithetical relationship with clinical theory and practice have elevated a bloodless secularism to triumph over the human concerns of understanding grounded in shared meanings. The drama of life probes deeper and fuller.

Simply stated, my faith is a belief that what pass as clinical problems are at core a search for meaning. That meaning gives purpose to life.

FAITH AS JOURNEY

Alison Cheek

I WAS BORN AND RAISED in a small rural village on the outskirts of the city of Adelaide in South Australia. It was very beautiful. Although suburbia grew around this fertile parcel of land, we lived in such a tight-knit, ordered community that it was very much a subculture with an ethos of its own. There were the landowners who grew fruit or vegetables; there were the workmen, and the tradesmen, the post office and the general store. That was it.

In the center of town there were two churches—a Roman Catholic church and a Methodist church. About once a month a priest came in for mass at the Catholic church and the Irish gathered for worship. The bulk of the people, however, attended the Methodist church. Here the minister also came in from the neighboring town.

My earliest memory of church is that everything was different there. It was a special place that radiated kindness and goodwill. My childish restlessness and my inquiring mind were tolerated with amusement by all but my parents, whose pride and self-image I sorely tried. But an even more powerful impression was the sense that in that building social caste fell away and everyone was on the same level in the presence of something greater than ourselves. Without any of the aesthetic surroundings, the visual symbolism or ceremony of the Catholic church, there was in that plain little Methodist church an unmistakable awareness of the numinous.

As a child I followed my father around, sharing his love for the land

---

Alison Cheek, M.Div. was among the first women to be ordained to the Episcopal Church. She has been trained in pastoral psychotherapy and has practiced in Washington, D.C. and Philadelphia, Pennsylvania.

—the land which he and his forebears had tamed and cultivated and planted with vines and fruit trees. I learned the cycle of the seasons and what must be done in each month of the year. Sunday was never a work day. On Sundays my father would frequently walk around the Garden, as the eighty-four acres of orchard and vineyard were called, casting an eagle eye over it all, savoring its beauty and making note of trouble spots where spraying needed to be done, or watering, or somebody's poor pruning needed to be corrected.

I learned to distinguish between a leaf bud and a fruit bud, to prune, to plough a straight furrow; I learned how to control the course of an irrigation channel, to pick and pack fruit without bruising it, to recognize green aphids; I learned not to spit chewed up licorice root on the ground because it rooted and propagated with runners; I learned some of the dynamics of the law of supply and demand in the wholesale market, and a myriad of other things little girls customarily were not taught. But overshadowing it all were the ceaseless forces of nature at work, benign and destructive, and my father in the middle of it all, sometimes able to direct and control and protect and sometimes helpless and railing. From that experience, I absorbed a sense of the smallness and frailty of human beings in the face of natural phenomena, and of the power and greatness of the human spirit. Above all, I drank in the deep and passionate love my father had for the land and for life. From him I received my tenacity, determination, sometime patience, rootedness in the land, and the irrepressible expectation that after winter comes the spring, after death comes resurrection—a deep love of life in all its moods and aspects.

At an early age, I began to branch out and to move freely between worlds. My father's parents lived in the homestead on our property in the Marion, but my maternal grandparents lived four miles away at the seashore. The world of this grandfather was another world entirely, and one into which I entered joyously from as early as I can remember. I loved my grandfather Whiting with more tenderness than anyone else in the world. I remember him as a white-haired, scholarly man with stooped shoulders. He was self-educated, with a keen intellect sharpened by his masses of books. He was interested in everything and forever discussing something with someone. By himself he was shy, but not with an adoring and responsive little granddaughter who soaked up everything he had to say like a sponge, seldom understanding a word of it.

It was Grandpa Whiting who introduced me to the myths and

legends of Greece and Rome, German folk tales, children's encyclopedias, and the world of books in general. As we walked along the seashore he would recite poetry, identify shells and sea life, pour out his heart and his knowledge. He was critical of much of his religious heritage but did sometimes preach at the Unitarian church. He died when I was in my early teens and has never ceased to be present to me. The faith that comes from growing up in the Marion is deep and primal, personal and experiential. The faith I inherited from my grandfather Whiting is expansive and all-embracing, a Renaissance faith.

While the majority of children in the Marion went to the public school in the neighboring district, a few of us went to a private school. The school was at Brighton where my grandparents lived, and we went there by train. In this world I learned to round my vowels, call England "home," and to absorb knowledge at my own pace. Beyond kindergarten there were no grades. When we finished the first grade primer we went to the next, and so it was with every subject. I left this school at ten, having read most of Shakespeare and the novels of Charles Dickens.

My next school was in a suburb of Adelaide, a Methodist girls' school that was as disciplined and structured as my beginning school had been loose and free-flowing. Somehow the boundaries eased my anxiety. I learned easily and flourished. Almost by osmosis I absorbed a broad understanding of a Christian tradition. Scripture was a required subject, usually taught by one of the professors from the nearby theological college, and each morning at Assembly we read aloud from the New Testament. But in my teen years I became a rebel. My world was too small and constricted, and not all the field hockey or tennis or swimming or horseback riding in the world could take care of my energy. I became acquainted with the city and looked forward to the time when I would go to the University of Adelaide.

About this time, close friends of my family built a house not far from ours. Auntie Doll and Uncle Bert were retired, although Bert worked the land around the house. They were gracious and unhurried. Bert introduced me to the world of classical music and I spent many hours there listening to music and exploring thoughts and ideas in leisurely conversation—in fact, just being. From Bert, too, I absorbed a sense of self-worth. He broke through role stereotypes in a way that was out of step with his environment. Gentle and courtly though he was, he had strong sentiments about the equality of the sexes and believed that girls should be given every opportunity offered to boys. He encouraged me to be who I am. Conditioned to feminine stereotypes that I anxiously tried to live up to, I hung back and dragged my feet at Uncle Bert's lesson.

It was my mother who decided that I should go to college. Nobody in our family had more than a high school education. It was her gift to me that she made me believe I could get my B.A. and pursue a career.

My college years were expansive, stimulating, enjoyable, lonely, boring, miserable, exciting, affirming, intimidating, gregarious, isolating, but, best of all, there were men there, a welcome change from my Methodist girls' school. In high school I had been introduced to economics. The subject became a symbol for me of a larger life in the outside world. It beckoned me, and I majored in economics and history. But most of my intellectual probing and endless hours of discussion took place outside of the curriculum in the field of theology. The Australian Student Christian Movement at that time attracted some of the liveliest minds in the university. It was thoroughly beyond me. But I wandered along on the outskirts of it all, intrigued, stretching my mind and greatly stimulated.

In my final year, I married my economics tutor and opted for domesticity. I thought my mother would be disappointed, but apparently a part of her dream that I have a career arose as a counterpoint to my being first a tomboy and then an intellectual. Her other wish for me, that I should get married and have a large family, was one she imagined coming later. Nevertheless, I always felt supported by my mother and am grateful to her for making legitimate the notion of an independent career in a cultural setting where marriage and a subordinate role were expected of women.

Bruce, my husband, won a scholarship to Harvard the year following our marriage. During our three years in Cambridge, I twice had the lovely, exciting, absorbing experience of becoming a mother, and we returned to Australia with two small sons. Now we lived in Canberra in a little house of our own. A third son was born and my life revolved around home, friends, neighbors, church, and community. Bruce was a research fellow in economics and I read Albert Schweitzer's theological works, struggling to get inside forms of thought and a world-view so alien to my own. I feel that I mentally vegetated during those years, until I remember the strange, disturbing, alluring, intellectual effort to read and understand Schweitzer.

It was in Canberra, in a beautiful old pioneer church, that I was confirmed in the Church of England. The bishop with his crook, resplendent in cope and mitre, sat before the altar in his bishop's chair as we came two by two to kneel before him for the laying on of hands. And there for the first time I knew in a tangible way that there is a Spirit, congruent with, yet greater than, the spirit of a man or woman. It was a strange, moving, unexpected experience which still stirs me deeply and brings tears when I recall it.

In 1957, Bruce accepted an appointment in Washington, D. C. and once again we said good-bye to Australia and embraced another culture. A year later our daughter was born; the family felt complete. I took great joy and delight in my children. Mothering was a very important part of my life. I blocked out most of my negative feelings.

When our daughter went to kindergarten, I entered the Virginia Theological Seminary on a part-time basis, one of the first women to be accepted as a candidate for the degree at that Episcopal seminary. I was a pioneer and regarded by many students with fear and suspicion. My seminary years were profoundly happy for me. They led me, however, to a conflict where I was required to choose in order to come of age.

My two years on a parish staff after graduation in 1969 were important ones. Deep bonds developed with members of the congregation. Without churchly orders, my identity was a confusion to them. At times of crisis my inability to function sacramentally was disappointing to many and frustrating to me. During this time I was training with the Washington Institute for Pastoral Psychotherapy. Here was my growing edge. Here I was fully challenged and completely responsible. I grew into a special ministry and left the parish.

In January 1972 I was ordained deacon and began to assist on the staff of St. Alban's in Annandale, Virginia. With joy I began again to function liturgically. I was a fish in water. Carefully I distracted myself from the painful awareness that my male classmates were already priests of two years' standing while my own call to priesthood had to await the good graces of men in power.

Sometimes I had to face reality. Consciousness once raised has a way of becoming ebullient and refuses to be lowered again. With the existential knowledge of oppression comes the pulsating and throbbing of pain and anger, pain and anger. I served on the Board of Examining Chaplains for the Diocese, and thoroughly enjoyed it though I knew each year that the moment would come when I would recommend those men for the priesthood, and inevitably would re-live the painful humiliation of categorical exclusion.

Once I accepted an invitation to the ordination of a man almost young enough to be my son. I liked him and wanted to be there—or so I thought. Before the procession began, the Ordinary made certain I understood that only presbyters, not deacons, come forward to lay on hands. I still feel the embarrassment, rage and grief that flooded through me as I stood alone in the pew, while my brothers went up into the Sanctuary to lay their hands upon the new priest.

It was not until I worked as a psychotherapist with women helping to unravel our oppressive conditioning and claim the whole of ourselves, that the full enormity of the way in which my church double binds women began to bear down on me. My conflict grew, my integrity eroded, as I stood up each Sunday as the official representative of an oppressive regime. I could not tell whether it was cowardice or my calling that held me in bondage. All I knew was that week succeeded week and I did not leave. I saw no hope in working politically for change. The writing was on the wall yet I could not uproot myself.

Some of my sisters, in the center of church life, did much better. They fought with spirit to claim the validity of their call and the fullness of their personhood and that of all women within our communion. Finally, three courageous bishops met their faith with an act of love and justice.

When those three bishops without jurisdiction in Philadelphia agreed to ordain women qualified and called to the priesthood, those of us who presented ourselves for ordination had to stand over against those in authority in our diocese. I expected to be deposed for my action, although I knew I would fight against that. Still, I had to be willing to take the full consequences of my action myself—alone. I had to define myself in terms other than the church had previously defined me. The authorities in my diocese had said that, although fully qualified with an acknowledged vocation, I must wait for an affirmative vote by the full church at the next Episcopal General Convention before I could be ordained a priest. I therefore had to refuse being defined by the church as an inferior whose sexuality needed to be voted upon by a gathering of church politicians, predominantly male, meeting in convention.

I had not always been capable of making such an autonomous decision. It was a moment when the gains of my own psychotherapy pilgrimage, my theological education, and my faith all came together. I am using the word "faith" here to refer to a life-stance, an attitude toward God and world and self. I had suffered the pain of conscience as understood in the Greek world of the first century and in the writings of the New Testament. In this usage, "conscience" has only a negative connotation. It is the pain that follows an action which transgresses the moral limits of one's nature, the pain suffered when we violate our integrity. In retrospect, by allowing myself to be open to this kind of pain I was able to challenge my tradition, to act autonomously, to risk separation and rejection, and to enter a new heritage with like-minded people.

How can one talk about the benediction of the Spirit? The phone rings. It's always ringing in our house. But this time it is one of my sister deacons to tell me about the ordination and to ask me if I want to be part of it. It staggers me. My heart says, yes, O yes; my body registers panic; my head begins to compute the risks. I take time to ponder all the implications. I find myself asking, "What is worth living for, what is worth dying for?" I rediscover my integrity. The gospel comes to life. The decision is made; peace and fear co-exist, strange bedfellows. The family is supportive. Those who care deeply for the church and for me try another route to ordination. It is blocked. On a hot, sticky day, with the support of my rector and the blessing of my congregation, I journey with my sons to Philadelphia, the city of brotherly love.

If at that time anyone had asked me why I was doing it, I would have said: "To be faithful to myself and my vocation, to affirm the dignity and full personhood of all women, and to name ourselves as appropriate persons to represent before God the people of God." That was the best I could do then to articulate it. It now feels much more complex.

I recall again and again the bishops who ordained us. Their inner strength and fortitude, their gentleness, their non-coercive, self-giving love has renewed my vision of what Christianity is and can be. I am talking of my encounter with these men, person-to-person. I had met none of them before. I'd had extensive telephone conversations with one of the bishops since the middle of July, had forwarded him my credentials, and now we all sat together to be examined by the men who were to ordain us, and to decide together if we were convinced that this path was God's will for each of us. It was an extraordinary meeting. We were such a diverse group of people discovering that we were bound together by one Spirit in allegiance to one Lord. My chief memory is of the peacefulness of it all, and of the harmony of the ebb and flow of conversation as each one probed the seriousness and the implications of what we were about. Each felt fully responsible for his or her decision and for the consequences of it. Past and present fused together as this disparate gathering shared together their understanding of the Christian pilgrimage and their love for the church, and experienced together unity in diversity, a oneness in Christ.

Later that evening the eleven women met together, explored their differences, and affirmed their respect for each other's integrity and individuality. Conformed by the Spirit, external uniformity was unnecessary, even undesirable, in the minds of the eleven. We experienced in microcosm the marvelous, joyous, creative diversity of the macrocosm of the Church, the Body of Christ. I also experienced the respect, the trust, and the love which does not seek to control, of my brothers who ordained me and of those who presented me for ordination. How then can I possibly doubt that God the Spirit is alive and well and active in the church? How can I help but be responsive and responsible?

On July 29, 1974, with pain and joy, with soberness and peace, and with a whole heart, I was ordained a priest in the Church.

In August, the Episcopal House of Bishops stated that in their opinion the necessary conditions for a valid ordination had not been present at Philadelphia. My own bishop subsequently ruled that in the Diocese of Virginia I was to be a deacon, not a priest. The eleven women, knowing ourselves to be priests, went about living out our vocations in our own ways. I did not function publicly as a priest until late that October when, along with two sister priests and supported by women from all denominations, I concelebrated Holy Communion at Riverside Church in New York City on Reformation Sunday in a service in celebration of women in ministry.

As I travelled to New York for the service, I experienced a primitive terror and panic, so that I could hardly move my limbs. I felt as if I were about to break some deep and ancient tabu and indeed I was. As soon as I arrived and met with the other women and began that service, I felt calm and happy. It felt natural and right and good to do what I was doing. But the prelude—the terror—showed me how fragile at that time was my new-found autonomy and how deep are the unconscious factors which deprive us of realizing our full potential.

Since that celebration have come years of turmoil and confrontation. They were heady, growing, exciting years, painful, joyful, embittering, enlightening years. They are still hard to write about. They include the experience of standing over against a seemingly immovable institution, participation in two public ecclesiastical trials, much publicity, many church services and speaking engagements, and all the while maintaining a private practice of psychotherapy. Many people helped to keep me sane and stable during that turbulent period. But, above all, I was aware, as at no other time in my life, of paying constant attention to being who I was, and of my determination not to be influenced by what other people wanted me to be. The events I was caught up in demanded that I respond to them, and yet I lived solidly out of my past even as I grew and changed. I know it was an important period in my faith journey, although I have yet to sort it out. I think that in the midst of it all Jesus became for me, not merely Lord, but Lord and brother. It was a time of continuous interchange with women without any church connections and women who were struggling to be both feminist and believers. The struggle continues.

In February, 1977, the Diocese of Virginia formally and publicly acknowledged me as a priest in good standing, in a service at St. Paul's in Charlottesville. Bruce had longed to see me recognized by the church, and I am glad that he had his wish. Two months later he died. He had always supported me generously, but I didn't realize the extent to which I lived out of his love and companionship and spirit until a heart attack claimed him unexpectedly and suddenly.

The walk through the pain and grief of the loss of Bruce has been a journey all in itself. At the time of his death many devoted friends helped our family to deal with the separation. We had the particular guidance and support of the Rev. William Wendt who was rector of St. Stephen and the Incarnation in Washington, D.C., where I had first officiated as a priest in an Episcopal church. In 1975 he was brought to ecclesiastical trial for inviting and allowing me to perform priestly duties over the godly admonition of his bishop. We had lived through a turbulent history together.

Now it was he who was there for us, enabling us to buy a plain pine coffin, telling us of a funeral director who would be sensitive to our needs. It was Bill who suggested that we might like to dress the body ourselves, and never will I forget the sight of my sons and daughter-in-law gently, awkwardly clothing their father's body, faces filled with grief and tenderness as they put on the favorite red turtleneck sweater, navy slacks, and beloved velvet slippers. We were bound together that day in a bond of love and sorrow that has weathered some later storms. It was Bill who gathered into one whole the friends who came to the church the night before the funeral and encouraged them to share their stories, their memories of incidents in their life with Bruce. We laughed and cried, were warmed and moved, and ended up singing "Waltzing Matilda." Our daughter, still recovering from surgery earlier in the day, was brought to the church by friends just as the others were leaving. Our young grandson, aged nine, was there through it all, and the next day was a torch bearer with his mother at the funeral service, and threw his shovelful of dirt into the grave. I hope that later on we will be able to talk together about what it all meant to him. I know it was helpful and healing for him to be very much a part of all the acts and feelings of the adults around him in his first brush with the death of a beloved person in his life.

It was Bill who suggested that I talk about Bruce at the funeral service. I didn't think I would be able to speak of him without tears, but, having warned the congregation that I might break down but would surely go on after a bit, I found that I could speak in my own voice. As I began to say the things that I wanted to say about Bruce to do him honor, for he was a very human person, I felt such a connection with the diverse collection of people present that it seemed as if they were extended family. As a last gift to Bruce I wanted to say the requiem eucharist. My rector stood at my side in case it became too difficult for me, but I had surmised rightly that in this moment I would be immersed in doing a familiar work. Three sister priests distributed communion with me; others cried out the traditional concluding verses of victory over death, and we sang "The Battle Hymn of the Republic," Bruce's favorite hymn. I read the committal at the graveside and then, as the dirt thumped onto the coffin, my rector took me in his arms and I sobbed. Others around the graveside embraced their neighbors and mourned with me. Bruce's death was a powerful event, a time when resurrection faith and the bitter grief of loss and separation were expressed as a whole, all of a piece.

Now I have had to learn to be on my own. Slowly, I have made changes in my life, letting go of some old secure ways, broadening my work commitments, and freeing myself to be open to the options of a future unknown but beckoning. Life is always unknown, but the illusion that it will go on as before has left me now.

Often I have been asked whether there was any conflict between being a priest and my work in psychotherapy. There has not been. Christianity has to do with wholeness. Even the impossible New Testament injunction, "Be ye perfect," is a translation from a Greek word meaning whole or complete. I see the discipline of psychotherapy as an endeavor to uncover, understand, and claim the whole of oneself in order to grow into full maturity.

Some years ago I began to work with a new patient. Anna was very quiet and often unable to speak, her essential self mute and held in bondage. Somehow, without many words, we made contact. I liked being with her but soon felt out of my depth. I sought the help of a supervisor with many more years of clinical experience than I, and, after the three of us had met together, he said to me, "With this person you'll have to go by faith." I was startled to hear a secular psychiatrist use such a phrase, and sobered by the implication that I had started on an uncharted journey.

I spent a long time with Anna. She and I brought to each other the fruit of our respective training and life experience, our fear and dread and not knowing, our persistence and our desire to overcome. Our growing respect and love for each other sustained the relationship. Anna slowly, slowly blossomed and grew and made some changes, and inevitably changed me too. I ponder the mystery of the faith which makes possible the therapeutic journey: it is faith-in-relation. I reflect on my part in that faith relationship, elements which arise from my own particular life. Often during our time together I drew on images of nature and have come to realize how intertwined is my faith with my rootedness in the land and the community of my early years.

Now I am inclined to think that every venture in psychotherapy, the healing of the soul, whatever else it may be, is indeed a journey into that faith which opens itself to the mystery of the individual psyche and to mutual relation. Many of my patients do not share my particular faith or world-view. That has never mattered, for I have discovered that when human spirit touches human spirit, the journey with another can begin.

BETWEEN FEAR AND JOY

Michael Eigen

THE SOURCES OF FAITH seem to embrace one. Something in my very fabric grows from and through faith, a kind of soil and air. I can reach into it with a breathtaking intimation of limitlessness. A cut-off point is also part of the experience, a vague boundary beyond which words, thoughts and usual sensations grow silent, a zone where a sense of limits and boundlessness seem to converge.

At times this underpinning is like the sea. It snaps into focus in the form of a moment suddenly heightened which, in some way, is crystal clear; no room for questions as long as it lasts. My first memory of such an epiphany is of seeing the starlit sky when I was a little over two. I was on the way to the hospital with appendicitis. My father carried me in his arms. I looked up and felt shock wave after wave and kept asking, "What is it? What is it?" "Stars," my father said. My heart burst with awe.

Something like this feeling occurred a few years later when I saw a beggar play his clarinet in the country. He laid his dusty hat on the ground, put together pieces of black wood covered with silver keys, and played so fully I tingled all over and laughed, wept, danced, sang. It was the star feeling again, in sound. I wanted to play like he did. It would be like making stars, a heaven in sound, all around, anytime. Yet earthy too: breath, wood, linked with timeless experience.

The same feeling occurred again most strongly in adolescence when I kissed my love, Laurel, goodnight for the first time. Stars

---

Michael Eigen, Ph.D. teaches and supervises psychotherapy at the New Hope Guild and at the Institute for Expressive Analysis. Dr. Eigen practices psychoanalysis in New York City.

shined all through me and I danced, sang, shouted all the way home —pure joy.

Such moments were highly sensory. There was no question of this being another world. It was this world that so lit up. At the same time it was my soul that so lit up. William Blake says it in *The Marriage of Heaven and Hell,* "If the doors of perception were cleansed everything would appear to man as it is, infinite."

However, another experiential thread did feel like another world. One way I most fully experienced it, as a little boy and in adolescence, was through reading. At certain times I was so completely immersed that coming back to everyday life was a bewildering let down. Unlike the boundless sensory moments involving starlight, music, or a kiss, stories and the images that came with them definitely belonged to a world within. Reading was a way to make contact with the sense of immersion itself. Such moments were comforting and quickening, a venturing into a mysterious elsewhere. The vast inside world, like the vast outside one, could be blissful or horrible. So often there was the problem of coordinating such seemingly radical, different aspects of Reality: each claimed to be more real than the other.

A dramatic instance of polar currents coming together for a time was meeting Socrates the same week I had my first sexual intercourse. Through Socrates, words like Truth and Goodness felt genuine. In my experience they were usually used hypocritically and manipulatively. Not so Socrates. Here was the thing itself. I experienced an instant conversion. The star-music-kiss feeling took the form of an unfolding direction: Know Thyself—experience and know with thy whole being. At the same time sexual feeling seemed endlessly wondrous.

The visual and sexual worlds that opened up could not be counted on to dovetail. Battle appeared. Each claimed primacy at the other's expense, often ripping each other mercilessly, almost all the time enriching one another secretly. Of course there were beautiful, harmonious moments, wherein primal joy permeated all claims. For me Vivaldi's "Four Seasons" most perfectly expressed this unifying joy.

I am not sure exactly when God became consciously linked with such powerful emotional currents. God early became associated with fear and terror as well as joy. Many prayers in childhood were tied to fears of injuring or being injured. However, there were prayers of joy too. I am forever grateful that teachers read psalms to begin the day in public school. How otherwise would they have become part of me, and how poorer my life without them! Hebrew school was a mixed blessing. I suspect the sound of the Hebrew language coupled with my musical training was decisive in evoking and strengthening a sense of the fullness that invisibly permeates everything. However, I never learned to understand Hebrew. It was something like speaking in tongues. The precision I knew was there remained out of reach. Only the Mystery was palpable.

Certain Biblical phrases were decisive, perhaps above all: "Thou shalt love the Lord thy God with all thy heart, with all thy soul, and with all thy mind." Among other things, this gave some form to my sense of intensity and indelibly inscribed the idea of living with one's whole being. This "commandment" acted like a time capsule. I can't imagine what would have become of me without it. Very gradually the painful self-consciousness I suffered turned more and more into a profound appreciation of the mysterious depths of awareness as such and the miracles that go on in experiencing.

During my last two years in college I began reading about dream interpretation. I have been a devoted student of dream life since. Dreams mirror our positive and negative feelings, in finite and infinite keys, in seemingly endless combinations. Dream distortions often heighten a state of being, to such a point that it becomes difficult to escape realization of its presence. They express our struggle for meaning along with the obstacles in our way. Through them each night an astonishing reading of our concerns becomes possible, mysterious perspectives on the pulse of our development. As pure experiences they help fill us out, adding resonances, echo after echo. Because they stand over-against-within us, they may quickly bring us face to face with core ambiguities which pervade our relationship to ourselves.

I am by no means advocating dream worship. Dreaming, like breathing, is part of everyday experiencing. However, it may become impoverished. A patient who also works with profound religious feeling and a strong interest in dream life recently commented that dreams offered her an opening to the Holy. It then suddenly struck her that she didn't have to dream or, more accurately, need any meaningful relationship to dreams. That is, many others with tragic backgrounds comparable to hers suffered dream impoverishment as a result of trauma: so many did not relate deeply to their dreams. Then thinking of the particular lifeline her dreams provided she appreciatively added, "It didn't have to be this way. I'm just grateful it was."

At the time I was graduated from college in 1957, there seemed little prospect of pursuing my interests academically. It took some time before my life and my awakening to the meaning of dreams caught up with one another. It was a good eight years after college before I felt able to begin formal training as a therapist. Throughout this period I was immersed in my own personal therapy which, among other things, dramatically brought home my concern with babyhood, and its startling link with faith.

The infantile psyche is now seen as important enough to warrant research and reflection in its own right. It is crucial in understanding the roots of human identity. Today, some sectors are as intent on decoding babyhood as they are the origins of the universe.

There are a growing number of models of what the early mind is like. Images of baby life proliferate. Indeed, a bridge between the secular and sacred is being made by means of visions of the baby's possible experience, a new, breathtaking frontier of the human imagination.

In therapy, many patients develop the knack of creating images of a baby self ever coming into being. One lives in an atmosphere of creative activity witnessing and aiding the incessant reconstitution of self and other. At least in imaginative vision we can experience ourselves as starting fresh, over and over. Such psychic work can lead to far-reaching alterations in the quality of experiencing and in one's sense of underlying wholeness.

In one instance, a woman reported feeling like a monkey and crab combined. She felt crouched and crowded, to the point of feeling suffocated. At some point both images seemed to be inscribed on a fetus in pain. A painful sound penetrated the fetus and it contracted. It could not get rid of this hurtful, attacking sound. The space it was in felt too small and the relentless sound made it even smaller. The sense of constriction was limitless. The patient began to make unearthly, high pitched shrieks, followed by tears of grief, pleasure and relief. "This is the right sound," she explained. "It ripped my insides so. At last I can give it a voice." In some sense the sound she made was an unborn scream, a premature scream perhaps, one she once hadn't the equipment to make. In therapy this mute but ripping sound within could begin to find a voice to express it.

In this case the baby she experienced seemed damaged, crippled, withdrawn, cramped. After linking a voice to the dumb sound within, the baby appeared fuller, richer, more at ease. My patient's actual appearance corresponded to her own sense of this baby self. She moved from looking pinched to warm aliveness. In empathic resonance I could feel my own baby soul move from a kind of frightened, apprehensive trembling to an open smile. The monkey now seemed to be a tricky baby, the crab a withdrawn, pinched, irritable one. Through them both emerged a baby with a fresh, radiant smile, the home base of the human self.

But, baby consciousness is not simply animal consciousness. The advent of a human smile in response to a face at two or three months of age signals a new dimension in the course of evolution. This radiantly expressive smile at the heart of human consciousness reflects an ineffable awareness of self and other. The sense of self and other spontaneously emerges with areas of distinction and union. The sense of self and other is the primary creative act of humankind and most basically evokes the experience of wholeness. The sense of wholeness is ever threatened by shifting imbalances and conflicts between the tendencies toward distinction and union. However, genuinely harmonious and unifying moments do occur throughout one's lifetime which function as reference points for faith. Our sense of self and other spans a variety of experiential worlds. Little children are interested in their sense of the Infinite.

Creating is always co-creating. Something, something else, and the relationship between them create one another in a seamless unity. We do not know how this is done, although it forms the possibility of our sense of self; an irreducible sense of mystery is a founding dimension of experiencing. Our relationship to Mystery, in part, represents the quality and meaning of our Faith.

Only by profound immersion in the faith dimension can one properly meet rage in psychotherapy. Rage is tied to the vicissitudes of faith. In an ultimate sense, rage bears witness to a sense of violation, rightly or wrongly. One feels things ought to be different, better. At basic levels faith, demand and expectation are inextricably mixed. Hurt feelings, fear, rage play a seemingly ubiquitous role in the problems of living. That rage may be reactive does not make it any less basic. Explosiveness seems to be a part of life and cannot be wished away. I do not believe that detachment nor a nurturing attitude can act as proper containers for someone involved in fury. Another sort of perceptiveness must be tapped and cultivated.

I believe that all-out rage, when properly met, culminates in a fresh sense of what self and other can feel like. The raging subject aims at the destruction of the object on which his own existence depends. He must be both frustrated and relieved if the object (the

Other) does not collapse or retaliate. In the moment of rage the self imagines the destruction of the other only to discover, if all goes well, that the other survives (and, of course, the self as well).

The other is realized to be beyond the limits of one's control. In an important respect one realizes one's total destructiveness to be a fantasy. Surviving that destruction opens the way to value and love.

One patient I worked with, Ann, seemed caught in trying to destroy God's love for her, a kind of testing of that love. She used herself as bait by placing herself in positions she regarded as sinful to the extreme. By falling as low as she dared, she tempted God to see if He would save her. Each time she would perform some new, self-obliterating act she would feel, "Now I've done it. This time I've really gone too far. Now I've really lost Him." Yet each time after the experience settled, however traumatic the aftermath, God would surface again. Each time she lost God and was found again, she wept and laughed with gratitude and lost Him again, over and over, until the reality struck home. God's recognition of her was outside her control. It persisted although she tried to distort herself beyond self-recognition.

In certain instances, while working with primitive feelings, patients' rage, often at my lapses or failings, are so intense that enormous perceptual shifts take place. At such moments some patients have seen my face as a penis or anus, spoiled, relentless. Such states can bear witness to more than a kernel of truth, inasmuch as therapists fail patients incessantly. Nevertheless, with persistence and care, a reversal tends to occur. My face then may be seen as ineffably glowing and whole. The "good face" resurfaces through the holocaust.

It is as if the patient said, "I see you but not just you. Rather, it's a more real, perfect version of you, a light that glows radiant and fluid. I can go in and through you yet feel more myself than ever. I can enter and pass through you without resistance and feel new and restored."

Something of this experience may often take a more mundane form. One patient who luxuriated in virtually unmitigated rage for over a year finally said, "I'm glad you held out. I always wanted to let go without having to make up for it. I mean, I didn't even know I always wanted or needed this until it happened. It felt so good to just let you have it without placating you." In this instance my patient was able to enjoy her rage without being bombarded by another's love demands. She felt grateful for being able to experience herself in this way. She attacked me for many things I was and wasn't. In some sense I emerged a very different sort of person than she could imagine, as someone who, one way or another, would allow and work with her rage. This both confirmed her and threw her off balance. Her fantasy that I was someone who ultimately would give up on her kept exploding, while simultaneously I bobbed up as someone in an important way beyond her control and real, if also unknown. In this case the love she felt for me would not have to be based on shutting herself out.

It is the fantasy world that is "continuously" destroyed at the same time that the real is "continuously" born. Both of these happenings are necessary for the real as such to be experienced. If there were no fantasy there would be no occasion for a fresh sense of the real breaking through, and the reverse holds as well. From this viewpoint, fantasy and the real require and feed each other. The object is being destroyed in fantasy and *as* fantasy and is felt as real because at the same time, its realness makes fantasy destructiveness possible. The realness of the object comes into being as a fantasy being destroyed at the same time it participates in an order beyond fantasy.

One patient summarized an aspect of this experience by saying, "You never are quite who I thought in some way. I rage at you for being one thing and you turn out to be another. I'm often right too. But the fact that we can sit and thrash it out turns it into something different. We both become more than what we hate about each other, something fresh, more real."

The "real" here is a total movement of the self-and-other, feeling past representational barriers, a floating freely in a joyous shock of difference. At this moment one is enlivened through the sense of difference. This may be somewhat akin to Job's wrath turning into joyous appreciation of God's mystery, a new-found trust, wherein anything outside of the faith experience at that moment must seem unreal. The real here is self and other feeling real to one another.

Adaptation is irrelevant to the kind of self-other awareness at stake in the moment of faith, where all that exists of importance is the fact that we are real together, living in the amazing sense of becoming more and more real, where destructiveness makes love real, and love makes destructiveness creative, and where mastery is unnecessary. The continuous recreation of the sense of the Other secures the possibility of growth.

Faith makes creative listening possible. It is an attitude as fundamental to science as to art or religion. Without faith one closes off the flow of experiencing. It takes faith to tolerate the buildup of experiences with their tensions, demands and ambiguities, including the discovery of the forms of expression most suitable for the emotional meanings at stake.

The psychotherapist has faith that emotional truth is possible, even necessary as a principle of wholesome growth. Strictly speaking, the emotional truth of a session is unknown and unknowable. However, we experience intimations and develop convictions about it. At any moment we may be wrong and this helps keep us humble. Nevertheless, the way we reach for the truth about ourselves affects the quality of our lives, in some sense *is* that quality. Our attitude toward the unknowable is a principal element in our mental health.

The attempt to contact the unknowable emotional reality of a session is facilitated by the inner discipline of memory, desire and understanding. The wish to remember, help, and comprehend can overly preoccupy the therapist and saturate his mental field so that the emotional reality of a session may be avoided or obscured. A certain "controlled openness" must be maintained in order for the emotional reality at hand to have its impact or be duly registered, and to enable interventions which mediate its evolution.

Attachment to usual sensual reality may obscure perception of psychic reality. Faith is needed in order to tolerate the suspension of one's more usual "realistic" orientation. Such an eschewing may be painful, uncanny or even dreadful at times, especially at the outset. One is continuously challenged to strengthen one's ability to experience and imaginatively perceive emotional reality in face of the awareness that certainty is beyond certain grasp. Faith in this enterprise paradoxically leads to the exercise and growth of the capacities needed to sustain it.

What is at stake here is not simply the knowledge about emotional reality that usual understanding and memory can supply. Such knowledge may at times prove useful insofar as it intersects with the emotional reality of the moment. However, what is most basically aimed at in psychotherapy is transformation in the realm of who we are rather than what we know. Through faith, we make contact with who we are and begin to become one with it. Within a context of the primacy of faith, knowledge can play its proper role in helping to generate patterns which grow out of, reflect and extend the emotional reality at hand. In such a venture, faith and knowledge cooperate, but faith is the explicit center and structural ground for the proper use of knowledge.

I am reminded of St. Augustine who begins many chapters of his *Confessions* seeking with all he is to know his God. Each time his discursive drive reaches its limits, he dwells in a profound, inexplicable love. Yet, at no point does he feel his need to know and his faith are contradictory. Quite the opposite. They feed each other. His need to know increases the intensity of his faith and his faith keeps his drive to know honest. William Blake conveys this differently in his vision of heaven as war between all the competing voices that make a person. In heaven none of the voices within the soul defeats or devalues another. All increase each other without compromising the integrity of any. The same is so when all goes well in therapy.

In therapy I do not have to know the answers or even wish to know them. Yet everything I learn may be put to good use. Knowledge provides a background which imagination draws on in accord with sensed requirements of a situation, possibly leading to further knowledge. However, without faith, knowledge corrupts or becomes a mere intellectual exercise or game. It may be a long time into a session or a case before one has any sense of what really is going on. In time one learns to wait in the darkness. The darkness may even come to be relied on as a friend (as well as enemy) from which unsuspected responses arise.

I am thinking now of some of my early work with schizophrenic children. In one instance, a little girl led me to the balcony which overlooked the school gym. She proceeded to play on the bars of the metal railing, even moving along outside them, with nothing between her and the gym below. Of course I should never have allowed this to happen. I was scared to death but could not refuse without feeling I was entering the kind of power play she was used to. At the same time I knew there must be a helpful way to stop her. On the other hand I was not convinced that I should do so, although it certainly would be practical. I realized the quandary I was falling into reflected the double binds that made up this girl's life.

At some point my awareness of what was happening physically began to fade. The next thing I knew I was seeing a light over the place where the little girl was, somewhere over her head. I became engrossed in this light, half sensing it was hallucinatory. I gave myself up to it and my fear vanished. I began to feel comfortable and renewed. At some point soon the girl took my hand and led me away from the balcony and we joined the others. For the moment she stopped torturing me.

I do not recommend such a course of action. It happened quite spontaneously and I am lucky it turned out well. However, I was tremendously impressed by the depths of interaction which are possible and began to get some inkling of what it means to open up to faith. Here the knowledge I gained was an awareness of entirely new possibilities of experience to be explored. Over the years this light has become a genuine source of inner communion.

These ideas contribute a certain unity to my life and clinical work. The psychospiritual dimension that holds everything together is faith, ever open to enrichment of being and meaning. The paradox of feeling whole thriving on divisions, a faith in travail, a differentiated faith is a state of affairs existing in mystery. It is in and through this mystery that we incessantly discover who we are and are not.

In this faith, criticism is essential in the same way that intellectual perception adds nuances to feeling. For me, in some sense, faith remains blind, even dumb. At the same time, it offers itself as an inexhaustible container for everything I can know or be. My drive to know quickens my sense of who I am, heightens the intensity of experiencing. It is faith which keeps knowledge aimed at the core, at the heart of being, and knowing which gives us our medium of access to faith or to anything at all. The more I know about how faith works, the more I appreciate its necessary elusiveness, its own way of seeing. I become less willing to compromise my (or anyone's) complexity. Complexity is movement, reaching out, fidelity to saving differences, the facts of resistance and permeability.

The breakthrough in our awareness of processes which characterize the infant self, I believe, will have dramatic consequences. The foundations of both sacred and secular experience swim together in infancy and, one way or another, remain intertwined throughout adult life. Faith and meaning are forces and we are the convergence of such forces. This is metaphor and more than metaphor. In human life, sacred and secular require each other, although they may enrich or mutilate one another. The vicissitudes of faith span both dimensions in the heat of therapeutic struggle. Without secular irony, faith would be naive, certainly the poorer.

To a degree I've emphasized the relationship between faith and knowing, inasmuch as faith and knowledge have been devalued in our times. I could also say the same about feeling. Faith lives in the tension between agony and joy. It has taken me a long time to begin to deal with the fact that faith thrives on being tested. Psychotherapy works at the limits, where pride and vulnerability converge. Throughout a lifetime one faces major disasters, loss of loved ones, threats to one's own health and sanity, the vast deserts and tundras of existence, the silent erosion of hopes, bitter loneliness. Even in a happy marriage one may have to learn to work with dry periods or areas of the self, when the other or oneself seems unreal, a big mistake. Joys become more valued, more resonant. Associative networks thicken. Coming through becomes a way of life. Faith is chastened, warmer, more alert.

A SPIRITUAL ODYSSEY

Laurence Sterne

I SOMETIMES THINK that my background is more varied than is usually found in a psychotherapist. Both my parents were converts from Judaism to Christianity. Yet, in an Old Testament tradition, at my birth they dedicated my life to healing and service in their new faith. My life has been a search to fulfill my parents' dedication, but within a context uniquely my own. In recent years I've moved towards an amalgam with roots in Jewish culture, Christian spirit, and Eastern thought.

From the age of two on I was schooled as a healer, and by my mid-twenties I had lectured and helped establish church and religious youth groups in many parts of North America, in Europe, and the Far East.

My odyssey in those years while working my way through college and after, included jobs on the swing shift in a factory, deckhand on tankers and freighters to Europe and the Far East, a stint in the Marines during the Korean War, a year of law school, a degree in economics, another in the teaching of English and English as a foreign language, and jobs as a newspaperman and magazine editor.

In my mid-thirties, while working on a degree in English and Comparative Literature, I became disillusioned with institutionalized religion; I left my church and went through a ten-year period of agnosticism and atheism.

Laurence Sterne, Ph.D. has come to the practice of psychoanalysis from an academic background in English Literature. He maintains a private practice in New York City.

Looking back now, I realize that in the late 1960s I attempted to fulfill my birth commitment of service and healing by way of university teaching. Unknown to myself, I was "healing" by simply listening to students when very few teachers or administrators seemed to be hearing anyone.

Actually, it was reading Carl Rogers on student-centered teaching, incorporating his ideas into my own teaching, and getting into encounter groups and humanistic psychotherapy that turned me around. I changed almost too rapidly. I had been one of the more structured department members and a kind of fair-haired boy in a conservative institute of technology. I had also been looked upon favorably at the institute because I had risen to Major in the Marine Corps Reserve, but now my clean-shaven appearance was replaced with long hair and wild beard. Because of my rapid changes, I soon lost my assistant professorship for what was then considered radical experimental teaching. In my therapeutic journeys since, I've learned how I contributed to that painful period.

Although I continued teaching part-time at various universities, I was beginning to realize that my forte, within a structured teaching situation or not, seemed to be in listening to others—really hearing what they were feeling. I was still antagonistic to anything that was tinged with the "spiritual," but unknowingly, I was moving steadily within my life purpose. I became a candidate at a psychoanalytic training institute which for years recognized the richness that a broad humanistic background can bring to the healing arts. Since the institute was comprised mainly of Jewish Freudians, I had to come to grips with my own Jewish origins.

Entering the mental health field by way of humanistic psychology, I was at first very resistant to the more subdued "traditional" psychoanalytic approach. Eventually I came to appreciate how a thoroughgoing understanding of the human psyche can help the analyst deepen his respect for the uniqueness and integrity of the individual. I think my feeling for the individual had been primed by my long association with literature and writing. It's my belief that from the beginning of civilization, the artist has expressed from the core of his being all of our basic emotions. Freud actually came along with his observations rather late and codified what the artist had been saying all along.

About five years ago my life took a twist which again seemed to bring me back to my original life purpose: service and healing. While on vacation, a copy of Ram Dass' *The Only Dance There Is* was given to me by a friend. Ram Dass, born a Jew (Richard Alpert) and trained in psychoanalysis, spoke in a vocabulary I could understand, including the idioms of the Judaic/Christian heritage from which I had become estranged. Ram Dass further awakened me to the enrichment of Eastern thought with which I had had a brief flirtation many years before as an undergraduate.

Within a short time after reading Ram Dass I was involved deeply in meditative and spiritual practices and, because of what seemed like conflicts between spiritual and psychological approaches to healing, I nearly turned my back on my psychoanalytic training and growing practice of psychotherapy. But, now I realize that the conscious and unconscious mind is still a most important medium for communicating with others in the sensory reality. And it's the emotional pain of that reality that appears to bring patients to therapy. They want to discover their own wholeness, a wholeness which allows them to fulfill their own life purpose, and also permits them to engage in a successful long-term relationship with a "significant other" whose wholeness they can accept.

Working through one's own, and the acceptance of another's, wholeness is an important laboratory for also accepting one's own spiritual integrity in relationship to a "supreme other." But it saddens me that among many in the spiritual community for whom I have come to feel great affection, some individuals want to avoid the important lessons to be learned in long-term relationships in the sensory reality. I feel, from the vantage point of my own marriage of almost twenty years, those individuals lose out on a rich human experience, as well as an important laboratory for relating spiritually.

Now that I'm at the latter end of a decade in private practice, I look back and see a gratifying by-product of the work many patients do for themselves with me if they choose to remain in treatment over a long enough period of time: they learn to sustain a successful long-term live-in relationship with a "significant other." Learning to negotiate such a relationship seems to take place with two different kinds of patients.

One kind of patient is already in a sustained relationship, such as a marriage of some years. But when the individual learns to look at the relationship honestly it appears that each of the partners has often been an unconscious co-conspirator in supporting the other's weaknesses and destructive patterns. When the patient sees those patterns, again and again, and then chooses to change them, what happens is that the patient and his partner gradually substitute more positive behavior patterns. Now, consciously and unconsciously, partners are in alliance to support each other's strengths and creativity.

Learning to negotiate a successful live-in relationship over a long term can take place with a patient who enters treatment never having had a sustained intimate relationship with a lover of the opposite or same sex. What I've observed is that such individuals first try out a capacity to remain in relationship with me, the therapist; after a while, outside the therapeutic hour, the patient may make a try or tries at a relationship. The first attempts are often as disastrous as before entering treatment. The patient has not yet experienced the all-important differentiation and individuation necessary for mature relationships. In time (not necessarily a short time), the patient moves on to new "trial" partners and relationships, which may range from one-night stands to weeks or months, with each new relationship resembling previous ones, but each possessing more and more potential for change and growth. Finally a mate is "selected" (although much of the selection process is unconscious from both partners) who has approximately the same potential for change and moves at about the same rate of change as the patient.

This is not to say that in any relationship one partner isn't for a time out of synchronization with the other nor that either partner is free from the never-ending alertness required for maintaining the relationship. But it is the awareness, alertness, and the willingness of each partner to work that represents the basic health of the relationship now being utilized for positive adjustments, for strength rather than weakness, for love rather than attack.

I bring together my Freudian training and my spiritual beliefs in treatment when I meet patients at the point of their experience of pain. That's the apparent focus of the treatment. Yet, because of my affirmative spiritual convictions, I've experienced a significant change in the way I think of the patient. With each patient I hold on to a view of reality that transcends the distortions and limitations of the human mind.

Even though I hold a transcendent view of reality, I rarely use a "religious" vocabulary. Such words antagonize the non-religious patient and give hiding places to the religious patient. I also try not to become trapped within psychoanalytic dogma or that of any other therapeutic system. To prevent such entrapment, I explore new dimensions of my own personal struggles; I also try going beyond the sensory reality and the consensus realities of our society. For example, I do not have to accept the "consensus reality" that I must be a victim of urban life's problems. From the various forms of meditations I've taught and used through the years, I've returned consistently to daily meditation in order to rejuvenate my sense of the spiritual reality of life.

Many people who will not seek professional help feel omnipotent about being able to solve their own problems. In the womb and very early in infancy, when all our needs are met "magically," it's appropriate for the infant to feel omnipotent. Later, the infant learns that physical and psychical survival depends on another, almost always—mother. If the mother's sensitivity to the infant's development is off, the infant can experience a new awareness of utter dependency on the breast/mother as humiliating after the earlier period of feeling absolutely omnipotent. Now the infant senses that mother can withdraw her physical or emotional presence, leaving the child feeling small and powerless. Again and again the infant strives, in vain, to regain the lost paradise, the state of feeling all-powerful like mother. The baby's humiliation (and rage) is very great. In order to cover over the humiliation, in the primitive unconscious of the infant, he or she "becomes" omnipotent like the mother as the child had experienced earlier.

Unfortunately, unconscious infantile omnipotence often remains quite alive well into adulthood and seriously interferes with relationships in love and work. Some members of the spiritual community of any religious persuasion, while convinced that they are working on their problems through spiritual means, may be using spiritual practices to avoid facing emotional problems often bolstered by unconscious infantile omnipotence. These can, in some cases, be masked as helplessness, or even hopelessness. Since it is painful to have those old hurts brought back to consciousness, the person hesitates to ask for help from within or outside of the spiritual community.

With a non-religious person there are sometimes fewer convenient defenses against this particular syndrome; it may be easier for the therapist to help such a patient name the omnipotence and make the choice to give it up. "But I don't want to go back to the past," say those who object to analytic psychotherapy, "I want to live in the present." My response is, "That's just the point. So long as our feelings from early life are alive in the unconscious, we cannot live in the present; we are forced to replay the scripts from the past."

It is the unconsciously covert, devious, infantile omnipotent ego state, puffing itself up as if it were God, that therapists try to "shrink." Even in systems declaring that mind and body are delusions, where the goal is at-one-ment and merging with the "All," almost always there is a place for individuality within the unity. The models from nature are clear: each molecule of water retains its own special entity within the ocean mass, each snowflake its own unique shape within the snowfall. Each of us is unique, but we are not God.

Often prospective patients are looking for a kind of magic from the therapist, instead of assuming responsibility for their own work—with the therapist providing a facilitative, safe enough healing environment. This environment parallels what a good mother provides so the toddler can take the first steps in physical, mental, and emotional safety; but the mother does not deprive the child of the right to walk separately, alone.

In spiritual means of healing as in psychotherapy, I believe a miracle happens when the person is prepared to receive the healing by uncovering the problem which often has been hidden from consciousness; then assumes responsibility for a more constructive mental pattern. At this point, the healing or "miracle" occurs because of the patient's good faith and receptivity.

The therapist really does not "do" anything and certainly does not "cure" the patient. The therapist only provides the safety for the patient to go through uncovering and making new choices which will lead to a fuller life. The miracle that takes place is the emergence of the "true Self," more of the whole Self that the person was created to be, had the original environment—family, school, friends—been sufficiently nurturing, caring and supportive. The therapist facilitates the process in two important ways: (1) the therapist nurtures the patient's unrealized wholeness; (2) the therapist's vision helps the patient to unlock healthy potentials from their imprisonment.

One of the spiritual tools to help free a patient from self-imprisonment is "visualization." For example if a patient has felt stuck in an occupation for years, and consistently begins to visualize functioning in a new one, within a reasonable amount of time that is what can come about. The kind of mate one would like to have, too, can come to one who clearly visualizes that person's characteristics. However, problems relating to work and relationships usually require ongoing professional help because negative visualizations are present as well, often deeply embedded in the unconscious.

Another spiritual tool I make available to patients involves "positive affirmations." Embedded in the unconscious are numerous negative affirmations and what we affirm is what we experience. For example, we may be affirming negatively, "I deserve to be poor," and when we replace the negative with a positive affirmation, "I deserve to be prosperous," we have a very different experience. Both the processes of visualization and affirmation, though seldom called by these names, are part of traditional psychoanalysis, which generally disdains anything that sounds like mysticism.

My meditative and spiritual practices attempt to go further than my long personal psychoanalysis and psychoanalytic institute training were able to take me. But all of it combined is the basis of my belief system and influences my practice. Also, group training experiences were important in testing my uniqueness, my own Self within the powerful emotional coherence of each group, each an emotional reproduction of my childhood family.

Just as the group experience was an important environment for my own personal growth, so, too, each individual patient becomes my environment for additional growing, evolving. In fact, every patient represents some part or parts of me and the patient cannot be cured until I, too, am ready to give up—"forgive"—those elements in myself no matter how hidden, split off, disassociated, or denied. For example, unless I feel comfortable with both the active and passive aspects of my own feminine and masculine self, a patient, whether male or female, heterosexual or homosexual, may never experience the therapeutic environment as safe enough to work through a comfortable sense of identity. Similarly, I must be in touch with my own dependency needs in order to work successfully with the addictive patient.

In the past year I've explored my own Self further: some months of work with a hypnotherapist and more recently with a sensitive psychiatrist, who combines bioenergetics, rebirthing, primal, and gestalt. But I believe there are realities beyond the self. To explore these realities, I meet regularly with other therapists and non-therapists who share similar convictions in the "transpersonal."

But the self can become unbalanced when it spends too much time in the head; in recent years I've balanced out my sedentary habits with a good deal of camping, with using my own hands to build a weekend mountain retreat, with bicycling to and from work, and with training for and running in various marathons. I search for ways to return to sensory reality better centered, better equipped for creative service and healing for myself and others.

In my own explorations as a psychoanalyst, my patients and I risk in order to grow and change. I try to go deeper into my core Self. It's that intuitive Self that communicates more to the patient than the words I speak or the brand of therapy I practice.

BE AT PEACE

Kenneth Wapnick

ELEVEN YEARS AGO, writing this piece would have been unthinkable. My marriage of five years had just broken up, with much unresolved bitterness and hurt. I was a psychologist with no faith in psychology. However, with no real faith in anything else, I had no choice except to continue in my profession. I was twenty-eight years old and had no idea where my life was going. Something was wrong, but I did not know what it was. If I had looked back over those twenty-eight years, however, I might have discerned a pattern that would have clarified my situation and the direction my life was about to take.

I grew up in a Jewish home in Brooklyn. Although my parents were not truly religious, there was a strong awareness of our Jewish identity. Not surprisingly, I was sent to a Yeshivah—a Hebrew parochial school—for my elementary education. I did not like it at all. I had many friends and did well in my English subjects, but resented learning Hebrew and did very poorly in it. My parents did not force me to remain, but by the time I realized how much I disliked it I was almost near the end. I completed the eight grades and then went to a public high school, wanting nothing more to do with the Jewish religion. Despite these negative feelings, the eight years had given me a solid foundation in all aspects of Judaism. We had studied the Torah—the first five books of the Old Testament—three times, and the remaining books at least once. I knew all aspects of Jewish reli-

---

Kenneth Wapnick, Ph.D. wrote his doctoral dissertation on St. Teresa of Avila as part of his graduate training at Adelphi University. He is a practicing clinical psychologist-psychotherapist in New York City.

gious and cultural life, and could even think in Hebrew, not to mention read, write and speak it fluently. It was not for many years, though, that I would feel good about this education.

While a junior in high school two developments occurred that shaped the course of my life. The first was discovering Freud. I had heard about psychoanalysis in school, and one day while in the psychology section of the library I picked up a book which gave a clear and succinct statement of basic psychoanalytic theory. Captivated by it, I quickly began to devour everything I could find on the subject. I read many of Freud's major works, as well as those of the neo-Freudians. How much of it I really understood I don't know, but I did know I wanted to become a psychologist. I never questioned this decision until I was midway through my doctoral studies.

The second development was on a different level. My mother decided to expose the family to classical music, and so she joined a classical record club. The introductory offer was the Toscanini recording of the nine Beethoven symphonies. It was love at first hearing for me, and it began a romance that was to continue for many years. Classical music, and especially Beethoven, opened up a world I never knew existed. It was not an outer world, but one within, beyond the normal range of my feelings and experiences. Over the years I felt myself increasingly drawn into this world, and music became the most important influence in my life. When I would hear the late music of Beethoven or the mature Mozart, I knew its depth was still beyond me, but it acted as a guide for an inner development I intuited but did not understand.

In my undergraduate years I became distinctly aware of this inner and outer dimension. On the one hand I was fascinated by the different psychological theories, understanding that each reflected some aspect of human behavior; on the other I knew that none of the theories could address my experience of listening to music. These theories, in fact, seemed to have nothing to do with it. In my senior year I attended a lecture by B.F. Skinner, the leading exponent of behaviorism and a man I greatly respected. Answering a question after his formal talk, he made the comment that if he were given an infant at birth, with total control over every aspect of that child's environment, he could make a Mozart. At that point in my life I did not believe in heaven, but did know Mozart's music was not of this world and that environmental or psychological manipulation could never produce Mozart's sublimity. Strangely enough, despite my clear awareness of the duality between these inner and outer dimensions, I felt no conflict between them. I was quite comfortable following these two paths simultaneously.

This pattern continued into my second year of graduate school, when for the first time I began to question what I was doing with my life. I was finding the study of psychology increasingly irrelevant to my real interest in music. However, I had no musical ability to speak of, and certainly was not interested in studying music from a theoretical point of view. Therefore, I finally resigned myself to finishing my studies, but was now painfully aware of the inner tension between these two worlds.

The first serious attempt to integrate the two came in my dissertation, which began as a study of the spiritual dimension of Beethoven's music. It did not take me long to realize that this subject would never pass a doctoral committee. As I proceeded, I also realized that I had no real investment in the actual subject of the dissertation. My concern was only that its central idea remain; namely, that psychology (this was in the 1960s) tended to ignore or distort this inner dimension of human experience. I ended up with a dissertation on the 16th Century mystic St. Teresa of Avila, a most providential choice. Especially interesting to me was my strong, positive identification with Teresa at a time when I was not only not a Christian, but did not believe in God! However, even though I did not believe in God, He certainly was around. Without God's help the dissertation could never have been completed and accepted.

The two years after receiving my Ph.D. in clinical psychology were difficult ones. I struggled unsuccessfully to integrate the inner and outer worlds into my personal and professional life. The completion of the dissertation had strengthened my faith in an inner world, but that placed a strain on my external functioning. I went along as best I could, but my fear was still unknown to me. I knew only that "something" inside me needed protection, and that this concern must come before anything else. Unfortunately, it did. Two years later, in the summer of 1970, my wife and I separated, and our one-year-old daughter remained with her. I moved to upstate New York and took a job in a state mental hospital.

Despite this upheaval, a marked change for the better began to occur in my life. A striking experience made it clear that this abstract inner world was far more personal than I had thought. I suddenly knew there was a God, and things began shifting into focus around this new Person in my life. I had never known such peace or happiness. There were difficult moments to be sure, but I learned how even these could easily pass when turned over to God. Moreover, this acceptance of God also brought with it an acceptance of Judaism. I felt God transcended the religious forms themselves, but for the first time I felt comfortable within them and grateful for the thorough Jewish education I had received.

Without any conscious awareness of what I was doing, since I was ignorant of such customs, my life became increasingly monastic in form. I lived within an ordered schedule, which would have seemed ascetic to an outsider but was pure joy for me. Nothing really mattered but God. Aside from my time at the hospital I lived practically as a hermit. By the close of my first year I felt that music, having led me to God, had taken me as far as it could. It was no longer needed to fill the place in my life that God alone now filled.

Circumstances took a turn for the worse, as I found my living schedule increasingly more difficult to maintain. Thinking I was spiritually lax, I applied myself more diligently, and for a time was able to continue my basic life style. After a serious case of influenza, however, I found it impossible to continue any form of spiritual activity or discipline. This state of internal disquiet remained for several months. Throughout it all, though, I never lost my faith in God. I knew that all I needed was to hold His hand and somehow He would get me through. I had read enough of the mystical literature to recognize I was going through a dark night of the soul, a spiritual crisis that often foreshadows a significant change in one's life. I had no idea what that meant.

Finally some light broke through my darkness. A series of steps led me to the books of Thomas Merton, a Trappist monk who, after a startling religious conversion, entered the Abbey of Gethsemani in Kentucky. Astonished to find that there were people actually living a life totally dedicated to God, I arranged to spend five days at this monastery. The fact that these monks were Christian never occurred to me as a problem. I knew they loved God as I did; everything else seemed unimportant.

Things began moving more rapidly now. Despite my lack of concern with Christianity, I thought it would be helpful to have some knowledge of the Catholic Church, especially since Merton had written so ecstatically about his own priesthood. Therefore, I attended early morning Mass regularly. Much to my surprise, I had the same feelings I once had when listening to Beethoven. I knew these experiences were of God, but who would have thought I would have them in a Catholic church?

I soon did something I had delayed for some time. I gave away all that I owned and took a furnished room on the hospital grounds, hoping that divesting myself of possessions would magically bring me peace. Although that was not to be, I felt good about it, and eagerly awaited my trip to the Trappist monastery.

When I arrived at the monastery I had the strangest feeling that I had come home, hardly something a Jewish boy from Brooklyn would expect to feel. I was so caught up in the monks' life that during the following morning's Mass, a special day of Mary, I decided that God wanted me to become a Catholic. Strongly associated with this was my desire to become a monk. I was not concerned by my lack of interest in either Jesus or the Church. All that mattered was my certainty that this was God's will. I talked with some monks and this strengthened my decision. On returning to the hospital I spoke to the Catholic chaplain, and soon thereafter was baptized a Catholic.

I now felt it was time to leave my job and spend some time alone. My plan was to wait the required year, and then enter the Abbey of Gethsemani as a monk. It all seemed so clear. However, I thought I should first go to Israel, for reasons that were not clear. Trusting what I felt was God's direction, I left and soon found myself in the heart of Jerusalem, unexpectedly feeling I was in the holiest place on earth. Though not yet fully identified as a Christian, I nonetheless felt something very special about the Christian holy places. Curiously, I also felt no less a Jew. Most important, I was at peace for the first time in months.

To my surprise, my next stop was the Trappist monastery of Latroun, outside of Jerusalem. Thinking to spend only a week, I spent three and a half months, a time that solidified my desire to become a monk and an opportunity to consolidate all that had happened in the preceding year. It took some catching up.

When I thought it time to go home for a brief visit before settling into this monastic mountaintop, I was returning to repair injured relationships, especially with my family, to see old friends and patients, and to look up a certain book on spiritual development that had been mentioned to me before I left. I accomplished these things, never imagining their ramifications. That period proved significant for three major reasons.

The first was a necessary correction to my own personal theory of spirituality. Until this time I believed that only by being alone could I find God. My way to God was through the monastic life, and the more solitary the better. From the moment I left Israel, however, everything turned upside down. From a quiet, isolated existence I found myself traveling a great deal, hardly ever alone. To my great surprise, for the first time in my life I found God to be as present when I was with people, living a "worldly" schedule, as I did when I was by myself. This was a revelation, and freed me from a dependency on the monastic regimen. I realized I could be at peace anywhere, as long as I was where God desired me.

Secondly, I was able to see the book on spiritual development, called *A Course in Miracles.* It was the very thing for which I had unknowingly searched, as it resolved a seemingly insoluble problem. While I was never happier than when I was in the monastery, there was a thought that had always gnawed at me. I knew that becoming a psychologist had been God's idea and not my own, and that it was only through His help that I had completed school. I knew, too, that I valued my work with people and found it rewarding. Remaining a monk, however, would have meant ignoring that part of my life. It did not seem right to me, but I also did not see how psychology could be reconciled with spirituality in any meaningful way. The Course provided the answer and so I once again changed my plans and decided to remain in the United States. The monastery would be a nice place to visit, but was no longer to be my home.

Finally came the most significant event of all. I had been a rather peculiar Christian. I found great nourishment and solace at the Christian holy places, participating in many of the religious practices and living the monastic rule which was decidedly Christian. Throughout it all, however, Jesus remained a non-entity for me. I consciously spent very little time, if any, thinking about him. Yet, during the past year or so, I had become increasingly aware of a more personal and direct presence in my life, guiding and comforting me, providing helpful answers to my specific questions. I always identified this presence with God and never thought too much about it, other than feeling grateful for its gentleness and love. To my great surprise, during a visit with my Trappist friends in Kentucky that summer, I realized for the first time that this presence had a name, Jesus.

That moment of realization was truly the happiest and most joyful of my life. I suddenly knew that Jesus was more than a symbol or historical figure who lived once and then no more. He was a real person, alive within me. I knew with a certainty that has never left, that not only was Jesus there, but that he would always be there. With that awareness, a chapter of thirty-one years came to a close. It had been a period of running away from Jesus, at the same time he was leading me to him. Now that we had at last met, we could begin our new life together and my preparation for the next stage in my journey to God.

That stage specifically involved *A Course in Miracles* (Tiburon, CA: Foundation for Inner Peace): learning what it said and, more importantly, seeking to implement its teachings on forgiveness in my personal and professional life. The Course is an inspired set of three books, written over a six-year period beginning in the mid-1960s. It consists of a Text, which sets forth the concepts on which the Course's thought system is based. These ideas provide the theoretical framework for the Workbook, a series of three hundred and sixty-five lessons which are the practical application of the Course's principles. The Manual for Teachers, written in question and answer form, addresses some of the more likely questions a student might ask. In addition, there is a companion pamphlet on "Psychotherapy," which rapidly became my therapeutic Bible.

In our age of psychology and renewed interest in spirituality, the Course provided a unique blend of both worlds. It integrates the insights of psychology with the timeless truths of spirituality, presented within a Christian framework. The Course's central theme is that the way to remember God is by undoing guilt through forgiving others and, therefore, ourselves. In the healing of our relationships, our relationship with God, seemingly ruptured by sin, can be healed. As I slowly resumed my professional life, I began to realize that psychotherapy afforded me countless opportunities to be healed of my sins, providing specific applications of the principles of forgiveness that the Course sets forth. My practice of psychotherapy, therefore, along with my understanding of its healing potential, is based on ideas from *A Course in Miracles.*

I had seen Sister Annette for about two months. She was fifty years old and had been in religious life almost thirty years. She was also one of the angriest people I had ever worked with, filled with a silent hatred toward those in authority. Over the first few sessions Sister Annette was able to begin questioning some of her attitudes toward her Order and her desire for revenge. She no longer seemed as committed to the retaliative steps she had contemplated. Or so I thought. Then one day Annette walked into the office with her face coldly exhibiting the wrath of God. Her convent coordinator had done something she judged as being beyond forgiveness. Sister Annette was hell bent on war, absolutely closed to any suggestions she do otherwise.

That same morning I had come down with a very bad cold and felt miserable. My prayers and meditation did not help, and I sat before Annette feeling utterly helpless and discouraged. I knew that if she left me as she had come in, she would be making an irrevocable mistake she would regret the rest of her life. Yet nothing I said could budge her, and my growing frustration only made my cold worse.

What added to my difficulty was the belief that Annette had been sent to me from God, and it was my responsibility to help her. I was obviously failing. Midway through the session, my desperation led me to remember that I was not the Therapist, and that I could not be more concerned for Annette than Jesus was. Even as I was talking and listening to her, in another part of my mind I began to pray for help, asking my Lord to provide the words that would heal her anger and fear, and restore to her awareness the love that was her true identity.

The response was immediate and I suddenly became available to the help that was there—for me. A warm surge of energy rose from my chest, through my lungs, nose and throat, and I could feel my cold being healed and my head clearing up. At the same time I began to speak. I don't recall what I said, and doubt if it was anything too different from what I had said previously. Only now I was different. I no longer saw Annette as separate from me, a patient in trouble whom I, as therapist, had to help. She now was my sister, and by joining with her I was joining with Jesus. I had become the patient as well, and together we received healing from the forgiving love of God. By the end of the session her softened face reflected the shift from anger and fear to forgiveness and love, as my well-being reflected the same shift in myself. I had learned my lesson that day.

Psychotherapy is essentially a process where two people, regardless of their religious persuasion (or lack of it), join in God's name. Though separate on one level—one to be healed, the other the expert who heals—in reality they come together to communicate the only healing message this world needs: Be at peace, for all your sins have been forgiven you.

Nothing happens accidentally in a world where God is present, and the two people sitting in a therapist's office have found each other in order that both may advance in their journey to God. Patients believe they have problems which condemn them, responsibility for which they usually project onto another. Therapists may believe they have special knowledge or ability differentiating them from their patients, whose problems they must somehow alleviate. But in truth, patient and therapist are the same. Each of us wanders in our world of guilt and fear until we can join with another, undoing the belief in separation and alienation that is the basis of all guilt. In the therapists' joining with their patients the office becomes a temple, where two persons come together to worship at the altar of forgiveness. In that joining are all dreams of separation and inequality dispelled, guilt replaced by forgiveness, and God invited back into our united hearts from which our own fear had banished Him.

Our guilt can never be undone in isolation. Coming face to face with the emptiness we believe is our true reality is overwhelming, as is the terror of confronting the wrathful God our guilt teaches will punish us for our sins. To escape from this awesome specter of oblivion or annihilation we must first repress the guilt and then project it onto others, choosing to see our wretchedness in them rather than in ourselves. By attacking our projected sins in another, separating the sin from ourselves, we hope magically to be free of the burden of this guilt.

This dynamic of projection has been graphically depicted in the Bible, where the Children of Israel are given a procedure for the Day of Atonement whereby their sins can be absolved. On that day the high priest would place a goat in the center of the camp and "lay his hands on its head and confess all the faults of the sons of Israel . . . and lay them to its charge. Having thus laid them on the goat's head, he shall send it out into the desert . . . and the goat will bear all their faults away with it and into a desert place" (Leviticus 16:21 ff.). Thus the sins of the people are transferred to the goat who is driven away, symbolically acting out the way we falsely seek to free ourselves from guilt.

But, the judgments we make on others are in reality the judgments we have first made against ourselves, and these projected attacks merely reinforce the guilt we have tried to escape. These mental manipulations bind us in a prison of guilt and fear. Yet there is a means whereby we can be released. Forgiveness offers us this key. Through forgiving others the sins we have projected onto them, we are in effect forgiving our own sins, for they are the same. Each of us shares this prison and the need for forgiveness, and each of us offers the other the opportunity to be freed with us.

I recognize in patients the answer to my unspoken prayer. My patient's "problem" is a disguised form (and sometimes not so disguised) of my own secret sins and hidden guilt. Those who appear at our door are those on whom the temptation to place our own form of unforgiveness will be strongest. In them we see our own sins, which we attack and judge against, made manifest. Our conscious recognition of this process is not necessary. All that God's plan requires is our willingness to join with others that we might see their symptoms as a screen hiding their spiritual reality from themselves. It is the same screen within ourselves. Our defenses are chosen for their capacity to cloak heaven's light in the darkness of our own particular hell.

Our function, for the salvation of both of us, is to look past the darkness of the patient's life to the light that is never extinguished. Seeing beyond the specific illusions of the ego the patient has adopted, we correspondingly see beyond our own, even as we minister to these illusions by whatever therapeutic model we follow. Through this process, which is an expression of forgiveness, our belief in our own darkness is undone and the light in us released. Our patients' acceptance of the light we offer reflects their forgiveness of us and of themselves, and joins us in the one light of God.

With Sister Annette my own self-attack was reflected in hers, and there it remained unforgiven while we remained separate. My prayer for help was really for forgiveness, asking to be joined with the One whose love unites us with Him. In that instant I was expressing my willingness to be free from darkness and walk in light. In that same instant I was healed, along with Annette. My faith in her restored my own, allowing Jesus to lead us both away from guilt that we might accept His love.

As psychotherapists, our great temptation is to play God, believing that the successful outcome depends on us. Only guilt can result from this form of arrogance, for we have usurped a function that is not our own. A patient's progress becomes a brief source of pride and self-glorification, while apparent failure signals our own as a therapist. Either way our guilt is reinforced and both patient and therapist remain enshrouded in darkness. Our real responsibility is not to our patient, for of ourselves we can do nothing. Our task is only to let the Spirit of God heal through us as we join in His name. We step back and let God lead the way, trusting that He knows that way better than we do. Perceiving God's truth instead of the illusory self of the ego makes this healing possible. Through this forgiveness, we find fear, guilt, attack and judgment are set aside and we merely love the image of God we see in another and in ourselves. Thus we learn we are loved by Him who is not of us but is in us, and we are all made one in this love. That, finally, is what psychotherapy is all about.

THY FAITH HATH MADE THEE WHOLE

Barbara Jo Brothers

I BELIEVE IN THE PROCESS between my patient and me. I begin with a strong belief that authentic expressions of who we are to one another will have healing effects. This authenticity will not come automatically nor easily, but in beginning that process we move toward growth. Adhering to a process of authentic and congruent communication creates a context for personal growth. Being real with myself, about what I'm feeling and thinking, and being real with my patient is a cornerstone in my system of values.

I stay out of the way of the unfolding, in order to identify and help dislodge barriers. I believe knowing "the truth" of each other makes freedom with each other. In the freedom, growth takes place. My patients are free to see from perspectives beyond those taught by family, free to love without being inhibited by fear, free to see a personal "truth" apart from what parents said was true about them. This freedom comes from nurturing the truth between us, becoming real and exchanging genuine feelings and opinions. The truth builds trust and trust is freeing . . . and trust is believing.

Trust is believing with some experience in the background, some basis for belief. Faith is the starting point, the belief before there's been time to gather the evidence. When I start with a new person, I begin by believing the therapeutic paradox works even while I'm not necessarily knowing how to make it work for me-as-patient. I may be involved in what seems like a hopeless maelstrom in my own

---

Barbara Jo Brothers, M.S.W., A.C.S.W. is Associate Editor of *Voices: The Art and Science of Psychotherapy.* She is a clinical social worker who has a private psychotherapy practice in New Orleans, Louisiana.

personal therapy. I may be experiencing no evidence from that switch in roles to suggest there exists the hope I see so clearly from the vantage point of me-as-therapist.

What do I do about those hopeless impasses when I am sitting in the chair of therapist? As therapist, I use a kind of faith in the system as a take-off point to get us out of impasses. I free my patient and myself by switching out of, "What do I do now with a hysteric, a schizophrenic, or an obsessive-compulsive?" "What technique should I use?" into the other part of my brain that whispers images and fragments of images. I stop "thinking," and, for guidance, focus on the emerging images. During one particular session, I had that "what do I do now" feeling, reached into that image-producing part of my brain and came out with: "I feel like somebody who just slammed a door on a small child's finger." To my surprise, my patient lights up with the glow of having been completely understood and we go on productively the rest of the session.

To find the connection point, I must be able to float for a while, trusting that an answer will emerge from me, trusting my own good will toward the patient, trusting the inner flow to which I can have access . . . like trusting water to hold me up if I relax in a swimming pool. My faith in the therapeutic process is new with each new patient. What we do together is a new creation; before it begins to unfold, I can only believe that it is possible for our particular history with each other to begin.

I see my own version of faith in the therapeutic process as an extension and extrapolation of my faith in the human process, ongoing life, and my faith in the Process of Love. I did not come to this version which is now my own easily. I never was one to accept outside authority, for solace or for guidance, without question. Often, I think I believe now only because of the love and trust reflected from a patient's face.

My religious background is not prepossessing, odious as it seemed to me from time to time. Also, I did manage to fashion it all into something that spelled Truth to me once I got enough years on me to give me some perspective. Ironically, it might easily sound no more radical or unusual than the Apostles' Creed now that I've got it hammered out.

I suppose what makes my traditional religious faith feel unorthodox to me is my own agnostic way of believing. I was a source of consternation to many a Southern Baptist Sunday School teacher in my early adolescence. The young therapist emerged as early as 13 when a certain Mrs. Smith told my class that God had told her in a dream that dancing was a sin. I inquired for the details of the dream and subsequently pointed out to the good matron that, by her own description, it had clearly been her own mother who "came to her in the dream" bearing that message and not God at all. Nor would I submit to baptism as I refused to confuse any real "calls" from the real God with simple small town social pressure. This was heretical behavior in a person of my age in the 1950s. Trying to explain that I simply had too much respect for God to behave in such a hypocritical manner seemed useless to me at the time. Instead, I allowed myself to be known as one of the "unsaved," though I remained a continual puzzle to the "faithful" by continuing to be found in their presence and by my singularly moral behavior. I'm glad I managed it. The integrity I cultivated by so doing has been much more useful to me than the comfort of fitting in with the crowd—not to mention the determination I had to develop to maintain that stance.

Once I sat on the outer edge of faith in life, with a patient in the half-dark, arguing on her behalf in the face of Death. She had called the night before; she felt like stabbing herself in the stomach. Flipping past everybody's theories in my mind's file on how to deal with suicidal patients, I decided on something simple and direct. "What have you got in your house that's sharp enough to do that?" "A kitchen knife and my sewing scissors." "That's all?" "Yeah, that's all." "You're sure?" "Yes, that's all." "Meet me at my office tomorrow afternoon at 5 and bring them both with you . . . and call me back if there is any problem with making it till then."

It turned out that the person from whom I sublet my office was using it at that time. Instead, we used a bare, lampless room with a large window and a carpeted floor. The fading daylight added an ethereal quality to an already between-worlds sort of ambience. We sat in silence for much of the session. At one point, she asked me what reason there was for her to live. I thought a while . . . it was not unusual for five minutes to go by between our responses, then said simply, "Because I want you to."

The silence had by no means been empty. I had vacillated in my head, "Should I just arrange for her to be hospitalized and get this over with? Am I not just being omnipotent? Why do I want to keep all therapeutic responsibility for what happens in this? I'm a social worker and we have excellent excuses to pass this kind of thing on to somebody else."

Besides the fact that she had been employed in most of the mental hospitals in town on a professional basis, I knew that hospitalization was unlikely to work well for her. Who, besides me, would be able to tolerate these stony silences without erupting into some fit of allegedly therapeutic activity? Much later she told me how grateful she'd been that I permitted those silences. They had represented some kind of refuge for her that I still don't fully understand.

Yet, her life may well depend on what I did that afternoon in the half-dark. Or was it what I did? No, it was more my being there with her in the struggle. Forget about my own anxiety about "what a good therapist would do in this situation." She sat there with the knife and scissors in a paper bag on her lap. She said, "Are you going to take them away from me?" "No," I said gently as possible. "You are going to give them to me." "But what if I want them to kill myself with?" "That's why you are going to give them to me, because we don't want you to do that." "Are you going to put me in the hospital?" "No."

As the session ended (or, rather, *forming* an end to the session, I had determined to be there all night if necessary until I could be clear that Life had won out over Death) she handed the paper bag to me, and said, "When can I have them back?" I said, "When we know it's safe for you to have them." "Suppose I need the scissors to sew something?" "Then you can come by and pick them up, then bring them back when you've finished with them." The reason she needed them turned out to be a Christmas present for me . . . a lovely white satin butterfly-shaped pillow.

A year later, a patient told me of persistently being "told" to drive her car off the road. This followed my having waited one night on the phone while she flushed down the toilet all substances with which she had considered overdosing.

This struggle, this suffering, this wearing down, couldn't go on. I had to figure out a way to stop it. And yet, so often, all I knew to do was to sit there, watch the process, wait for an opening, try not to fall asleep, try to stay alert. Part of God's creation might hang on what I, the lone witness, would do. Evil is whispering destruction in her ear while I, on the other side, repeat, "No, don't listen, that's not truth; *Life* is truth."

All too agonizingly often, I feel more full of doubt than faith. It's easy for me to measure and recite the dimensions of my catalogue of doubts. These I can easily find, remove from my inner shelves and examine at will. I find them tumbling through my consciousness of their own accord, clattering past whatever I had intended to accomplish, clouding my issues, blurring my visions.

My doubts are so crystal clear and familiar; they are so well established and grounded. I can enumerate and tell anybody the infinite reasons for their origin. They are not ephemeral. They are quite concrete. Clear sentences come streaming out of each one with little variation. Their predictability and reliability are beyond question. They also frame my faith.

I'm not going to launch into an isn't-it-wonderful discourse on duality with that thought. I don't think it's at all wonderful. I would much prefer to find the reassuring glow of faith without having first to go through an inner maze of elimination.

Still it happens like that. It's that kind of process. I journey endlessly into the night, wilderness all around, before sliding into a depot station I recognize and seeing the lights of home.

I have concluded that the appearance of my faith would be much rarer were I not involved in the profession of psychotherapy. It's not only that I know that therapy requires a belief in humanity, I do know that. However, with me, the process feeds back from the opposite direction: my patients provide me with the faith. This comes through much more profoundly than philosophical notions about "belief in humanity," however valid such beliefs might be. I don't mean my patients are all such deep and wise people that they are able to provide support for me in those areas. From time to time, those aspects in them do surface, but the source of my believing comes more indirectly.

For example, there was a period when I'd reached a thick, dark impasse in my own personal therapy. Nothing seemed to "work." I felt like I was going in ever-deadening circles. I even came down with a serious illness which I've not yet interpreted as to cause, effect, means-by-which, or simply process. I'm not even sure at what point I would place the illness in terms of chronology since there seems to be such a non-linear effect in operation as I see life these days. In about the third week of my convalescence, I began seriously to consider giving up the whole quest of therapy for myself at the moment. Still puzzling over the meaning of becoming ill suddenly when illness hadn't even been a frequent pattern until my therapy intensified, I decided it really might not be worth reaching "mental health" if I died in the process. Realize that this is profound doubt talking, but realize also that I had endured a pounding, unrelenting, violent headache for fifty-five or so hours at the onset of this viral meningitis. At two in the morning after a couple of days of that, a person will consider conceding a lot of things. At that particular point, my psychological condition started looking not so intolerable when I set it up against the rodeo going on inside my skull.

The week I'd recovered sufficiently to begin seeing patients on a limited basis, I got a phone call from a prospective new patient. She wasn't even referred by somebody who knew me. She got my name out of the Yellow Pages. By the third time I'd seen her, I was clear that I might as well be looking in a mirror. This person was presenting me with a picture of my own dynamics with unmistakable clarity. In startling detail. Her issues were my issues. Her defenses were my defenses. She even had some of my more redeeming features. There she was, showing up in my life as soon as I could get out of bed.

Of course, many things could be made of this set of circumstances, ranging from my name being close to the beginning of listings on out to the mystical ranges of possibilities about "Why me?" One thing, however, was immediately obvious to me, regardless of my prevailing degree of cynicism, agnosticism, etcetera: there was no way I could put a lid on my own issues and accept this patient for therapy at the same time. And if I wouldn't accept this young xerox of myself into treatment, what kind of patients was I going to accept? I'd have to change professions and get out of the whole business. Even if I stubbornly wanted to believe in randomness and coincidence and not admit she was sent by the Universe to my office, I still had to see that she provided me with the reason for going on with my own struggles to free myself of my early childhood bonds.

That sort of event is a major source of faith for me. The obvious thread connecting my own growth with that of other human beings forms ensuing patterns which are hard to deny. I still didn't see any way out of my own impasse, but I did stop thinking about giving it all up. In the middle of all my uncertainty about my own direction, I could see quite clearly what this patient needed and where it all started for her. While not even believing in the therapeutic process, I was presented with a phenomenon that, in effect, restored my faith. My response was by no means, "Hallelujah." It was closer to, "Oh, shit." But I got the point.

I don't like experiencing what I perceive as the flip side of faith. When I don't fight my inner flow, I know there are no flip sides. The doubt is just another aspect of life. The Universe goes on, whatever I might not be engaging in. In my better moments, I'm quite relieved I can't stop the world when I want to get off and even get into being reassured by the certainty the sun really will rise tomorrow, however heavy the cloud cover. The faith is defined by proceeding as if it were all true while not really knowing at all.

It is also remarkable to me that I often do my best work when I come into the session feeling the worst. No hope for my own life, no change in my own relationships, no trust in the therapy I'm receiving, no sustained feeling of communication and trust . . . a gray, somber world. My patient says, "I feel so guilty. My son was shot by the police. I know he was on a suicide mission because I had given him nothing emotionally for the past two years." I don't try to correct her; she's probably right about her connections. I just say, "Even if all that is true, is there no way to forgive yourself?" I'm offering hope and I don't even know where it's coming from. An hour ago, I didn't have any. I can only conclude that the hope was born somewhere in the process between this woman and me. By the time I said it, I noticed I was believing it for her. What happened between us had generated faith in me in the benefits of therapy. Eventually, that same faith will catch on with her. I believe that because I have seen it happen in my other patients. In fact, two others in the group spoke up to confirm that belief, telling the new group member how badly they had felt when they first came to the group.

A basic aspect of the essence of faith is to feel no hope at all and to proceed as if I did, the willingness to go on, to allow the generative powers to work, to begin before all the evidence is in. I have to open myself to the pain of the other person and be willing to let it roll around inside me, touching all my own tender spots which might recognize its particular nature.

Only a few days before, my own friend had been shot and killed. No matter that this woman's son could have, in theory, been my friend's killer since he was shot during an armed robbery attempt. The resonating feeling was that jagged pain I'd felt. How much greater might that kind of pain be if the loved person had been a son? To go back into that pain for a moment in order to meet this person in hers . . . it even might have been accounting in part for my own depression that day. Go back into it. Then, strangely, when I did, tender feelings for this grieving woman predominated. Yes, I believed she probably had placed the seed of self-destruction in the boy, but nobody grows from a point of self-loathing. There must be belief in one's own worth. Another flashback to my friend's death: who could make any sense out of that kind of event? Even the priest at the funeral mass had admitted that. The only reasonable answer seemed to be a shift of focus away from destruction and toward whatever might be life-giving and life-enhancing. All the tears, self-recriminations, and guilts, justified or not justified, in the world would not bring back that boy or my friend. All that can be done is to search around for what possible remnants of caring between people there might be lying around.

I hadn't been particularly interested in contemplating, "Is that all there is?" I wasn't feeling all that philosophical or spiritual that week in that particular juncture in my life. But Life didn't ask me whether I was ready or not to think about Life and Death. Suddenly, the question rang out, splintering my winter afternoon . . . receding footsteps leaving me with the horror and the sorrow and the question.

All that seemed reasonable to do was to turn away from the destruction.

When I left the group, I noticed I was feeling entirely different from when I arrived. Replacing my feeling of depression and deprivation was a feeling of well-being and a singular feeling of openness. I don't know how much that particular session did for that patient, but I certainly benefited.

> ". . . Daughter, be of good comfort. Thy faith hath made thee whole. Go in peace."
> ". . . Daughter, your faith has made you well; go in peace."
> "Daughter . . . It is your faith that has healed you—go in peace."
> ". . . My daughter, your faith has cured you. Go in peace."
>
> (Luke 8:48)

Further exercises in trusting my own intuitions born of my own life experiences have often come in the form of my mirror image mentioned earlier. She has a way of sitting in frozen silence for long periods of time, feeling anxious the whole time because she's not producing, not "doing what's expected." I don't find these silences impossible to deal with because I understand what is happening. However, I do know that I am dealing with a very young, sensitive, and frightened child who is interpreting and reading the very flickers of my eyebrows for signs of impatience or criticism. It is a sensitivity too refined to be accurately labeled paranoia; it is that kind of exquisite awareness that sensitive children who survive abusive parents develop. In order to follow what is going on in this patient, I cannot rely heavily on words. I have to let myself slip into that intuitive space where I observe my own process for clues about hers. Occasionally, I make a misstep, yet often don't know if I have made a genuine error or just uncovered a new way of relating to this delicate person.

I also keep forgetting how suggestible she is. One day after one of the long silences in which she said, "I just can't talk," I said, rather offhandedly, "We could play jacks." Several weeks later, she walks in with a Scrabble game! I think to myself, "Many therapists would call this resistance, but I think I'm going to put it in the category of play therapy and go with it." After all, she did enter her first institution at age 11.

What I really hadn't considered is what an excellent access that particular game would present for dialogue with her right lobe, bypassing the mine fields in the more direct paths.

The first word she spelled out was "women." (Her initial session she had talked about her decision to have a woman therapist, her rejecting mother.) Indeed, "women" had been the starting point. Just to keep an air of balance, I responded with "him." She reiterated with "her." I said to myself, "O.K.," and added "net," because I wanted to avoid "nut." We progressed on with me sticking with words like "new," "lit," and "dawn." At one point when she had spelled out "quota" and "steal," I rather clumsily said, "You think you have to steal your quota; that's too bad." She made an impatient noise and said I better watch what I said or she'd stop playing and spelled out "near." I said, "Oh, of course, I'm sorry; 'steal' goes with 'near.' " I spell out "run," feeling like I'm communicating by telegraph. She spells out "home" and says, a little sarcastically, "Is it 'run home' or 'home run'?" I replied I was sure either would do. She said, "I almost don't want to make this next word," and spelled out "rage," following "ooze" and followed by "cry."

I treat my messengers from the Universe with a special respect and a bit of reverence. I know this kid has lots of wisdom for me. For both our sakes, I treat her gently. Not wanting to tread on unseen flowers, wanting to weave a kind of safety net beneath her, wanting to put new pictures into her self-image and replace her old self-destructive tapes with new beginnings. I'd like to think she will eventually be able to "run home" to me with the "rage" and "crying" instead of the painful way it "oozes" now. If I can stay with her well enough so that she feels safe enough to "steal near," that may happen.

What she doesn't know is that we met that day on the spot my own mother left me . . . playing together. As I go back over that spot, I heal us both, picking up the dropped threads to weave them back together.

My faith feels more like a result of my choice of career than antecedent to the choice. I did have a framework of faith when I began the course toward becoming a therapist, but I have always been more of a searcher than someone convinced of holding the last word. I have never been able to accept the more simple solaces of religion any more than those offered in therapy to me as patient. It has always felt arduous and like an odyssey in which I do reach my intermittent harbors, but through many perils. I have always had to re-write all the Holy words, re-examine all the concepts, and, in the darkest hours, throw them all out and simply crouch and wait with a kind of remembering of faith more than actual feeling of faith. After a few years of what I begin to think of as solidness, I find myself again suddenly walking a knife edge of belief with doubt plunging down on both sides. Then I'm back looking at all the "answers" all over again.

I have always been a searcher. Even before it became fashionable, I was suggesting ecumenism in my Southern Baptist Sunday School classes as I was growing up. My intellect was offended by the notion that this relatively small body of "believers" could have a corner on the truth market. Fortunately or unfortunately, that attitude has characterized my faith. First I have to stay open to all available data, then I have had to try it out. If it works, I keep it. Through all my years winding my own way out of my own halls of depression, fashioning the heritage of my own particular family pathology into something that works, I have felt a continuing Sustaining Presence. Sometimes It's been like a faint cry across a sea, sometimes I've felt like I've had to hold my breath to hear, It has felt so barely audible. There have been panicked moments when I really couldn't locate It anywhere and have somehow been "rescued" either by my own desperate reaching out somewhere or by a well-timed call or intervention coming into me from some individual in the outer world.

I didn't really get into the business of therapy because of my faith (again, unless there's something that God knows and I don't). I do often think therapy keeps me in my faith.

I was drifting through the barrancas in Northern Mexico and landed on a ledge before a cave. A community of luminous beings were clustered there and I felt a rush of peace and joy. They were glowing with a white light. I looked down at myself and saw large gray un-lit patches in myself. I glowed unevenly, unlike them. I said, with profound sadness, "I guess I can't stay; I'm not glowing like the rest of you." One of the beings stepped (or glided) forward . . . they were neither male nor female, but this one seemed to have a feminine air about her. She said, "Oh, don't worry about that; you will pick up the glow from us." After she said that, I had a rush of peace that felt as if I would never have to worry seriously about anything throughout all eternity.

When I woke up, I recognized a revelation which sounds obvious, but which had a freshness about it that felt like a certified Message from the Universe. Isolation and my old familiar paranoia is not really the truth. There is a fellowship of some kind out there in the world which holds the design for wholeness and completeness. God knows, I don't mean a church even in the Universal Church sense. This, of which I caught a glimpse, was Limitless in scope. The direction was: don't be afraid to love; it's the way to fill in what seems to be missing.

FROM DARKNESS, LIGHT

William Crosby

IT MAKES A DIFFERENCE whether we live in the light or in the darkness. Psychotherapy is the journey through the darkness and into the light. Faith is that deep affirmation from the core of our being by which we perceive that light and live in harmony with it or adjust to the darkness. The light is basically love, and the darkness is basically fear. Although psychotherapy is a gradual process of growth, in the unfolding of that fear, love and fear are mutually exclusive. Love casts out fear.

This testament conveys my understanding of psychotherapy as it relates to faith; it expresses my own journey out of the darkness. As I wrote, I observed my own eclecticism. The ideas represent a collage of what I have been and what I have done, channelled into who I am and what I am doing today. In this particular stew can be found my years (hopefully waning) of lovelessness, as well as the more recent years (hopefully waxing), in which I am discovering the various realities of love. New understandings emerge as the light of love illuminates itself, as the darkness becomes apparent. What I have always known as metaphor, I begin to know in experience.

First, there was my childhood Protestant upbringing, a puritanism as much responsible for my darkness as the confusion and fear in my family. Then, the gentler Episcopal Church which superficially rescued me from a God of wrath and pain. There is my sense of priesthood which began when I was a child, that I briefly lived out ec-

---

William Crosby, Ph.D. was ordained to the Episcopal priesthood before receiving his training in psychology. Dr. Crosby has practices both in New York City and in Woodstock, New York.

clesiastically and that I now enjoy in the psychotherapeutic cure of souls. And there is my Franciscan sense which also began in childhood and which keeps reasserting itself in various forms in my life, in my new spirituality and in my work.

Also included in the stew are my many years of healing and growth as psychotherapy patient, succeeded by a few years as a spiritual seeker. During my short priestly stint, I recited nearly every day a portion of the Gospel which says that "the light shines in the darkness but the darkness does not comprehend it." My therapists were extraordinarily loving people who worked with me very skillfully so that I could begin to open my heart and to unfold my life. Only toward the end of my therapy did I begin to comprehend this as I started to relate to others more lovingly. A new dimension of life began to open. During the past few years, my spiritual pursuits have begun to show me the inner wasteland of my lack of self-love and to begin a deeper transformation. An inner light intensifies slowly and creates a new kind of universe for me to live in. I now understand why the story of the exodus of the Jews from Egypt is so important. I have gone from the slavery of my own personal bondage, through years of wandering in the desert of my own barrenness and only recently have sighted the promised land of my lovingness with all the milk and honey that it implies.

The process of illumination in the light of love continues slowly. At times it seems illusory as the old darkness returns for long periods, or else there is a twilight time. It is nurtured by those few whom I have allowed to be lovingly close to me, helping me to extend that love. I begin to yearn for networks of communal love. In spirituality, I find that a more impersonal love (Unconditional Love, or Divine Love, or the Force, or Shakti) is just beginning to shine into hidden recesses of my personality, slowly transforming a part of me from demanding and condemning judgment to constructive and supportive evaluation. I begin to know the heart as the point of balance, the place of integration between the mind and the body, the masculine and the feminine, the flesh and the spirit, heaven and earth.

After I finished seminary and before I was ordained, I revolted and was alienated from religion and the priesthood. My own pathology had been reinforced by the pathology in the Church, and I then began a process of redefining my beliefs and the Church's beliefs so that they were consistent with what my life (my therapy was a major part of my life) was teaching me. But when I began work as a psychotherapist, my work as a priest suffered in comparison so that I dropped it completely. I knew a lot about piety but nothing about spirituality in those days. Psychotherapy was vital and alive, and it seemed to suit me to be engaged in it. The Church seemed to be stuck in a rut that no longer interested me.

Like many therapists of our time, I have been watching the emergence of a new spirituality within myself and within our society with suspicion at first, and then with a kind of amazement. I had little hints over a period of time, usually in some altered state of consciousness, that another dimension was beginning to emerge in me. Shortly after I began to take this seriously, I learned about Swami Muktananda, and for over two years was his enthusiastic follower. As I learned about Hinduism through his kind of yoga, I learned something more about Christianity and something more about psychotherapy. Most important, I began to learn to love myself. Perhaps it was the beginning of self-love that made me separate myself from him, as I kept reacting to aspects of his path that reminded me of my Protestant origins. Since then I have benefited from a variety of teachers and guides who have led me to grow and unfold and evolve.

A two-week conference with Brugh Joy was one of the most powerful and effective spiritual experiences that I have ever had. Besides a wealth of teaching and very profound personal guidance, the conference was designed to help us open the heart center, to experience the flow of "Unconditional Love" and to channel that "energy" as we work healingly with others. Somehow he was able to get around my formidable defenses and to begin a subtle process of change which is still continuing and which I still don't really understand. For months later I had a sense of radiance from my heart and the palms of my hands. At times I was able to see physically that "energy" extending like rays from the tips of my fingers.

I don't know where it is leading me. I have a fantasy that my work will one day achieve new dimensions and new power through spirituality, so that I can give as effectively as I have been receiving. My eclecticism seems to reflect my Episcopalianism. The Episcopal Church prides itself on its ability to include and to integrate (not always comfortably) Catholicism, Protestantism, and indeed many religious points of view, under one ecclesiastical roof. Likewise, I sense within myself the beginning of some integration of all that I have been and all that I have learned.

Faith is not the same as belief, and it is not the same as religion. Belief is more mental, the assent to a set of ideas, but faith is a total human response to an experience of life itself. Belief is more typically conscious, whereas faith can be totally unconscious. Beliefs are, at best, a projection of our past experience onto the unknown, whereas faith is an attitude which either opens or closes us to the experience of the unknown. For example, a person can believe in purgatory, heaven and hell because of knowing the kind of purificatory psycho-spiritual growing pains that have been preparation for a fuller and more joyously loving life, and because of experiencing that other kind of pain, the empty pain of lovelessness and isolation. A person also can believe in reincarnation by looking back toward childhood at what seems to be a succession of lifetimes punctuated by distinct periods of death and rebirth. Both of these phenomena become beliefs possible to affirm and project beyond this lifetime. Beliefs, as mental phenomena of both patient and therapist, are grist for the therapeutic mill.

Religion, on the other hand, is that system which is meant to reveal the light, a kind of incarnation of that light and love in the world, revealing to us our linkage, our at-oneness with the light. The light equals love equals God. But in practice, religion is too often opaque and irrelevant, or a distortion which can cause or reinforce fear. It can be an unwitting servant of darkness. For this reason, the new spirituality of our age is emerging outside the institutions of religion. Faith is essential to psychotherapy, the progression from faith to faith.

Religion can be a friend or a foe of that process. If religion were truly effective in making real to us our at-oneness with the source of all wholeness and health, healing and vital renewal of life would be part of our ordinary religious experience. Today, religion seems impotent, or a force that creates and compounds the problems. Yet, its function is the same as that of psychotherapy but on a higher level (the cure of souls, personal transformation and rebirth). It could render psychotherapy irrelevant and unnecessary if it were doing its proper job. The very existence of psychotherapy reveals the inadequacy of religion in our culture. Perhaps psychotherapy is also preliminary to a renaissance of true spirituality which, in turn, may deepen and hasten the process of therapy.

There are manifestations of darkness, just as there are manifestations of the light. When a person is deprived of love and resides in fear, it manifests itself in behavior patterns that we call symptoms. This is certainly most clear in neurosis which is based on anxiety, a form of fear. Usually the darkness relates to the rest of the personality with a loveless judgment and often sadistic punitiveness that perpetuates the fear, resulting in contraction and inhibition. As a result, the self-concept is diminished and negatively distorted, and the drives and emotions are not permitted the freedom to find their natural harmony in the personality. Perhaps all "mental illnesses" are forms of fear, as fear is the hallmark of a certain kind of faith. Thus, in psychopathology, there is an inner universe for each person which has a transcendent aspect, usually quite unconscious, which, to some degree, causes fear and which inhibits the development and flowering of the personality. In turn, this is projected, also quite unconsciously, onto the universe so that "God" or whatever we call the Ultimate, is a God of wrath rather than a God of love, and human existence becomes contracted in shame or fear of transgression or imperfection.

Traditional religious beliefs may teach us that God and our world and ourselves are loving and harmonious, but religious institutions rarely lead someone to experience a deep faith that is consonant with those beliefs. The inner universe has its origins in our early experiences of our parents as infants and young children and the childhood universe of our families. We absorb and perpetuate within our own personalities, not only our own experience but the deep patterns of faith within our parents and our families as well as those of our culture.

Love and fear, darkness and light, psychopathology and normal human functioning are each exclusive of the other. Carl Jung has pointed out that all of us, no matter how well adjusted and harmonious, have a "shadow" within the unconscious, a personal and collective condensation of negativities which may emerge under stress or crisis. Conversely, no matter how deep or pervasive the psychopathology, there is love and light somewhere to be brought forward and to be allowed to expand and permeate the personality. Despite our distortions, there is a balanced spiritual ecology in our personalities as they emanate from the Source. It is by faith that the particular relation exists as it does in each person.

By a change in that faith, the relation can be reversed. Perhaps that is the mechanism by which love casts out fear. We are who we are, and life is what life is. By faith it can be the hell of lovelessness and all the fear-related negativities which the darkness spawns. But by a positive faith, our same selves and that same life can have the qualities of heaven.

The task of psychotherapists can be understood from a number of different levels. We can work at the level of the symptom, as in behavior therapy. We can work at the level of the personality dynamics, the pattern of positive and negative emotions and drives that produce the symptom, as in psychoanalysis. We can work in relation to the bodily or energetic patterns which these inner dynamics manifest.

Any effective way of working psychotherapeutically, since the human being is an organic whole, will cause changes on all the different levels. Thus, any therapy can produce changes in the faith of the patient. Perhaps the working-through process, which is so much of our work, is really that gradual transformation of faith as psychotherapeutic experiences gradually reveal the love—perhaps first in the unconditional acceptance of the therapist, then in the process of therapy as affirming and enhancing life, then in relationships as the old patterns dominated by fear recede, then here and there in the world. Finally, the patient can be free to let go, be vulnerable and trust in a universe that emanates from love and a sense of self permeated by love. Fear, anger, cruelty, guilt and all that a negative faith produces become energy transmuted in accordance with the affirmation, self-actualization and confidence that emanate from love.

When understood from this point of view, psychotherapy and spirituality are related, but they are not the same. Spirituality is the tendency of the personality to extend itself into experiencing the Source or Essence from which it emanates. Psychotherapy works for growth within our human personalities. A spiritual path takes us from the level of personality to an identity that transcends personality. But the two overlap, since spiritual growth can involve a healing and an integration of personality: body, mind and emotions. And psychotherapy, by that progression of faith from fear to love, can bring us toward what is spirit. Nevertheless, the focus and purpose of each is quite separate.

I find the Hindu notion of Maya useful in understanding the distinction. Maya means illusion. Illusion is part of our human condition. In India, Maya is personified as a goddess because it is not "bad," but a part of the structure of our existence. It is caused by God the Concealer who, for his own purposes, creates human life so that we do not know our true identity as beings who are one with God. In that same Hindu system, God is also the giver of Grace by which our identity is discovered as the veil of illusion is drawn away and we know and experience that oneness with all that is.

In psychotherapy, the path is towards the self. Spiritual paths take us from the self of personality to the transcendent Self. For all of us, the veil of illusion covers the self in some of its aspects, the illusion of being inadequate and the goal is the discovery of our real human identity, our wholeness and health. The casualty of darkness is self-esteem. The aspect which produces the casualty is almost always the superego which therapy must transform into an agent of love and grace, rather than the perpetuator of the illusion. Thus, psychotherapy might be considered a preliminary or first stage in spiritual growth by which we are released from the negative impact of superego so that the personality can expand and find the natural balance and harmony in all of its aspects. Only with this kind of psychological health is spirituality truly grounded.

Spirituality, then, for those who so choose, continues the expansion into the light in a similar way. The Maya of illusion is that the self of personality, no matter how well integrated and soundly functioning, is our whole identity. The goal is the experience of ourselves as the Self, integrated and at one with the Absolute, and with all that is, since everything is at one with the Absolute. The self-esteem that psychotherapy works so hard to strengthen is an aspect of the limiting definitions that we impose on our sense of identity that keep us from experiencing ourselves as we truly are, from knowing that Self which is at one with the Absolute. The Self is the Absolute. By psychotherapy we proceed from darkness to light. By spirituality we experience that we are, indeed, that light. By psychotherapy we transform our faith from negative to positive and in so doing begin a transformation of our personalities. By spirituality that transformation is deepened, perhaps infinitely, as we journey beyond the personality into the infinite, beyond the merely positive into the light.

The role of the psychotherapist can also be understood on a number of levels. If the focus is on the symptoms, then the therapist is a kind of technician. If the focus is on the dynamics, then the therapist works with his own personality by withholding or expressing it in the relationship. At the level of body and energy, the therapist is a catalyst for unblocking and transmutation. At the level of faith, the therapist is a companion and guide facilitating the journey from fear to love, from an inner world (and, by projection, an outer world) that, to some degree, is in shadow and darkness into a world characterized by light.

To understand one's work to be part of this transformational process of faith means the "transpersonal" therapist is a technician who works within the context of the therapeutic relationship, but is like a navigator leading a ship away from the shores of fear, across the uncertain waters of change with all of its resistances and seeming perils, to that other way of being. Insofar as the therapist has made the journey already, both shores as well as the way are known. This level of therapeutic work is in paradoxical contrast with the others in that it involves not a filling up with techniques and learning, but an emptying of the therapist in order to be a channel through which the unconditional love, the real facilitator of the journey, is expressed.

The therapist-guide who works within the dimension of faith is guru, priest and shaman at the level of personality. In Hinduism, the guru has a trinitarian relationship to the devotee and to the Ultimate. Everyone is an incarnation of the Self or the Ultimate, but the guru knows that he is and lives his life accordingly. If the guru's mission is to manifest, reveal and effectuate that incarnation, then he is a Christ figure. The devotee's sense of the Self is very much like that of the indwelling Spirit. Deep within the self lies the Self, and at the level of the Self, guru and devotee are not two but one. The Transcendent God has an aspect of guru (Satchitananda), and at the level of the Self, God, guru and devotee are not three but one. The word Guru is made up of the two Sanskrit words Gu (darkness) and Ru (light), and it is his function to guide the devotee out of darkness and into the light.

At the level of personality, the therapist has the same characteristics and the same function. The therapist, often despite unresolved personal problems, manifests love, understanding, acceptance, forgiveness, as well as wise and firm authority. These same qualities ("Good Parent," "Loving Superego") lie deep within the patient, beneath the pathology. By consciously or unconsciously identifying with this aspect of the therapist, therapist and patient become at one in that love and it is reinforced and nurtured in their relationship. If that loving relationship does not reflect the harmony of life itself, then we are leading our patients, Pollyanna-like, down the garden path. Our experience tells us that there is, indeed, such a harmony in life at one with harmony within the microcosm of personality. As the therapist guides the patient into light, it is accomplished by that trinitarian oneness of love within therapist, within patient, and within the transcendence of life.

A guru, by definition, is a "perfected master," a being who has already gotten there. A priest makes no such claims. He does his best, but his mission is to be a channel of grace. A priest is selected and ordained by a community (in the case of Christianity, the Church) to be its representative person (parson). His vocation is to be one through whom the power of God can flow in certain situations (in Christianity, notably the sacraments), despite his shortcomings. Therapists have the same function in our society as it seeks a kind of psychological redemption. The old distinction of grace and works applies here. Psychotherapy has a kind of sacramental function. The therapist as priest, in his stance of unconditional positive regard, becomes a conduit of grace, of that more impersonal love flowing through the personal relationship. The patient needs the "ying" characteristics of openness, receptivity and the allowing of change as well as the "yang" qualities of effort and action. Insofar as the therapist functions as priest and therapy as sacrament, the work of therapy in the sessions is the outward and visible sign which makes possible the inner grace of light and love communicated and transmitted in relationship.

The shaman seeks power to help and to heal. Whereas the guru's work springs from within and the priest's from the community, the shaman knows the Ultimate through nature, worshipping the earth as mother and the sky as father. The wisdom and power of healing and of transformation come from the earth, its plants and its creatures. By surrender and attunement to the earth and its processes and forces, the shaman is healed and transformed, and becomes empowered to likewise assist others. The shaman is properly on a power trip of the heart seeking skillful means to be of service to others. The therapist is shaman insofar as he works experientially. The shamanic aspect grounds his work. He seeks natural phenomena that can enhance healing and transformation.

The various therapeutic methods use techniques that are natural phenomena, and these are all part of the shamanic aspect of psychotherapy. For example, psychoanalysis relies on the everyday phenomenon of "transference" by which we often perceive and react to people and situations in terms of significant people and situations of the past. Group process is likewise a natural phenomenon that psychotherapists use as a tool.

As shaman, guru, and priest, therapists are empowered beyond themselves to guide patients from darkness to light. If there is a new spiritual awakening beginning in our generation, and if the new transpersonal awareness arising here and there in psychotherapy is part of that awakening, then a new emphasis on faith unleashes super-conscious potentialities.

When we deal with matters of faith, we are forced back to the very first stage of growth, basic trust. Our journey is from basic mistrust to a fuller and firmer trust in life and ourselves as expressions of that life.

AH! SWEET MYSTERY

Cooper C. Clements

ABOUT FIVE YEARS AGO, I knelt by my bed praying and had a view of the glory of God. As I looked up above the bed I saw the Messiah, the Christ, as if riding in a chariot pulled by horses. The light and glory were so awesome I could tolerate the power of it for only an instant. But I'll never forget that glimpse into the supernatural world. I was overwhelmed by the incredible glory with its bright light and radiant power. It was too overwhelming, and at first I just wanted it to stop. After a little while, I began to realize that a wonderful thing had happened. I felt very blessed.

For about five years prior to the vision, I had been praying, meditating, and studying many avenues of metaphysics and spiritualism. I was no longer a scoffer or cynic about the existence of a spiritual dimension and another world. But my direct personal experience was minimal and I wasn't a practicing Christian at the time. Thus, I was surprised and amazed by the vision. Primarily, though, it served as a powerful confirmation of a deep reality. To believe and to know are different.

In the weeks following the vision, I changed. Something had been established; some foundation of faith was now built inside me. It was like a bedrock in the Spirit that I knew could never be removed or destroyed, no matter what happened in life from then on. By now the vision has taken on even deeper meanings, but that first inner certainty still remains. This foundation, confirmed by the memory of seeing Christ riding in awesome splendor, has held firm since then.

Cooper Clements, Ph.D. is Associate Professor at the Eastern Virginia Medical School and is in private practice in Virginia Beach, Virginia.

My earliest awareness of God was in the First Baptist Church in the small Mississippi town of Calhoun City. I remember the preschooler Sunbeams singing, "Jesus loves me this I know, for the Bible tells me so." I was puzzled, though, about people loving each other because there seemed to be a wide gulf between the only two churches in town: the Methodist and the Baptist. They were right across the street from each other, but the two congregations seemed to feel as estranged from each other as Arabs and Israelis. The Methodists were inclined to look with scorn at what they considered the over-emotionality of the Baptists. Meanwhile the Baptists were very concerned that those Methodists baptized by sprinkling instead of immersion, and weren't at all sure they'd make it to Heaven. Since my father's family was Methodist and my mother's Baptist, I wasn't sure where my appropriate loyalty lay. Fortunately for me at the time, neither of my parents took part in this battle.

Although my father was part owner of the local newspaper, times got hard and very little money came in. He took a job in Claremore, Oklahoma, working for a newspaper owned by a Cherokee which lasted only a few years. Although I only lived in Oklahoma for two years, they were very formative and significant ones for me.

Around that time I was ten years old and the realization of Jesus being crucified for my mistakes sunk in. This was such a wonderful and undeserved gift that I was overwhelmed with the wonder of it all. Realizing that He had conquered death in coming back to life brought hope as nothing else ever could. I received Jesus Christ as my Savior and was baptized in the good Baptist way of full immersion.

The day when I accepted Christ, I experienced the most love and joy that I have ever felt. Through all the years since then I always looked back to that day and knew that something more important than any other event in my life had happened. No matter how agnostic I later felt, I never forgot that time of love and assurance, that time of feeling close to Jesus personally and experiencing His loving and compassionate Presence.

During the time in Oklahoma, our money ran out and I was sent back to Mississippi to my grandmother's where I stayed for a year. While with my grandmother I went to the Baptist church which she attended. I also joined the Boy Scouts which was to be a significant experience for many years. Attaining Eagle Scout was my first peak experience. A Mr. Swaim lived at my grandmother's house as a boarder. He served as a grandfather to me and we were very close.

Mr. Swaim was over seventy and about a month after I left to rejoin my parents, he died. I returned for the funeral, but it wasn't until many years later, during my personal therapy, that I was able to realize the terrific shock his death had been to me. Only then did I see how much it had hurt me and made me afraid that someone I loved might die.

The family reunited in Jackson, Mississippi. Our first apartment was near the Capitol building and also close to the First Baptist Church where I grew spiritually. Several times at church meetings, I rededicated my life to Christ and each time felt blissfully enveloped in love and very close to Jesus.

Unfortunately, not all was well between me and the Baptists. While the regular minister took a positive approach, we would sometimes have visiting preachers who were hell-fire and brimstone screamers. They seemed to be filled with hate and bent on scaring people into Heaven. I got the impression that sex was sinful and dirty. They probably meant we were not to do it unless married, but I interpreted the avoidance and prohibition as entirely negative. I also became aware of race issues as I got older and this was very disillusioning to me. Many of the prominent leaders who came to church on Sunday were community spokesmen enforcing segregation during the week. And, of course, the only Blacks to get into the church building were the two janitors. As a result of my increasing disillusionment with church, I began to drift away near the end of my high school years.

I viewed these Christians as hypocrites. I figured they were playing it safe; just in case there was a boat leaving for Heaven, they wanted to have a ticket. In a few years, at the height of my doubts, I felt I had seen through the whole phony scheme of huckster preachers and wondered how they could pull it off; I reasoned that not even the slickest used-car salesman could get away with having people buy something that wasn't delivered until after they died. Of course, by then I was rarely listening to that still, small voice of the Master within. Somehow, though, I always knew that I was born again and that I couldn't go back and be unborn in the Spirit anymore. Deep inside, that memory of bliss stayed with me and I always believed that God is great enough to handle anything and more than able and loving enough to forgive me any mistakes and misguided notions. The old Baptist teaching of "once saved, always saved" has been a comfort many times; though the lambs may wander off, God never gives up on us.

After high school I won a small scholarship and attended Millsaps, a Methodist-affiliated college in Jackson, for one term. I was restless, though, and knew I'd need the G.I. Bill to finish college, so I joined the Air Force for three years. While in service, I read some inspirational writing by Harry Emerson Fosdick, then pastor of Riverside Church in New York City. I wrote to him about trying to decide my life's work. He answered with encouragement to pursue Christian work. I was still disillusioned though, and went to Veterans Counseling Service to take some vocational tests. My counselor was a psychologist and he decided I looked like I'd be a fine psychologist. I wasn't certain, but enrolled in a liberal arts course at Millsaps rather than go to Georgia Tech as I'd tentatively planned. There I ended up majoring in psychology.

Although my undergraduate years were spent in a Methodist college, it was no longer under church control. The remaining religious aspects were required weekly chapel attendance, two religion courses, and no modern dancing on campus. I was fortunate to have an excellent teacher for a religion course who was a handsome, well-built ex-football player from Harvard. He led us into serious consideration of philosophy and personal religious issues and had us record our questionings in a personal journal. This teacher was intelligent, educated, and caring enough so that I was willing to consider the notion that a religious life could be meaningful. I considered going to a seminary, but my eagerness to learn clinical skills and be a therapist won out and I entered graduate school at Indiana University.

I was surprised when I began my graduate psychology program at the contempt shown for open thinking such as using the word "mind." I soon learned that the two acceptable viewpoints were those of B.F. Skinner and J.R. Kantor. Skinner said all we needed to look at with people was the stimulus and response; inside was an empty black-box which we didn't have to know anything about. Kantor agreed that it was a black-box but said we needed to know all we could about it; however, its contents he defined as not-psychology. Wisdom being the better part of valor, I adapted and soon joined enthusiastically in the crusade to save the world via Behaviorism, and I became an expert at building automated Skinner boxes and running rats. Incongruously, we had a clinical psychology training program, a Psychological Clinic, with some warm, humane clinical professors. There was coexistence as the clinical was quizzically tolerated over in the rat lab. We had many bright professors and a thorough study of learning theories turned out to be a good foundation for intellectual clinical observations.

At the same time, campus life was exciting. By the end of my first year I met and married a psychology major, Jackie, and we worked our way through graduate school and traineeships. Although religion was off-campus at this state school, we found lively outlets for our humanitarian impulses. Most of the psychology graduate students were strong proponents of social justice. Finding out that a Black graduate student had been denied service at the only bar near campus, we did a sit-in protest and carried signs outside the bar daily. The President of Indiana University, Herman B. Wells, wouldn't endorse drinking for any students, but sent a memo to every public place in the city stating that any facility not open to every student would be declared off-limits to all students. This settled the local segregation issue. We also took a stand against the extremism of the "McCarthy era" before it was safe to do so. When a textbook commission recommended banning *Robin Hood,* we formed a group known as the Green Feathers and put up "Don't let them burn your books" posters all over campus. Except for the local Unitarian fellowship, as far as I know, most churches around town were silent on these issues.

I was committed to go back to the South after graduate school and found an opening on the faculty of Emory University in Atlanta. Emory was Methodist-affiliated, but the only visible influence to my cynical eye was that absolutely no alcoholic beverage was allowed at any campus or college-related function. This earned our students the nickname of Tea-sippers from the Rambling Wrecks of Georgia Tech.

A year or so after our arrival in Atlanta, *Life* magazine ran a series on religion which described the orientation of various churches. Because Jackie and I had grown up as Christians, we felt some desire to find a church. We concluded that the Unitarians sounded closest to our thinking. We looked them up in the phone book, started attending, and felt enough at home to become members. It was full of professors and liberal intellectuals and it was the only predominantly white church in the area that had Black members at that time. Our Unitarian church attracted people who were disillusioned with traditional churches. We found mutual support in working for social causes and reviewing the faults and failures of the nominally Christian church groups.

Those were vibrant years to be in Atlanta. The city was turning from the past and becoming one of the major cities of the nation.

Thanks to the wise capitulation of Governor Ernest Vandiver regarding integration of the universities, the brilliant editorial writing of Ralph McGill in the *Atlanta Constitution,* and other leadership, Georgia did not suffer as much disruption as other southern states. Our Unitarian church received a few bomb threats and the Reform Jewish Temple down the street was bombed once. We attended a few social functions where bomb threats were made because Blacks were in attendance. Although I had no doubts about the brotherhood of all people, I did have empathy with some of the resentments about the self-righteousness of certain amateur civil rights activists in those days. Their tones of hate reminded me of the Baptist brimstone screamers.

By the mid-sixties, Jackie and I were materially and professionally prosperous but spiritually impoverished. I left Emory University to practice clinical psychology full-time in private practice and she soon joined me in this endeavor. Through the years I had become more and more active in mental health projects and was constantly serving in local, state, and national positions. During this period, at the height of my doubts and unbelief, I remember thinking that there probably was no life beyond the grave and that our functioning was no more than electrical impulses traveling along neurons. Given this view, the most meaning I could see for my work was that at least I could help people to have pleasant neural impulses rather than painful ones. Spiritually, I ended up feeling about as empty as Skinner's black-box. Except, of course, Skinner's box wouldn't know it was empty.

Studying the behavior of organisms, mostly through the hooded rat, hadn't done it. Most people were just as miserable as if nobody had ever studied them. The permissive child-rearing craze was a tragedy. While the causes to which I'd devoted so much of my life had some good results, it looked as if society and the world were going downhill or falling apart, rather than following the gradual higher and higher and better and better American dream.

While feeling this way, one day my wife Jackie came home with a copy of *Autobiography of a Yogi* by Yogananda. She'd bought it for herself but suddenly said, "This isn't for me; it's for you to read." It was not like her to hand over a new book. She usually writes her name in books before she gets home, lest there be any doubt as to who gets to read them first. Reading Yogananda's autobiography served as a primer on the spiritual world and brought me into the reality of the unseen. Yogananda's guru happened to be a specialist on Jesus Christ. I was able to regain my perception of Jesus as the Son of God by means of this viewing of Him in the context of the supernatural world described by Yogananda and his teachers.

Meditation was another avenue of significant development in the spirit for me. I practiced Zen meditation for awhile. Later I learned Kriya Yoga techniques and still later, Christian approaches to meditation. Eventually, as I became somewhat knowledgeable about the spiritual world, I came to see tuning in to the spiritual as very similar to turning on a radio. No longer doubting that spiritual forces are broadcasting, I believe it is vitally important to discern which "station" we are receiving when we open ourselves up in meditation. A number of Christian writers emphasize the need to listen for God's answers after we have done our talking in prayer.

Eventually, I took the most drastic step of all and read the Bible! I mean, I read the entire Bible. From beginning to end, every word. This brought revelation! Of course, I had been taught about the Bible for years. I had read parts and learned to find all the books rapidly in Bible games. Even during my most agnostic years, I sometimes quoted scripture to make a point. I realize now that I needed the words to teach a principle or truth I had learned from there long ago. Finally I went to the Source and there found the key. I found the answer to why just trying to be a good Christian wasn't adequate when I was an idealistic teenager. When I read how God promised Abraham he would be the father of many nations and kept this and other promises through almost four thousand years (and even provided a written, detailed record for us), I knew only the living God could have managed all this. Furthermore, now that my eyes and ears were beginning to open I noticed a crucial part of the story that had not been meaningful to me before.

When I was a child, mention of the Holy Ghost conjured up an image of the wavery-voiced, foggy apparitions in ghost stories. I never wanted to think about it. However, after seeing how God communicated again and again in varied ways, I wanted to learn all I could about the Spirit, as told by the Author. After reading about repeated brief visits by the Spirit through Old Testament times, I was excited to read where Jesus said it was expedient for us that He go away, so that He could send the Comforter, the Holy Ghost, to be with us and guide us. That was the missing key. After Jesus was crucified and resurrected, He told His people to tell all nations about Him, but then said to wait in Jerusalem until they were filled with power from on high. So they waited and prayed until one day a sudden sound came from Heaven like a great wind, and they saw something like tongues of fire and were all filled with the Holy Ghost. Now they had the power to act!

For me, this solved the mystery of why "being good" wasn't enough. We need the power to do God's work in this world. Now I knew what I was looking for! And I wanted to find some people who knew about this power. I could see the power of laying hands on the sick for healing, so I decided I could use that as a guide.

Actually, waking up to the Holy Ghost came over a period of years after we had attended a healing service in 1972. We had seen some apparent healings that certainly would be miraculous if genuine. I was very skeptical at that time but there were some people healed who had more than hysterical symptoms. One 33-year-old woman, who was born deaf, received her hearing. I was familiar with deaf speech and hers sounded completely authentic. The expression on her face, as she conducted the choir on stage to hear her first music, would have been hard to fake. There also was a four-year-old boy whose short leg grew five inches in a few minutes, to equal his good leg. This got my attention so I worked to find out more about these phenomena. I did my best to uncover the scientific bases for them, until finally the attempted scientific explanations became more incredible than the spiritual ones. Eventually I sought out people who were showing the signs of the Spirit. That following week two amazing coincidences (miracles?) happened. In unlikely circumstances I came in contact with two strangers who were filled with the Spirit and taught me more about this experience.

During the years of spiritual study and growth, my wife was simultaneously doing the same seeking, although our routes were individual ones. There was enough rapport that, while we sometimes disputed details, we did not accuse the other of being crazy. This was something we were thankful for; we saw other couples where only one was seeking and the other person could not understand what the seeker was experiencing.

Jackie got back to a Biblical belief before I did, perhaps because I'd had past negative church experiences which she never had had. During this interlude when she was a believer and I wasn't certain, there was subtle tension. She was concerned that I was still partly following pseudo-Christian paths. My worst fear about her was that she'd turn into a stuffy, judgmental person like some of the church women I'd known in childhood, but this was really alien to her personality. My more realistic fear was that she'd be an enthusiastic, fanatical "Jesus freak" and an embarrassment to me. I felt this way even though for years, as a therapist, I'd been an advocate of not being afraid to look like a fool. It seems strange to me now that no one looks askance if you're wildly enthusiastic about the Dallas Cowboys, foreign cars, golf, or even the latest therapy techniques, but you're supposed to be dignified and sedate about the Son of God and all the glorious, Heavenly events.

As I think about how my faith in the Spirit enters into my work as a psychotherapist, it seems to me that any successful therapy depends on the presence of faith and hope. *Faith* is basic to the therapy enterprise. As the letter to the Hebrews in the New Testament defines it: "Faith is the substance of things hoped for, the evidence of things not seen." This statement means to me everything is created in the spiritual realm before it manifests in the material. Just as Abraham believed in his spirit that he would be the father of many nations, so the therapist fosters health by believing in it before it is evidenced. Often the people who come for therapy have lost faith in themselves; beset with problems and armored with defenses, the client cannot see much positive potential. The faith of the therapist in seeing what the person can be plants a powerful seed for the person's own potentialities.

People often ask how I tolerate listening to problems all day. Sometimes they're asking indirectly whether I can listen to their problems, but they also are recognizing that it could be exhausting. I need faith even to begin the journey that lies ahead in therapy. Knowing that nothing is impossible with God, I am able to sit and listen. I know I'm not alone and can silently pray for help from God for us.

Sometimes a person describes such a tangled web of fears and defenses that I feel overwhelmed. I turn it over to God. Then I can sit back and wait. It is beautiful to see someone shift to a different perspective and begin to untangle the web. Believing that love is the greatest power there is helps me refrain from adding to a person's fears by trying to control, prevent mistakes, or judge their choices. Faith sustains me throughout the spiraling journey toward health.

Are psychotherapists secular priests to modern mankind? I think perhaps we have been because we have followed some basic spiritual principles. And, these principles work even if we are not spiritually connected to the Source. For example, meditation "works" as a means of opening us up to spiritual forces no matter which station we tune in to. To disown our Spirit is like trying to sit on a three-legged stool with one leg missing.

As psychotherapists, a fundamental aspect is the make-up of a person. The Scriptures tell us that a whole person has three essential parts: body, soul, and spirit. The Bible teaches us, often by means of case histories, the healthy and unhealthy roles for these parts. God always answers prayer. I'll admit I used to get disillusioned when God didn't answer "Yes" immediately! Looking back, I'm often thankful that the answer was "No" or "Not yet, wait." God is a loving Father and wants us to be healthy and prosperous. God gives many promises, so I never hesitate to pray for people that God will heal or prosper them. I know He always will, so I can turn over to Him how and when it will happen. God never said we wouldn't have trouble, but promised to deliver us from troubles.

Spiritual laws and processes are often similar to those at the psychological and physical levels, but sometimes we find they are quite different. Our God is a loving Father who has a perfect plan for our lives. However, I think He has given us free will to choose, the only way we could love God meaningfully as persons, not as robots. Inasmuch as we have free will, we can choose to follow God's plan, make one up ourselves, or follow someone else. Of course we feel frustrated when we don't know God's plan for us and yet want to do His will. God makes it easy for us by telling us a simple procedure. "In every thing give thanks: for this is the will of God in Messiah Jesus concerning you." We aren't required to know the plan. Our ego is likely to balk at giving thanks for things which look bad to us. But God says *in every thing.* He takes care of our questions by telling us that "All things work together for good to them that love God, to them who are the called according to his purpose."

One of the most practical spiritual principles that I have learned in the past year is that spiritual qualities are not as dependent on circumstances as are the emotions of the psyche. We tend to gain more pleasure from the pursuit of happiness than from its capture. However, qualities such as love, peace, joy, kindness, patience and faith are products of the Spirit and not dependent on our psychological or physical states. Thus, we can experience joy in our spirit even in the midst of trying circumstances or while going through a painful emotion. This is a great help to me during the nitty-gritty of everyday living. Since emotions fluctuate so unstably, they are not trustworthy indices of the true state in our Spirit.

These principles are sometimes received like a breath of fresh air, especially by clients who are jaded from various fads. However, sometimes people have been disappointed so much that they are not receptive at all. At times they may not be interested in anything spiritual. It's beautiful that God already knew that and told us through the prophet Isaiah: "So shall my word be that goeth forth out of my mouth: it shall not return unto me without fruit, but it shall accomplish that which I please, and it shall prosper in the thing whereto I sent it." This sure knowledge that God's work will bear fruit in some way (even if it seems to be futile) gives me the boldness to go ahead and present it.

One time I was seeing a divorced young woman who had often been hospitalized during psychotic episodes. She had already made clear that she was only interested in God as an abstract Force and not as a Person. She said she felt like a piece of garbage and I responded that she needed to get the garbage out by expressing her feelings. She had also complained that her lower abdomen was hurting and that she felt she needed a man of her own to comfort her. I handed her a Bible and asked her to read II Corinthians 1: 3,4 where God is described as the Father of mercies, and the God of all comfort. She started to weep and said in church she'd always heard people talk about the devil and sin as devil-worship. She hadn't thought of God as having mercy. Then she mentioned that she'd long ago had an abortion and wondered if that was connected with her abdominal pains. She was then able to grieve about her lost baby and to feel God had mercy and was not condemning her. She prayed for forgiveness and sat in silence for awhile. Suddenly she broke out in a beautiful smile and exclaimed, "I feel so different!"

Of course I don't push the Word of God on somebody if I sense that it would be too disturbing. Then, I focus on psychological approaches and trust that the Spirit will do its work another way.

I pray for my clients each day and often silently during sessions. Infrequently, people will request prayer for a specific crisis. I know people get well quicker now and I certainly feel my work is much more meaningful. There's nothing like letting the Head of the Universe be in charge!

It has taken time for me to begin to learn. I guess most people new in the Lord try too hard to do the right thing and follow the right principles. We all need to learn that it is through the grace of God that we are saved and not by our good works. He still sends the Holy Spirit with specific guidance for each believer who asks. The Holy Spirit provides the power for carrying out the work. As we grow in the Spirit we are likely to channel increasing power and be given varied gifts to apply in His name.

The basic spiritual principles on which psychotherapy rests include non-judgmental listening, forgiveness, and compassionate love. These are a good foundation for our lives as well. "And the greatest of these is love." That statement summarizes the mystery of life which baffled me so many years. It is love the world seeks and it is Love alone that rules.

MIRACLES OF ACTUALIZATION

Walter E. O'Connell

BEING NATURALLY HIGH, as opposed to using drugs or alcohol to achieve elation, involves more than therapy. It is a constant goal, a way of life, an instrumental religion, as well as a psychotherapeutic model. When achieved, it is holistic and sees all persons as active agents. Natural-high philosophy embraces the metaphor of Alfred Adler who saw all persons as the artists and created products of their own life-styles. Everyone is responsible for one's own self-esteem or sense of inner worth. Likewise, we all are responsible for our own level of social interest (state of universal inner belonging). Regardless of heredity and environmental conditions, each of us is responsible for how we feel about ourselves and how we fit into our world. Others can contribute for better or for worse; however, each of us is responsible for our own actualization (unqualified feelings of worth and purposeful belonging) or constriction (chronic depression and loneliness).

Over the last quarter-century, I have treated hundreds of clients with a combination of work and play. My treatment has worked in my own life. From a hopeless mixture of acting impulsively with inhibitions learned in childhood, I slowly, imperceptibly became a prince, still needing, even to this day, to watch out so that I don't return to froghood. At earlier times, I would devote tremendous zeal

---

Walter E. O'Connell, Ph.D. is a Diplomate in Clinical Psychology of the American Board of Professional Psychology. He serves as a psychologist with the Veteran's Administration and as Adjunct Professor at Baylor University. Dr. O'Connell is in part-time practice in Houston, Texas.

and patience to treatment, seemingly to convince myself and the world that my methods (and ultimately "I") did work. Now I often see my efforts as my contribution to evolutionary energies.

Alfred Adler said that he needed only an hour to learn all he needed to know about a client. By seeing the unfolding of invidious comparisons, demands, and the discouraging blame of negative nonsense time and time again, a perpetually-practicing-pupil (one who develops an awareness of mistakes and who practices loving-kindness as the royal road to inner actualization) could take half that time. One of my weaknesses is to assault zealously the inner workings of constrictive forces. When I anticipate and give others feedback about their possible ways of blocking my feedback, this maneuver is often successful in stimulating insight and outsight (SI). But my interpretive rush can be too sudden, before patient trust is earned. The lack of therapeutic trust precludes success. When I am not politely democratic with firm friendliness and gentle strength, I am seen as a dangerous person, intoxicated with demands to satisfy myself.

Later, these patients might learn I can also be brash and brusque with myself. I am (and will always be) far from perfect in the skills of actualizing actions. Yet with all my chipped edges and missing pieces, I can still unleash a splendidly uproarious sense of humor. Such is an integral part of natural-high theory and practice. Even constrictive addictions for power demand respect. They, too, are part of my personal pilgrimage. If need be, I will hang out with them and hear their "angelic" message. Addictive compulsions inform me of my human condition, giving me the opportunity to voice, record, share, and celebrate the constant contradictions which, when accepted rather than awfulized, become something else, the hallmark of the humorist, the swing between the poles of paradoxes. These perceptual swings are, to me, the *sine qua non* of the religious person, the actualized, the democratically-inspired. The humorist is involved but not attached to external games because meaning, for such a person, is anchored deeply within, beyond space and time within the humor experience.

Observing death and dying labs has taught me to understand the ultimate paradox: what I call the sad-glad perceptual swing. Death brings an inexorable end to relations in the world, hence the sadness. It stops the actualization opportunities in this lifetime for the deceased. However, the bedrock of my natural-high theory is any belief that enhances self-esteem (SE) and social interest (SI) is experientially true. It embraces the belief in a mysterious union of self with *S*elf, which releases an expansive energy responsible for SE and SI growth. In this larger sense, death can contribute to happiness.

Another basic tenet of natural high is the necessity for self-stroking (not judgmental ego-stroking). A giant step in natural-high actualization is encountered when one can go beyond meditation for relaxation, beyond meditation for stress-management, to the third stage of the fertile void. Here is the possibility for an unfolding of numinous symbols. If one stays with these symbols, honoring them, hanging out with them (without constrictive evaluation and judgments), high SE and wide SI ensue, generating even more expansive energy (at no expense to the immediate environment or to the universe). At this psychological place, one can honor the god-within, can self-stroke simply for being (no place to go, nothing to do, no one to be). Most natural-high pupils are not yet there and are never permanently there. Stroking for effort, but not for perfection, is the next lower spot on the actualization scale. There are group meditations, after which the leader of active imagination exercises reminds all pupils to stroke themselves for having allowed themselves the growth experience (or even a more extreme position, "Stroke one's self, for having creatively chosen resistance"). Most of us have only at fleeting times (on the mountaintop, the beach, in the forest) felt the strength of the deep self, spirit, or soul, beyond death's destruction. *The Tibetan Book of the Dead* warns us that even after death, the unactualized person's self still has the stigma of the proud, avoiding ego. The "bad trip" of death comes, we are told, from the self behaving like its controlling, departed ego. Hence, we need to experience the separation of striving ego from expansive self before bodily and ego death.

At times when I look back over my own life, I become paralyzed. I know it will not always be that way, though. My dreams have been sending me messages to look at my past and I am doing that. These moments bring me into a helpless vertigo, experienced as a sense of lessened worth and doomed isolation. I feel "less than" and "different from" others. On such occasions, I am without self-esteem and social interest, incapable of the miracle of change. Experienced continuity and stability are alien to me in times of attachment to my old addictive perceptions of being no good. Such perceptions are part of my early distortions defining and invalidating my best intentions. At such times, I feel the panic of being thrown defenseless into a brutally competitive world. Natural high theory states that the past attitudes, simultaneously constrictive and addictive, will surface at times when I feel of lessened worth and belonging. No magic pills, phrases, or pensions will remove this blight (or gift), part of the similarity of us all.

I have often called my psychology "Zen Adlerian," thereby emphasizing two neglected facets of the Adlerian focus on healthful cooperation-as-equals. "Zen" to me implies the practice of continuous paradox. Only through personal experience rather than rote behavior can one even approach a sense of personhood. In my self-learning, appreciation of two maxims is paramount: "Whenever you *OAF*, you never can loaf" and Alfred Adler's, "Everything can be anything else." *OAF*ing is an easy road to symptom construction and retention. By OAF I mean owning, awfulizing and fighting unwanted thoughts, affects, or actions. Take a popular event, the depression that most of us unwittingly trap ourselves into. (And I must add here that most of us do not remove ourselves from destructive psychological symptoms by increasing our self-esteem and social interest. Rather, we do so through elevating ego-esteem, even through an honest appreciation of our disabilities.) Psychological symptoms could be given up easily if they were not used for social power. Natural high students cannot learn what it means to give others support if they continue to use social interventions to gain power. The need for power appears to be compensatory, reflecting a sense of insufficient strength. Since we are made in the image and likeness of God (the external Self) and are an inherent part of the process of creation now, the need to prove worth and competence is totally unnecessary. We are all God-like and have latent abilities to free up our social belonging and self-esteem, wherever we want, and to contribute to the growth of others through the loving-kindnesses of courage. Destructive behaviors, on the other hand, are like tar babies; if *OAF*ed (owned, awfulized, or fought) they become part of us and can destroy us if they become the essential means of getting power from others.

A personal parable will share where I am in faith and intuitive knowledge now. In my first venture into psychotherapy thirty years ago, I recorded all memories that came to mind. I overlearned with great certainty that all my early recollections were prime examples of my Oedipal complex. Even to this day, when someone uses "why?" as a hidden means for communicating "don't," I say "Because my Oedipal complex makes me." So convinced was I of my unfulfilling fate that I drew a cartoon of myself with pencils and begging bowl and the sign "Oedipal complex" hung around my neck. Ten years ago, when I was learning Eastern philosophy, I unearthed these early memories. At the age of three, I already felt like an unredeemable outsider . . . the second of two with an older, infinitely more powerful sister. For eons, it seems, I would sit by the curb dropping pebbles into a catchbasin. I was totally part of the expanding ripples of stone against water. And the voice in my head thundered again and again, "Who was I before I was?" With nausea and vertigo, I'd move away from the catchbasin to visit a residue of my Celtic homeland, the silent pines.

It may be that I was denying my father; certainly being told I was an unacceptable number two in everything (except sickliness) generated anger and destructive fantasies. Yet, why that particular question, a Zen koan traditionally given to students by their masters? My family had no intellectual curiosity for cultures beyond that of the next block—and I still had not experienced a radio. Yet, the possibility of samsara, the reincarnation, the soul's journey through many lifetimes, appeals to me. My natural-high faith becomes deep intuitive certainty in states of expanded SE and SI when I can readily envision interlocking contributions across time and space, which exist merely as the stage for the dance of actualization to take place. The statement, "I am here in time and space" only vouches for my failure (with the help of others) to reach a state of actualization at the time of previous deaths. I do have that opportunity now to get off the wheel of samsara by sharing, keeping journals, celebrating and honoring wherever I am in my pilgrimage. To get off samsara, the eternal wheel of life and death, is utmost in my thinking.

I let perceptions and feelings flow by, after recording such presences. Be involved in each moment, attached to no-thing: above all, be who you are. "I am what I am" said God in true self-disclosure. My perception of anxiety, anger, or depression is not "mine." It is merely the result of a lawful process that asks me to recognize and record the feelings—then let them go. If you can't let the affect go, focus on its happening, without making demands, and it will of its own nature disappear. Even anxiety is not a real threat. What I feel are merely bodily signals, judged by a constricting sense as "good" or "bad," "sick" or "healthy." Record, share, celebrate, honor, humor the happenings and let them flow on by. I own nothing; for my undifferentiated self is not my actualized self. Nothing is permanently catastrophic to me if I can communicate with a Self beyond ordinary confines. Happenings are sad, unfortunate, unexpected, but there is no place for fight or tragedy in a universe in which anything can be anything else. Had I not experienced being the younger child, the sick one, I would not have opposed the narrow, negative institutionalization of persons (the less-than, the separateness) that so cripples human possibilities. Had I not been told that I killed my father (by running away from a feared operation while he chased me), killed my mother (by moving to Texas) and killed my first wife (by divorcing her), I would never have been so concerned about death. I would also not have been so concerned where contributions and responsibilities begin and end in personal interactions.

Were my phobias, which contributed to my insatiable curiosity about pathology and treatment, like my death concerns and alienations "good" or "bad"? Who "contributed" and who was "responsible"? All were; all "good" at times, were "bad" at times. It all was . . . so I choose actualization, self-realization and help model and create a strong support group. And stroke for being for personal reassurance or for effort until you die. And there you'll be, where you should be at that moment: perfectly imperfect.

Part of the humorist's redeeming social value is seen in the defusing of extreme black-and-white demands upon life and upon the people therein. Right-wing religions and psychologies interpret the world in terms of readily-available free will. Their left-wing opponents call for social awareness and look at people as hapless victims of social conditioning. Natural high, my sense of the sacred evolved by me, resolves the opposites; the extreme right and both sides in isolation are wrong: individualistic self-esteem and social courage are equally needed for evolutionary purposes.

The most elusive, most precious, and most paradoxical truth I like to call the paradox of perfection: as a person, where I am right now is the perfect place to be. I honor my constrictions, symptoms, and sins. I am made in the image and likeness of God and inherently belong in this purposive universe. However, human behavior is incomplete and imperfect in time and space. If we all were perfectly encouraging, time and space would disappear as we gracefully accepted our innate self-esteem and purposive belonging. If I devote my energies to prove my worth in the external world, I will only create more misery there. Accepting my worth and belonging, energy would naturally flow to awareness of the need for constant social loving-kindness. Perfection of behavior will follow perfection of self-worth and belonging, albeit by a fair number of millennia. Natural high, you see, is more than a therapeutic vantage point. It expresses my deepest beliefs.

FAITH AND THERAPY: MUTUAL ENRICHMENT

Sister Helen Szekely

FAITH IS CENTRAL to my life: my breath and heartbeat. It is not only the most precious gift I have, but also the only unbroken thread through the many passages of my life that gave me direction, meaning and vitality.

By faith I mean a personal relationship with a personal God who not only knows me but loves me and gives me the opportunity to respond to His love with every fiber of my being. The enduring element in this personal relationship with the invisible God is His abiding presence which draws me to respond. My faith response, however, changes as my life changes. It reflects the influences of my culture, my family, and my psychological unfolding.

I was fortunate to have been born into a culture where the presence of God was as real as the gentle breeze and warm sunshine. Our songs and folklore were filled with images of God who took care of the lowly, rewarded the good and punished the evil. My mother taught us to pray as soon as we learned to speak. When we were old enough to walk we joined in the festive celebrations of religious and national feastdays. These festivities are still treasured memories. They sprang from the heart of a romantic people, combining reverence with joy, honoring heaven while embracing the goods of this earth.

I never heard of unbelievers while growing up and I found it perfectly acceptable that people worshipped God in different ways

---

Helen Szekely, M.S.W., Ph.D. is a Roman Catholic nun who, as a clinical social worker, maintains a private psychotherapy practice in Orange, California.

as Catholics, Protestants, Jews. Among the simple people of my hometown, the faith of my early childhood was enriched by beautiful customs and rooted in an uncontested certainty.

Conflicts in my growth began in Catholic grade school. I became aware my father was not a practicing Catholic and concluded that he probably would go to hell. Prompted by love and fear, I did all I could to convert him. Little did I understand that he had a deep personal relationship with the "Lord of the Universe" but he was unable to harmonize his experiences with the attitudes of the Church of his day. I knew, however, that he was an honest, dedicated, creative person. He never yielded to public pressure; honor and personal integrity were his highest values. There was something amiss in the assumption that he should have to go to hell. My mother, on the other hand, followed the teachings and laws of the Church unconditionally and blindly. Doing what others considered right was important to her. Neither parent invalidated the faith of the other or tried to win over the children to a particular point of view. The conflicting parental attitudes towards the established Church, however, changed the unquestioning faith of my early childhood and I began a quest for truth and a search for meaning in religion.

As an adolescent, I became a relentless questioner of every article of the faith presented in religion classes. Fortunately, my teachers were challenged rather than irritated by my endless questions. I grabbed every possible opportunity to engage in formal and informal debates as I continued to define my own ideas about God, the meaning of life, tangible and intangible realities. Although I acquired quite a skill in debating and could deduct logically coherent arguments in defense of my faith, I could not change my father's convictions. This compelled me to continue my own search.

Becoming proficient in dogmatic theology, however, appealed only to the intellect. It seems that God seduced my heart in another way. During my early teens I fell in love with one of my brother's schoolmates, John. It was a delightful, innocent romantic affair. We played tennis, swam, skated, hiked and he taught me to love classical music by listening to the radio he built himself. I thought I knew what heaven was like when I was around him. My feelings overflowed in poetry, shared only with best friends. The heat of our love was tempered by a religious experience of my boyfriend after which he became a daily participant in church services. Following his example, I made a retreat and became a daily church-goer. What followed is difficult to describe. I began to enjoy the presence of the Lord Jesus in the Sacrament so much that I would remain in front of the altar as long as possible and then would run a half mile to get to school, out of breath, just before the teacher came to the classroom.

Those intimate moments before the altar had a profound effect on me. In an imperceptible but growing way, I began to desire to dedicate my life to God as a religious sister rather than to be married to the boy I loved. This strange new attraction surprised me at first. Again and again I would dismiss it. Finally, reinforced by the example of some of my favorite high school teachers, it prevailed over my romantic feelings. After two years, I had to choose between marriage and religious vocation. With mixed emotions, I buried my friend's love letters and souvenirs in a protected spot in our garden and wrote a "Dear John" letter to my dear John. I did not know how and when I would follow the call, but felt compelled to make the choice at that time.

Shortly afterwards I faced one of the greatest tragedies of my life and with it, the first severe test to my faith. Hungary became the battleground of German and Russian armed forces and the target of American air attacks. My father decided to pack up the family and fly westward to escape the invading Russian army. We left the place that was my safety, beauty and nurture for seventeen years. Danger and death became daily companions. The explosion of bombs and cannonshells drowned out the excitement of intellectual debates. Under pressure, my conformist mother felt lost and my idealistic father was frustrated. The turmoil of the war brought out the worst in people who professed to be Christians. The nagging question emerged in my heart, Is Christianity livable or only a story that fades away in the life and death struggles of hunger, cold and physical deprivation?

Doubting my Christian faith reached its crescendo one day during the month-long journey westward from Hungary to Austria. Short of food and without proper care for my sick grandmother, we depended on the hospitality of villagers around the highway. The task of begging for help fell upon me. On a particularly stressful day, a woman whose front room was decorated with a large cross, coldly refused my plea for help, while a widow honoring a large picture of Hitler in her small apartment received me kindly. In the silence of my heart, I wondered about the value of Christianity and could find no well-formulated, logical answers to ease the pain of disillusionment. Fortunately, I also met a few men and women who were not only prayerful, devoted Christians, but compassionate and caring human beings. Their influence was like a healing balm which I eagerly absorbed for my shaken faith. I came to know that a message lived is more powerful than a message spoken.

Five years later, having survived post-war and refugee camp deprivations and having obtained some training in social work, the desire to dedicate my life to God's service emerged with a new compelling force. Again the thought of an undivided intimate relationship with God drew me more than new romantic encounters and the promise of marriage. I was looking for a community I could join. Having been formed by a dual parental legacy of conformity from my mother and bold commitment to personal values from my father, it was not easy to find a community that would be fitting for a lifetime commitment.

In the midst of my search, I met a newly-forming group of plain-clothed sisters (counter-cultural at the time) who were being forced out of Hungary by increasing Communist pressures. I consciously shared their values of enlightened spirituality and thrust towards higher education. I was excited by the prospect of going with them to the New World and helping create a new religious family. Less consciously, I hoped that my new religious family would become a substitute for my lost homeland. Even more hidden was the fact that an instant, strong attraction to the charismatic leader of the group reflected adolescent dependency needs.

I willingly left my first job as a social worker and turned down a scholarship to an American university to embark on a life of dedication to Christ Our Lord. Nothing could have stopped me from finally following the call I had heard long ago. Soon I found myself in Canada with a handful of young women in their teens and early twenties, ready to take on a strange, new world and establish a new religious order.

With great enthusiasm, I became totally absorbed in the needs, values and norms of the community. The struggle for survival in a foreign culture welded us into a closely knit group around the leader. I learned to pray in new ways and became more deeply rooted in the personal love of Christ which has remained the principal source of my strength and joy ever since. I also learned to work hard and with discipline, and had major roles in launching new projects, opening new missions and training new community members. I shared with my sisters not only hard work, but play as well, and the demands of adjustment to a foreign culture were made lighter by the magic of familiar celebrations we brought with us from our homeland.

On the negative side, all life moved around and was contingent upon the strong, controlling leader. We succeeded in establishing a home for ourselves and grew in numbers, but the spiritual and intellectual frame of reference upon which the new foundation was built had limited capacity to expand. Our lives were confined to the perspectives of the past as we defensively protected our identity from all outside influences. As often happens with closed groups, the subtle demands for emotional dependency grew and were reinforced by religious ideals which were narrowly interpreted. The situation bred invisible seeds of powerful conflicts.

Perhaps my dual family legacy disposed me to be caught up in the conflict when finally the antagonistic group began to surface. My need for a sense of personal integrity compelled me to challenge the inconsistencies in the norms set by the leader. Indeed, it was an unacceptable move to make in a closed system! Soon I was dropped from trusted positions and, in spite of my clumsy attempts for clarification, I became the family scapegoat. In an attempt to resolve the conflict, I was sent to a graduate school of social work. Bewildered over the rejection and denying the rejection, I buried myself in textbooks, challenged by the new opportunity to study.

My career as a psychotherapist was predicated upon conflict rather than choice. Fear of failure and anger over losing influence, combined with the urge to learn and clarify issues for myself, motivated me to study hard. Once again, as in my teens, I needed to ask questions and seek answers to reconcile conflicting loyalties.

The atmosphere of a secular graduate school tested my faith. My whole philosophy of life was challenged by new schools of thought, strange epistemologies, and insistence on the scientific method. A long, slow, thorough process of integration emerged from these conflicts. For hours, I pondered the validity of new knowledge in the light of faith and the teachings of the Church in the light of new knowledge. Sometimes I ardently argued with a textbook through marginal notes. Other times I argued with teachers and fellow students.

Gradually, I came to understand the values upheld by the Church in a broader perspective. The rigid definitions of the articles of faith which I knew and taught yielded to a deeper understanding of the mysteries they expressed. I grew to treasure the spiritual leadership of my Church more than ever in the midst of conflicting values so characteristic of the pluralistic society I encountered. I think it is a singular gift that my personal journey from a constricted world view towards greater openness coincided with the renewal of the Catholic Church during the mid-60s. My personal growth and broadening world was validated by the new lifegiving movements of the Church, even though the small community I so dearly loved offered no support for my ideological expansion.

As my training progressed, I gradually accepted the career of psychotherapist I initially did not want. The more I understood the fascinating processes of the human mind, the more I enjoyed working with it. I found programs and mentors to accelerate my growth. Early in my practice I began experimenting with innovative techniques. Once my creative energies found an outlet within the four walls of my tiny counseling office, I embraced the career of psychotherapy as my own.

Meanwhile, personal psychotherapy became necessary because of the continued tensions at home and the demand for increased sensitivity at work. If graduate school forced me to expand my conceptual framework in order to integrate new knowledge with an old faith commitment, personal psychotherapy brought me face to face with more basic attitudes, deeper emotional conflicts. I had to face long repressed traumas, unfinished developmental tasks, intense sexual drives and strivings for power. I felt pain and confusion as the edges of my consciousness expanded. I not only had to question the traditional articles of my faith, but also the validity of my consecration to celibacy. At times, nothing that gave meaning to my life before made sense. God seemed distant and my prayer life was not comforting. Instincts, no longer repressed, clamored for satisfaction. Fortunately, my therapist was not only a skilled and compassionate guide, but respected my religious consecration. He encouraged me to stay in the struggle while searching for new meaning and new ways to relate to God.

Slowly, almost imperceptibly, new life emerged from the emotional and spiritual turmoil. I rediscovered the beauty of music, poetry and the arts. I learned to play again and to allow the splendor of nature to heal my troubled spirit. I experienced a sense of freedom to follow the attractions of worldly pleasures. Yet, as I pondered the meaning of my vocation, I discovered that it is a greater freedom to leave these pleasures behind for the sake of the Kingdom. My heart responded to this discovery with joy and devotion that was like a song; music played on the strings of my soul by her Divine Master. This new melody filled me with a joy and love I had never experienced before. I understood the words of St. Paul, "For the sake of my Lord Jesus Christ I have forfeited everything . . . so that Christ may be my wealth and I may be in Him." (Philippians 3:9) Discovering new passages of the Bible nurtured the hymn of love in my soul and my renewed consecration became a more authentic response of love to Love.

Psychotherapy enriched my life rooted and centered in God and gave me a new appreciation of my consecrated womanhood. Yet, complete reconciliation of my roles as nun and psychotherapist could not come about before another painful passage was completed. My first religious family, which I helped to create and loved dearly, could never accept me as a professional psychotherapist. For several years, I belonged to two different worlds. I shared my religious sisters' dedication to the Kingdom of God, but they could not share my vision of promoting the Kingdom through psychotherapy. I shared my striving and growing edges as a professional with fellow therapists, but the Kingdom of God was rarely a professional interest. The only place I felt whole and totally accepted was in front of the altar of God.

Ultimately, after numerous unsuccessful attempts to gain acceptance, I decided to leave the community and find a new religious order where I could continue to live my vowed life. It was as painful as a divorce, but finding and joining a larger and more open religious congregation has become a worthwhile re-marriage. I feel valued and supported as a woman sharing other women's visions to bring about the Kingdom, and as a professional psychotherapist as well. Mellowed by suffering and expanded by joy, I am more capable of appreciating the love and support offered to me by my sisters.

My rootedness in Christ and my emotional unfolding goes on its own course. My two principal avenues to foster emotional growth and a more complete response to God are prayer and the practice of psychotherapy. In the silence of contemplative prayer I see the meaning of psychotherapy in the context of my dedication. This motivates me to stay in the profession with total openness despite doubts and uncertainties. The closeness of God in prayer also gives me the courage to see the shadows of my personality and to expand self-knowledge and self-acceptance. Psychotherapy, on the other hand, provides the arena for this expansion in the intimate personal encounter with other human beings. The therapeutic process also gives me the opportunity to see God heal and transform other human beings and keeps me in touch with the reality of His abiding presence.

Psychotherapy as a profession and process gradually influenced my relationship with God. In the same way, my faith influences my practice of psychotherapy. The beginnings were marked by conflict. In graduate school during my first fieldwork placement in one of the worst poverty ghettos in Los Angeles, I was assigned to work with the family of two delinquent pre-adolescent children. They were Catholics and the family asked me to prepare their children for the reception of First Communion, an important step towards full participation in the Sacramental life of the Church. I happily reported the request to my field supervisor and to my surprise she firmly instructed me not to offer any religious instructions, but only "social-work intervention" to the family. I could not convince her that the two were perfectly compatible and reluctantly complied with her directive.

Other instances in graduate school reinforced the message that religion better be set aside and human problems be approached with a "value-free, scientific attitude." It was left to me to integrate the allegedly value-free orientation with my personal commitment. Eventually, I was able to see that to be fully human we need to accept our impulses, needs, emotions and all that we experience without value judgments. At the same time, to be fully human we need to set goals and define norms predicated upon temporal as well as spiritual values since only these values give meaning to our existence. Thus, I realized that a non-judgmental attitude and commitment to values are not only compatible but complementary aspects of life.

As the years passed, I became freer to follow my own therapeutic style and make all my personal resources, faith included, available to my clients. Two external circumstances that facilitated my own inclination to integrate my faith with professional work were my new religious family's wholehearted acceptance of my professional role and the professional community's increasing recognition of the spiritual dimension of human existence. As my two significant support groups changed, I experienced a greater acceptance as a woman consecrated to God and as a psychotherapist.

Occasionally, colleagues as well as the faithful challenge me with the question, "Do you bring religion into your work?" Sometimes I have the feeling that colleagues question my objectivity and the faithful probe my orthodoxy. I do not bring religion into my work explicitly unless the client asks for it. I hesitate to verbalize an experience that is so precious to me without an invitation. Besides, I don't want to impose my way of relating to God upon my clients who are vulnerable to my influence, for fear that I would interfere with their own authentic search for God. I am delighted, however, to share my religious experiences with clients when they ask me to do so. My faith resources, however, are latently present in each therapy session. At moments when a client's crisis and my faith experience synchronize, words about God, faith, spiritual values emerge simply and spontaneously.

The first to call for my faith resources were schizophrenic patients. Shortly after I graduated from the school of social work, I was working with a middle-aged, schizophrenic, paranoid woman who felt certain she was destined to go to hell. She had a network of some fifty priests to whom she turned for relief and reassurance, to no avail. After several months of working with her, she confided that she is married to the devil and therefore her fate is to be damned in hell forever. Having disclosed her secret, she began to worry about me. She was afraid that the devil might take out his revenge on me for divulging their secret. I spontaneously entered into her delusion and assured her that the devil cannot hurt me because I am married to God. Once she accepted that, I went a step further in trying to reach her. I proposed that I would marry her away from the devil so she would not have to go to hell. My proposal stirred fear, hope and excitement in her, and a momentary struggle followed. First she refused my suggestion, but I stayed with her in this struggle with my hands outstretched towards her. She suddenly grabbed my hands in a gesture of acceptance. After some moments of silence we sealed the pact with a simple prayer and entered our therapeutic marriage. This incident was a turning point in her condition. She began to get a firmer hold on reality.

In another instance, I was able to help a severely emotionally-regressed, elderly black woman who was an evangelical minister. She lived in parks and bus stations and talked about her congregation as if her role as a preacher were real. She called herself Sister Ann and would not reveal her last name to anyone. For some reason, she was willing to speak to another sister. Due to my faith, I was able to accommodate her need for a colleague with whom to communicate. Later on in the treatment, I even became her congregation and she prayed asking God's blessings over each part of my body and every piece of furniture in my office. It was not my way of praying, but I could sincerely accept her devotion and she felt my acceptance. Eventually, I was able to motivate her to apply for public assistance and she managed to get a tiny storefront church for herself, one corner of which became her living quarters. She was safely off the streets.

Schizophrenic patients with religious delusions, however, are not the only ones whose need calls forth my religious resources. At times I see a person beset by pervasive guilt. I tend to see such difficulty as psychological as well as spiritual. After addressing the underlying psychological conflict, I give an opening to talk about reconciliation in religious terms in order to help the person attain peace, joy and a new sense of freedom. In some other cases, a rigid religious view causes part of the dysfunction. Such a situation calls for a gentle approach. I do not deal with the distorted religious issue directly before the underlying psychological conflicts can be worked through because I don't want to invalidate the precious treasure of faith. This sensitivity is rewarded later. When the underlying psychic need for the distortion has been changed, a new religious meaning emerges with little or no help from me.

Sometimes I run across married people who rationalize their demanding attitudes towards their spouses by quoting the Bible, hoping to win a marital power struggle. Such attempts are short-lived in my office since I don't hesitate to put the quote back into its context and disarm the self-righteous contender. With this move, the demands lose ground and values presented in the Bible are clarified and reaffirmed.

On occasion, some of my clients expose their spiritual hunger by asking me to tell them how I talk to God. Such a question is usually an implicit request to teach them how to pray. Knowing where they are in their psychological development, I can translate my own experience of being with God in such a way as to encourage them to make contact with their Creator in their own unique way.

Clients most frequently find my faith a treasured resource during that phase of their growth when they have to let go of values and beliefs incorporated during childhood and young adulthood in order to establish their own. I can fully empathize with their fear, guilt, sense of insecurity and loneliness and encourage clients to stay with the process, to "launch out to the deep" and allow God to reveal Himself in a new way to them. When this occurs, I feel powerfully in touch with the person who happens to be my client. The verbal exchange is usually very brief, couched in some symbol spontaneously arising from the client's present experience.

Sometimes, metaphors serve to clarify a point or bring together paradoxical values; they have meaning only in a particular context.

Others fit more universally. For instance, with couples who want automatic happiness in marriage I tend to invoke the image of a gardener who does not expect to see fruits on his trees overnight. Nor would he decorate the trees with artificial fruits just to make them look better, but takes care of the trees hoping that fruits would come in due season. I tie this image to the old Catechism teaching about the "virtues" which we can cultivate in ourselves and the "fruits of the Spirit" which we can hope for in due season. Another image I often use to help modify a possessively caring attitude is Mary, the mother of Jesus, who did not attempt to take the cross away from her Son but supported Him in His suffering with her presence. I feel these metaphors have the flavor of lived experience and nurture us on our journey.

However, the times when faith and psychotherapy merge and mutually enrich one another usually occur with people who share my religious background. Clients of other philosophical orientations, however, sense my acceptance of spiritual values as well and feel free to discuss their quest for deeper meaning in life. My identity as a nun attracts some people and rules out others. Some patients have to work through the stereotype associated with a Catholic nun. The resistance can take the form of a blatant rejection: "What do you know about life—you are a nun and you don't have to struggle in the world?" This kind of resistance does not threaten me too much because I know if I can make contact on a deeper emotional level, the differences in life-style do not matter. I find flattery or unrealistic expectations more difficult to deal with. In this respect, I am vulnerable and can easily become inflated by such projections. Part of this unrealistic projection can be a subtle expectation that I will offer well-tested advice or easy answers and save my clients from conflicts and risk. Coming from a religious background where authority and obedience are highly valued, I easily can be seduced into taking on the projected role of an expert authority. I have to be on my guard so that the therapeutic process is not undermined.

My identity as a nun singles me out in professional gatherings, too. This is a blessing and a burden. I enjoy being approached by colleagues with spiritual questions whether they are related to their own personal search for God or to a problem with a Catholic patient. I feel the same sense of being totally alive, nurtured and energized as I feel when my clients activate my faith. My colleagues sense that something comes alive in me and enjoy the experience. I must admit, I really like talking about religion in a psychological context. On the other hand, there are colleagues who avoid me because I am a nun. Others place high expectations on me which I cannot live up to. The latter is a point of real vulnerability, and when unacknowledged hostility is mixed with high expectations, I feel hurt and defenseless. The greatest danger when colleagues relate to my religious role, however, lies in the possibility of hiding behind the role and not being touched by genuine human relationships.

The integration of faith and therapy as it relates to God and people is an unfinished task in my life. I have found an authentic expression of my dedication to the Kingdom of God in the practice of psychotherapy. For this, I am sincerely grateful. I am thoroughly convinced that psychological wholeness and emotional freedom are pre-requisites for a deep, passionate love for God and fellow-man. The more I possess myself, the more I can give of myself: the freer I become from fears and narcissistic needs, the more I can respond in love with my whole being. This sustains me in my practice on the dreary days when the burden of the profession weighs me down. To implement what I believe as a Christian and a psychotherapist in relationships with clients, colleagues, other sisters and friends remains a challenge. I am just a beginner.

WILDERNESS WANDERINGS

Carole A. Rayburn

I DEVELOPED A LOVING CONCERN for others and a deep religious conviction of God's everpresent love for all people from my maternal grandmother. A woman of great faith, she spoke often of being descended from the biblical House of David and of growing up in Tripoli, Lebanon. My grandmother expressed such a love of God and of humanity that those around her could not help becoming infected with her same ebullient, radiant, yet softly humble joy. I marvelled at the wide assortment of relatives and friends who frequented her home in Washington, D. C., arriving as early as 6:00 A.M. and not leaving until late at night. Each one was an interesting study in character for my young and inquiring mind. Rather than any specific lessons that my grandmother taught me, it was through observing her life of simple, devout, and humble faith that I began to want to serve God and people in some meaningful way.

My mother had thought of becoming a Roman Catholic nun at one time in her youth, but later she became attracted to the Methodists. Drawn away from the Syrian Orthodox religion of her parents, she chose the more egalitarian forms of religious expression. Her feminism was apparent even in the question of faith, to a degree uncommon for women in the early 1900s. Yet mother never officially joined the Methodist Church, declining total involvement in any religious organization because of a basic skepticism that there was any real

---

Carole A. Rayburn, M.Div., Ph.D. has held membership in the Ad Hoc Committee on Equal Rights and Affirmative Action of the Division of Clinical Psychology of the American Psychological Association. She is a Fellow of the Maryland Psychological Association and maintains a private practice in Silver Spring, Maryland.

and enduring goodness in people. Nonetheless, she sang solos in churches of several Protestant denominations, allowing me to tag along. At these churches, I found fascinating surroundings to add to my catalogue of interesting places and people. Somehow life seemed more beautiful and at peace in a church than anywhere else. Mother's cynicism was never able to counteract or to overcome the fervent optimism and childlike faith of my grandmother. Faith in God remained a very special part of my young life.

My father was not discernibly religious. His parents, as were my mother's, were first-generation Americans and strongly devout German Lutherans. However, he had had a traumatic experience in his early childhood which adversely colored his relationship with God. He had begun to question God when his boyhood friend was killed one Sunday morning while riding his bicycle home from church. My father agonized over this tragedy for many years, and he did not enter a church from that time until the day I was married.

But I was always drawn to religious people and places and I delighted in all kinds of people. I loved to be in churches, listening to the organ playing, my mother and the choir singing, and the minister preaching. I loved to draw pictures of children kneeling in prayer. At the age of twelve, I formed an "Upper Room Club" which met on Sunday afternoons. After reading the lessons from the devotional booklet, *Upper Room,* I preached and then we all sang hymns. At such times all was peaceful for an hour or more.

Somehow managing to survive a rough adolescence, I continued to take my problems—and sometimes my good experiences—to God in prayer. I never doubted that God heard and answered my prayers, and the Lord did not let me down in my childlike, trusting faith.

Influenced by my mother's musical abilities, I thought of studying voice when I entered college. This seemed to be one enjoyable way to be with people. However, though I was performing with dance bands and had my own radio show on campus, I did not feel this was serving people in a meaningful way. After taking the required courses in psychology, I decided that a more viable field of endeavor was to devote my life to working with others to help them restructure their lives on more solid and meaningful foundations.

This redirection in my life did not receive initial support from my family. Though my mother's favorite brother was a psychiatrist, she had her mind set on my majoring in the arts. Largely hindered in her attempts to achieve a greater musical career, she thought that she could realize her career goals vicariously through her only daughter.

My parents presented a stark contrast: my mother was a staunch and lifelong feminist, while my father was a classical male chauvinist. Although he was sure that educating me was useless because I would just get married and have children someday, he nevertheless lovingly humored me in my desire to study psychology.

Psychology fascinated me as much as religion did. Working with others in the intimate relationship of psychotherapy allowed that full expression of caring for others as my brothers and sisters in the family of God. The mysteries of the human psyche, with all of its intricate facets, was almost a religious experience of probing the world of the unknown and attending the birth of thoughts expressed anew or revitalized and brought into the light of more joyous awareness.

Though still intensely interested in others' religious concerns and in their relationships with God, I had long since given up any ideas about teaching Bible or expounding in a stirring sermon as I had during those pleasant days of my childhood. I was not one for doing anything half-way: I would either devote my time totally to the ministry or to psychology with no compromise. I focused most of my energy in those few select areas in order to accomplish the really important goals of life. If I was severely frustrated in one area of concern, I would pursue a path which seemed more viable in attaining my goals.

As my parents' only daughter, I would never have been encouraged to enter the male-dominated ministry, especially because of their skepticism toward organized religious institutions. Therefore, while I did not doubt the importance of religion in my own and in others' lives, I maintained my involvement in religious teaching as a concerned layperson throughout college. My focus was upon psychology and psychotherapy as tools with which to ameliorate people's problems.

While finishing my Master's degree in clinical psychology, I met my future husband at a Presbyterian Church social club. Both of us were Methodists, involved deeply in our professional pursuits and in church activities. While he was beginning his doctorate in biomedical engineering and I was almost finished with my doctorate in psychology, we discovered that he had cancer. Ronnie lived just twenty months after the onset of the carcinomas, just long enough for both of us to grow even closer together in the Lord.

In the excruciating sadness that followed Ronnie's death, I found that only God could fill the void left in my life. During this time, God made me especially sensitive to others' needs, leading me to desire to help them as I had been helped by the Lord. While working at a center for adjudicated juvenile delinquent children and adolescents, I was impressed with the youths' struggles to find answers to their problems through religious explanations.

Calvin, a fifteen-year-old whom I had seen in psychotherapy since his commitment to the institution at thirteen, was now seriously beginning to question some of the biblical information that the chaplain and the church volunteers had given to him. Sorting through the various Bible stories with his young, probing mind, he asked, "Dr. Rayburn, just what is all this stuff about Adam and Eve anyway? Is that really how sin started? Do you really think God knows or cares about my sins . . . about me, and that I can still get to heaven?"

Calvin was the only adolescent in the history of the juvenile center who had been committed on a real "sentence": the court would not release him until he had served five years of incarceration. Most adolescents had indeterminate commitments, with an average stay of six months to a year. Originally charged with homicide of a four-year-old boy, Calvin had escaped twice from the center and raped and robbed two women at knife-point. No one else in the psychology department wanted to work with homicidal patients. Further, intensive psychotherapy was understood to be reserved for the more tractable patients who had been admitted on less serious charges. Yet Calvin was one of God's children too, not ready for assignment to the trash-heap of life just yet. Some efforts on his behalf certainly were in order.

From the perspective of a religious psychotherapist, those who have committed a serious crime might well see their actions in terms of sinning, or in any event they may eventually experience guilt. I was never convinced fully that those whom psychotherapists see in juvenile centers were without conscience for their actions. More likely, years of defensive survival tactics built a coating on the exterior of the psyches of such individuals. The psychotherapist's task is to unpeel the many layers of rough hide to get through to the more vulnerable and caring interior person. It was not only my training as a psychotherapist which led me to hang on tenaciously to some hope for Calvin and for others such as he. It was my faith in the goodness within all people which could be tapped if we used our human skills with avid belief in the God who moves mountains. God could move mountains for Calvin, I was convinced.

Calvin was now asking me for spiritual guidance. This seemed like a breakthrough in his veneer of nonchalance. It proved to be just that. He had access to a chaplain, but he was approaching his trusted psychotherapist with whom he had been working in intensive treatment for two years. The ethics of working in a public setting prohibits the initiation of religious dialogue in psychotherapy.

One way for me to deal with the spiritual dimension would be to refer such discussions to the clergy. However, many persons who want and need psychotherapy do not see clergy regularly or do not wish to discuss these problems with them unless they had prior rapport. Also, individuals often view the religious or spiritual elements as an extension of other areas of their lives, not as separate ones requiring another kind of specialist. They sometimes want and even demand help of this nature from their therapists, and may consider denial of this aid as a betrayal. The whole situation was highly charged.

Although I continued to feel uneasy when my patients sought religious answers from me, I wanted to do as much as I could for them. However, I was anxious about crossing professional lines and not being fully qualified to provide such direction. Yet, the nagging concern that I might be denying them some beneficial avenues of approaching their problems remained. Would helping them sort out their religious thoughts, along with their emotions and behavior, lead to significant progress in their therapy? Even if the more essential aspects of religion were referred to a clergyperson, could not some basic discussion of the individual's beliefs, whether religious or philosophical, logically begin in psychotherapy? Nonetheless, though I continued to affirm God's love of all people who seek their Creator and to rejoice in Calvin's awakening of religious pondering, the forbidding ethical codes of my profession governing service provided for the public a formidable threat to doing more holistic therapy.

Shortly before my husband died, we had been reading our Bibles together daily and prayed even more than usual. Impressed with the sanctity of the seventh-day sabbath, I now became convinced of the authenticity of this day of worship. Both of us had heard our Seventh-day Adventist friends speak of the sabbath for years, but suddenly in the impending tragedy the teaching finally bore fruit. Later, attending an evangelistic series given by Adventists, I was impressed with the surety of their answers and their doctrinal soundness. They had very Bible-based answers, I thought, to questions that I had on death, on baptism by immersion, and on the way to live a fuller Christian life.

In mourning for my husband for quite some time, I did not notice at first something very important. Along with the rather pure doctrines, I had bought something else I did not like. One sabbath morning, I was jolted with startling awareness and my eyes were opened wide to a travesty of Christ's love for all people. That love, so beautifully expressed by Paul in Galatians 3:28, "There is neither Jew nor Greek, neither slave nor free, there is neither male nor female; for you are all one in Christ Jesus," was being denied at sabbath services. Looking up from my Bible, I realized that women and minority group members were strangely missing from the pulpit during the church service. Just an hour before church service, women superintendents and sabbath-school teachers abounded during the sabbath-school. It was as though an invisible curtain had come down to separate women from men at worship, and as though an inscription were engraved above the altar: "Church worship by white males only; others must not enter the altar area!" The only exception to this unwritten rule was an occasional female vocalist or instrumentalist who performed during the offertory.

Years of feminist upbringing by my mother suddenly bore fruit. I would not please any paternal authoritarian power-structure, particularly if this were at the decided expense of asserting myself as an equal member of God's family. My mother had taught me early in life to expect to be treated as others' equal, because I was equal to them. I was never a "flaming feminist," however, who awoke one day to discover suddenly that she had been grievously disenfranchised all through life in a sexist society. Encountering male chauvinism in my family and in graduate school, I had been aroused more gently to existing sexism. Then I took the matter rather coolly and calmly. This, no doubt, was attributable to my mother's instilling within me a basic self-assurance as a woman and as a person; I was not to be jarred by any mythology of male superiority.

I could not reconcile all persons being created in God's image—male and female, white and non-white—and still believe that that same loving God would segregate people according to gender and race during the worship of their Creator. Had Christ died for nothing? Did Galatians 3:28 ring falsely in the ears of Adventists? My world, idealized and ahead of its time perhaps, would be one which had competent men and women, who would not hinder each others' progress in any way, and would strive for the best possible society together by our loving God's grace and mercy.

To remain silent would be false to myself, to other Adventists and to my patients as well. I was helping my patients to speak out assertively against injustices in their lives and to become more competent individuals. To do less for myself and for other Adventists would jar my sensitivities as a person and as a psychotherapist. With such grave differences between how I envisioned that Christ's church should be and how my Church was, I knew that I had to help rectify the situation as rapidly as possible.

My concern that problems be approached in as holistic a fashion as possible, including the psychological and the spiritual aspects of the healing process, grew more intense. Sensing how painful it would be for women to be led down paths of sexism by pastors whom they trusted to counsel them wisely and fairly, I was more convinced than ever that all counselors and psychotherapists needed to exercise great care not to convey sexist thinking to those whom they treat. Individuals who suffer such disillusioning moments in pastoral counseling might well turn away from the pastor and the church and perhaps even all future psychotherapeutic intervention as well.

During this period of intense prayerful reflecting, I experienced a call to the ministry. One of my chief burdens was to help right the wrongs of sexism and racism in my Church. Studying for the ministry involved not only a tremendous financial loss but also risked loss of status in some quarters of the professional psychology community which had not been in harmony with the world of religion. Although I realized the prejudice in my Church against women in the ministry, I nonetheless began seminary.

I had grown more sensitive in my psychotherapy to those who experience helplessness and hopelessness when they come for treatment. Many have been maimed by continual discrimination in society. At times I could sense the pains of those who were struggling to overcome decades of prejudice and other faulty learning in their lives. Such assaults to the human psyche had imprisoned them from knowing deeper, more loving relationships with other people—and with God.

As a psychotherapist, I had often observed the influence that group members have on individuals in group therapy. After graduating from the Adventist seminary, I keenly experienced a giant bureaucratic structure resistant to inner reflection and to change. It was prepared to sacrifice the needs and rights of its individual members to stay as it was. Men were "chosen," women were not.

Beyond my sadness and anger, I am deeply concerned and even horrified at the lives of people that are being wasted. So many women are not allowed to light their little candles of God-inspired commitment to the Lord because of sexism. Instead they are permitted to stumble in the dark of noncaring coldness and indifference. Such insensitivity involves constant compromise for women and does violence to the truth that God loves all people.

Now, I am a strong feminist in my psychotherapy and in my personal outlook toward life. I am concerned about repressed men and women struggling to stay afloat in the stormy sea of prejudice. The important issue is that truth, and the God of truth, be made known by all people in all ways and in all places—even in religious institutions.

My wilderness wanderings into the desert of despair in the discrimination by the Adventist Church have not been without rewards. I still have a dream of a land where all will live in equality, peace, and harmony. This glory land is in the background of my work as I do psychotherapy. I will never believe the nonsense that God favors and upholds men more than women.

Through the trials and tribulations which I have experienced in my church, I have desperately held on to my faith in God. I have learned the painful lesson not to identify any religious group, however well-intentioned and godly it may appear, with the Lord of all creation. To do so, severely distorts a viable concept of God as does envisioning the God-head as being totally masculine or totally feminine.

Deeper walks with the Lord during these times have reinforced lessons learned long ago: people can be—and often are—infinitely able to cope with and adjust to or even change bad situations. Patients are never apart from ourselves; they are ourselves! My faith has provided me with a greater sense of humility. While a therapist and an erring human who is likely to stumble more often than I care to remember, I sometimes conveniently forgot the falls and side-steps. Perhaps this was an attempt to fantasize omnipotence and to persuade myself that knowledge of the psyche somehow renders therapists invulnerable to mistakes. Now I know that any such simplistic thinking overrates the prowess of the intellect and underestimates the webs that society can weave around any individual. My respect for those labelled "patients" by virtue of having problems and seeking treatment is more profound than ever.

My style of therapy is an active one. However, I have developed greater understanding and appreciation for the indirective approach of Rogerian therapy and counseling. An unconditional positive regard for others is necessary not only in psychotherapeutic, but also in religious settings. This sort of caring, nonjudgmental and unconditional acceptance is needed if the person is to grow in a relationship and to sense enough caring to want to cope with life.

My experiences with the church have also given me a better idea of how formidable the impact of group pressure can be on even a strong individual. As a therapist, I have grown quite concerned about those who would set themselves up as consciences for others. Clergypersons and psychotherapists are leaders within their fields of expertise, but they are not the captain of the ship. That is something that I want to remember in my practice. My faith has led me to be more egalitarian in practicing psychotherapy, recognizing that the therapist is sanctioned by society but not a puppet of societal mores which are questionable, immoral, or nonconducive to growth and viable learning.

The vast importance of the psychology of women has a deeper meaning for me now. While I have always regarded myself as a psychotherapist with a feminist orientation, I did not see so clearly before my seminary experience and the subsequent discriminatory events how much of organized religion represses women. Women, who as a group have often been as trusting as children in the male world, have believed in the dicta of men as though their demands and expectations were tantamount to scriptural commands. Just such a narrowed view hampered me as a child and an adolescent, overadapting to my father's demands and expectations. How unproductive is such thinking to the growth and development of women. My concept of God and of what God wants from me is no longer seen in such a restrictive framework. Nor do I see such thinking as viable for those whom I see in therapy—whether they be female or male. Through faith and experience in psychotherapy, I know that the scope of sexuality—including identification and roles—must be broadened for the most successful outcome.

My wilderness wanderings are not yet over. Before I get to the Promised Land of love and understanding laid in store for us by our great Provider, I must learn to forgive and to love more fully those who do not yet see the light of sexual and racial equality. With the help of my Lord, I will develop more patience and hope. All are equal in the love of Christ; our Saviour died that all might be saved. We will never truly learn to love the Lord if we have not learned to love each other. As long as God gives me the insight and the strength to fight for the truth, I will continue to do so.

If there is to be love for all God's children, if there is to be real understanding and empathy, if true harmony is to exist between sacred scripture and the tenets of psychology, my prayer is that God let it begin with me. I continue to long for the day when all people are able to actualize themselves through our all-loving God. Never will I want to turn my back on truth as I understand it. Whenever any authority—be it society or the church—contradicts the lessons from God, I will attempt to show that God is righteous above all else. It is God and the people God created that are important.

Because I have a strong faith, I appreciate the importance of a belief-system in a person's life. In my own life, my faith in God has helped me to focus on relevant issues in problem-solving. I think that people need something or someone to believe in beyond themselves and their immediate environments. Whether they call that in which they believe "God," "Buddha," "humanity," or "humanitarianism," they become more secure and serene when they have some anchor upon which to fasten their hopes and strivings. They must believe strongly in something outside themselves in order to want to learn to believe in themselves and to envision better days ahead.

My faith has given me a profound sense of the wrongs which are engendered when others are given derogatory or negative labels. In the religious realm, such pigeon-holing might include terms such as "heathen," "non-believer," and "unworthy." In the more social world, we find terms such as "effeminate," "castrating bitch," and "superman" or "superwoman." They are dependent on the vantage point of the beholder, who is usually inserting the value-system of the dominant group in society.

To me, it is very important that my therapy takes into account as much as possible the differences evidenced in human beings. How therapists interpret those differences, including the values placed upon them, is greatly important. My personal faith discourages me from being highly judgmental of others, either from a religious or psychological point of view. It is true that I would favor one solution over others for myself. However, just as I would not like to be coerced into adopting a particular way of dealing with problems, I would not want to have my patients forced into any molds.

God is to be glorified for the lessons that I have learned in this difficult situation with the Church and with my faith in my Redeemer. I thank God for all the insights given to me, in my psychotherapy with others and in life in general. Not everything in my relationship with my Church has been an easy lesson or a pleasant experience. Through the pain, though, I have realized many things. I have learned the importance of being much less rigid and far more accepting in psychotherapy, appreciating to a greater degree the role that society plays in either hindering or facilitating individuals' growth to self-actualization. My understanding of individual differences has grown.

Too, I have learned that most people need something upon which to anchor themselves and their aspirations. That something simply cannot be other fallible human beings like themselves. Others will eventually topple over if we lean too hard or too much upon them. People simply cannot be expected to fulfill our needs or even their own as can God. Focusing upon each other, whether in therapeutic or in religious settings, will not get us to the Glory Land. Although it is tempting and easy to say that we can believe only in that which is tangible, I believe that we must keep our eyes upon the Lord. We do learn by observing. As long as we observe the One whom we believe to be perfect, sinless, and ever-constant and all-loving, we cannot fail for long. When we become our own idols or lead our patients into idolatry by encouraging their worship of psychotherapists or other humans, however unintentionally and innocently we may do this, we are beginning to trek in the wilderness all over again.

As long as we flounder in a morass of ignorance, intolerance, discrimination, and suspicion, we remain in the darkness for a long while. We will learn to judge—rather prejudge—others by our own shortcomings and limited categorizing, choosing illusion and error to discovering truth and hope for a better world for ourselves and for others. As most therapists realize, even situations of pain to which individuals have become accustomed over time are less threatening than less potentially hurtful conditions with which they are not familiar. All of us desperately need to learn to trust, but to trust wisely.

As therapists, we do well to encourage patients to trust others wisely, but not to take unfair advantage of them. This is especially true when working with the persons who belong to groups which have been disenfranchised in society: the poor, non-whites, the persons of various ethnic minority groups, the women, and any others who have been placed in categories serving to cut them off from the mainstream of life. Before we as therapists can facilitate the emergence of others into the light of love and understanding, we must want to seek light ourselves. Some would recognize God or some other supreme being or prophet as their means of gaining enlightenment. Others might insist on making themselves their own deities, claiming that they pulled themselves out of darkness unaided by any "God."

As for myself, I know that only to God be the glory. Only my Maker has given me the courage to face the new light leading to love, understanding, and hope. Only through trusting in the Lord could I ever remain out of the darkness long enough to learn in the light those lessons necessary to help others on their exodus out of the wilderness. It is God and my faith in the Lord which will bring me home to the Promised Land.

A SPIRITUAL STRANGER

Paul Rom

ALL PSYCHOTHERAPISTS have a private faith of which they are more or less clearly aware. It may be important to the believer, whether a religious, a political, or a professional faith or belief; yet it is usually not disclosed to a patient or client.

The orthodox psychiatrist of a residential school for neurotic or delinquent boys of high intelligence once told me that one of the teenagers for whom I was to care became two if not more different persons. I did not share his psychological faith as I believe in the unity of the unique, socially embedded, whole individual.

When this boy then told me that I might be able to help him if I were a Catholic, I said: "That may be true; but about religious matters, you should talk with your priest who will absolve you of your sins and not with me as an unbelieving teacher." We soon agreed to discuss all those "sins" which worried him as "errors."

As a faithful psychoanalyst, the headmaster of this school meant to deprecate my scientific basis when he said: "You have helped this boy only by means of your friendship!" Indeed. However, my therapeutic human relationship with this "schizophrenic" boy (democratic and based on mutual respect) would not have been possible for me without using my insights and techniques as a very skeptical teacher who knew that we can lead a suffering person only from one error to another, yet a smaller one. And a neurotic orthodox Jew whom I told during our first session that as a man of learning I am a free-thinker said after some time of cooperation: "I wonder what

---

Paul Rom is Editor of the *Individual Psychology Newsletter*. Mr. Rom teaches and practices Individual Psychology (Adlerian) in London, England.

you will say when I tell you I now say my morning prayer with more devotion than I did before I knew you." I replied that we may consider this as a welcome result of our work. Asked about my faith, I would in summing up say: "I am a Humanist."

How did I arrive at adopting this label? Had not acquaintances of mine occasionally said I was a very "religious" person?

My father brought me up without any religious teaching. I do not know if my father ever believed in God. Having become a freethinker before I was born, he had left the Lutheran Church; and when in my school "Religion" became a compulsory subject, he had me excused from these lessons and I attended those given at a Free Religious Community, of which we were not members. A Catholic classmate went for his instruction to his priest, and there were no Jewish boys. My feeling of uniqueness manifested itself when beamingly I was told that during the first morning lessons of Religion, I could stay at home.

This young neurotic went however on Fridays to the nearby Thomaskirche where its famous boys' choir held public rehearsals. The spirit of Johann Sebastian Bach still lingered in this old church, and I often felt elated when listening to the hymns and motets sung by these lovely young voices or to the organ preludes and fugues. Now, near eighty, I sometimes feel "like in paradise" when listening to a record of Bach's *Musical Offering.* This mighty, unearthly, absolute music fills me with indescribable joy. Also listening in a Concert Hall to a performance of Beethoven's Ninth or in mass meetings to a workers' choir singing songs of solidarity between all the oppressed often lifted me up and even made me shed tears.

For occasional consultation, I read a German and an English Bible, yet I grew up with German poets like Goethe, whose *Faust* I used to read at least once a year. I now also have Walt Whitman's *Leaves of Grass* near at hand. I feel a spiritual brother of great poets and composers.

It was certainly before poets and composers had won me for a secular spiritual life that I had begun to believe in Socialism. My father and I thought that this, our ideal, would become the basis for general human happiness when the present production of commodities for the market will have been replaced by the production of goods to satisfy the physical and cultural needs of all men.

My political faith also includes Pacifism. We believed a war was no longer possible, for the internationally organized socialist workers would answer its declaration with a general strike. But alas! On that fateful August evening in 1914 when I was twelve, we learned that the majority of our social democratic members of the Reichstag had voted in favour of the war credits which the Kaiser had requested from Parliament; yet neither then nor ever in my life did I give up my belief in International Socialism as a valid guiding fiction which might prevent mankind from self-destruction.

After the escape of Wilhelm II to Holland, we believed that the Weimar Republic would achieve a democratic transformation of the warmongering system for which competition and profit-making were the basic motives. This turned out to be another vain belief.

In my student years in Leipzig in the early '20s, our professor offered as spiritual food for the educators of a new democratic generation, the teachings of Wilhelm Wundt (the father of experimental psychology); of Eduard Spranger (who with his book *Lebensformen* had developed a psychological typology); of Alfred Binet (interested in "mental age" and "intelligence"). Yet Gestalt Psychology was developing in Berlin and Psychoanalysis and Individual Psychology in Vienna. They dealt neither with mental atoms nor elements, nor with psychological types but with real, complete persons.

Later I read Freud and Jung, skeptically and with no profit for my personal and professional improvement. At the end of 1929, a physician who had recently returned to Dresden after studying Individual Psychology in Vienna with Alfred Adler, offered me a didactic "analysis" (which now I should call a "lifestyle interpretation"). This verily revolutionized me as a person. The often quoted poetic lines of a socialist workers' poem, *"Nach eitlem Ich du starkes Wir!"* (After the vain I, thou strong We) became the motto for my personal life. Adler had become my spiritual father.

Adler encouraged me indirectly when he agreed to publish an autobiographical paper I had offered him for his Journal. Its title was "A Case of Neurotic Abstention from Alcohol." I wrote this self-interpretation after understanding that my previous fanatical preaching of alcohol abstention and my looking down on all who, even moderately, drank alcoholic beverages was my trick to appear unique and admirable (at least in my own eyes,) and to attract other people's attention. I began to re-direct my childishness towards being more useful by modesty and cooperation. I started discovering more neurotic tricks so as to exclude them from my human conduct. Of course, one never becomes perfect.

I still believe that complete alcohol abstinence is the best social attitude and the right goal for the treatment of alcoholics; yet, as in other fields of life, I gave up my fanaticism. The Ethos of Socialism, Individual Psychology, and Humanism became for the "Unbeliever" indistinguishable and I devoted much time in helping to build the present International Association of Individual Psychology. How did this Ethos help me when I was still in Germany and Hitler had established his dictatorship?

I considered it an honor when the masters of the "Third Reich" dismissed me from my position as teacher in a secondary school which had operated an educational guidance center. They rightly labelled me "nationally unreliable" and also arrested me and many others to put us in "protective custody"—not to protect us against attacks by "Brown shirts," but in order to protect themselves against opponents of their system in the critical period of transition. I experienced this breakdown of my world where Nietzsche and Marx, Darwin and Kropotkin, Adler and numerous radical school reformers had been outstanding figures sitting in a prison cell. I did not know if ever I would be free again and developed a deep depression. This, however, I found inadmissible. I overcame it with the help of a fantastic, yet useful, fiction: I imagined that one day, after the downfall of Hitler, they would place him before me and through therapy I would transform this monster into a human being. After three months of protective custody they allowed me to go to France and as a grateful political refugee, graduating from the Sorbonne and publishing an Adlerian Journal, I nearly became a Parisian.

When the Hitler war broke out in 1939, I could but honor the French Foreign Legion by joining it, not for five years but "for the duration of the war." (The term "occasional Legionnaire" was for one of the old mercenaries the strongest insult he could find for me.) In the summer of 1940 the Hitler-Pétain armistice had been concluded and the new authorities sent us anti-Hitlerian legionnaires to a camp in the Sahara. Again through my belief in Individual Psychology my self-esteem remained unimpaired.

After the glorious autumn day of 1942 when we heard that the Allies had landed in North Africa I could join a British Pioneer Company in Algiers. Later, when the Allies had also occupied Italy, I had the good fortune of being loaned to the Army Education Corps where I taught Individual Psychology to British and American soldiers and held private consultations to solve personal problems.

Having settled in England after the war, I was a founder member of The Adlerian Society of Great Britain in 1948 and when in 1950 I became a British citizen, I changed my name from Plottke to Rom.

I feel a spiritual stranger amongst people practicing their denominational religion, even with my local Unitarian acquaintances when they indulge in their ritual worship. And realizing as a responsible citizen of my country that all great religious organizations as well as religious sects of all kinds rather hamper the development of people to become free, responsible, cooperative human beings, I became a member of the British Humanist Association.

FROM CONFUSION TO FUSION

Reuven P. Bulka

IN 1968 I WALKED into the University of Ottawa in search of a program fusing psychology and religion. One year earlier I had assumed a Rabbinical post in Ottawa, and since the Congregation was relatively small, I was blessed with enough spare time to contemplate furthering my education. But it was not education for education's sake; I was on a search.

For years I had been wrestling with the relationship between psychology and religion, and, more specifically, the relationship between psychology and Judaism. I saw that the study of the mind and of the emotions was becoming a scientific exercise, not divorced from philosophy but more the source from which the philosophy would emanate. The Freudian system, for example, was a scientific theory which became a philosophical attitude to life.

This probably would be innocuous except that psychology in its beginning and, in a lingering fashion up to the present, is perceived to be at loggerheads with religion. Even today, committed Jews have great difficulty in swallowing the word, "Freud." It is the very antithesis, the perception goes, of all that Judaism stands for. With no thought given to suspending the aspects of Freudian psychoanalysis which are incompatible with Judaism nor seriously examining psychoanalysis before jumping to conclusions, the general approach within the Jewish community has been to throw out the baby with the bath water.

Reuven P. Bulka, Ph.D. is the Editor of the *Journal of Judaism and Psychology.* He is the Rabbi of Congregation Machzikei Hadas in Ottawa, Ontario, Canada.

However, psychology purports to speak the truth about human nature. The search for the truth is fraught with dangers, with the possibilities of error. No one can claim to have grasped the whole truth, and can only hope to have latched on to part of it. Yet, the realization that psychology is concerned about the truth of human nature, about what makes us behave the way we do and what is most conducive to bringing out the best in us, forces even the most loyal religionist to take psychology seriously.

So I walked into the University of Ottawa in search of a fusion between faith and psychological truth. The University of Ottawa had worked at correlating psychology and religion, but had done very little in regards to Judaism. It was fortuitous that I was directed to a faculty member who had scant knowledge of Judaism, but who was keenly interested in exploring this possibility with a prospective student.

Unquestionably his initial interest and sustained curiosity was a decisive factor in my being able to embark on my area of study. We did not have the classical teacher-student situation, but rather were two individuals from different disciplines eager to see what further scrutiny would yield. I began by reading Viktor Frankl's book, *Man's Search for Meaning,* and was immediately taken by it. Most people are emotionally overcome by the moving description Frankl gives of his concentration camp experience. For me, Frankl's basic principles of logotherapy, his system of thought and therapy, really hit home. I seemingly had found a system that joined the wisdom of Judaism with psychological insight.

My professor shared my excitement but tempered it. "It's nice, but further research is necessary." He convinced me to contact Frankl directly, a task I approached with great hesitation. Obviously a famous man is busy; a busy man does not have time even to read my letter.

I was wrong. After writing Frankl, scarcely hiding my excitement, I received a letter back from him which mentioned that unfortunately, throughout his experiences in North America, the Jewish community was not receptive to logotherapy. It was therefore a surprise and a welcome antidote that a Rabbi, no less, should speak so glowingly about the system's affinity to Judaism. Of course, Frankl at no point espoused the Jewishness of logotherapy, nor would he identify it with any specific faith system.

The measure of the man is illustrated in his offer to meet me when he next came to the United States in Rochester, New York. A few days before our scheduled meeting, Frankl called from Boston. He had gone out of his way to locate my number to inform me that his schedule had changed. He would be in Rochester a day earlier and would have no time to meet me. My terrible disappointment was obvious in the phone conversation and I asked whether there would not be at least five minutes. He agreed to that and I met him for five minutes. It seemed like five minutes the time went so quickly, but actually it was four hours. It was the beginning of a profound friendship that continues today.

What is the essence of logotherapy that makes it so attractive from a Jewish point of view? According to logotherapy, "the striving to find a meaning in one's life is the primary motivational force in man." The meaning, potential and indigenous to humans, resides in the spiritual dimension. Humans are primarily spiritual beings, with the term "spiritual" signifying that which makes individuals human rather than implying any theological posture. The spiritual dimension is overarching, embracing other dimensions such as the instinctual, and potentially even raising instinct through the proper attitude to the spiritual level.

There are three fundamental philosophical notions which form the cornerstone of the logotherapeutic system. They are: 1) freedom of the will, 2) the will to meaning, and 3) the meaning of life.

The notion of freedom of will asserts that individuals are at all times free to search for and find meaning. Instinct, heredity, and environmental factors are seen as elements shaping destiny but not dictating it. In fact, freedom is contingent upon destiny. The host of restrictions surrounding the individual serve as the parameters within which choice is conceivable. "Man is not free from conditions but is and always remains free to take a stand toward whatever conditions he may have to face," says Frankl. Within the confines of destiny, the critical ingredient is the attitude taken to a specific trait. It is in human hands to decide whether the lust to spill blood translates into becoming a murderer or a surgeon. "Man ultimately decides for himself."

The will to meaning is the mediating principle between subject and object, between the individual and the world of values. In freedom, the individual *wills* to find a meaning, is not driven to do it. To reduce the search for meaning to an urge or drive is to make meaning the tool through which to release tension and achieve homeostasis. It would then be meaningless, a biological rather than human expression. Humans are not primarily concerned with pleasure or power. Pleasure pursued is pleasure eluded. In Frankl's view, pleasure cannot be a goal: it is the by-product of a meaningful life. Power also is not an end in itself, but the way to find meaning. People who lust for power are usually denied it or are destroyed in trying to attain it. Primarily, the healthy human expression inheres in willing to find and actualize a meaning.

Meaning of life, the third of these interrelated principles, posits the notion of the unconditional meaningfulness of life in all circumstances. Meaning is realized through values lived, be they the creative values of giving to the world, the experiential values of taking in from the world, or the attitudinal values, that is, the stance one takes toward an unchangeable fate or situation.

Meaning is objective. If meaning were subjective, it would be dependent on subjective feelings and thus compromise meaning's unconditionality. Being objective, the meaning is outside the individual, and demands transcendence of the self to be fulfilled. In Frankl's view, a person's humanness is realized in self-transcendence and not in self-expression. Self-expression and the desire for self-realization are self-defeating as goals. A healthy tension exists between the subjective "I am" and the objective "I ought." The interplay between them is a key to human life.

To be sure, there are times when one might be frustrated by what one feels is the meaninglessness of a particular situation. Frankl's notion of objective meaning asserts that "a" meaning is there to be detected. The conviction that every situation has its own unique meaning is the first premise of logotherapy, the underlying statement upon which logotherapy is built. Our inability to find the meaning does not negate the existence of it, and part of the task of a logotherapist in a situation of existential despair is to help the patient discover meaning. Beyond this, having ostensibly discovered the meaning, one never really knows if the meaning one has discovered is the meaning that is intended. Thus, one continually strives for an elusive, objective, quasi-mystical meaning, never knowing if one has reached it.

These three major tenets of logotherapy have their counterparts in fundamental philosophical notions within Judaism. The first major tenet in logotherapy, positing that each person possesses a basic freedom of the will, is remarkably consistent with the Talmudic principle that "Everything is foreseen but the freedom of choice is given" (Talmud, *Aboth* 3:15).

The will to meaning in Judaism, the second major tenet, is approximated in the dictum, "Let all your actions be for the sake of the name of Heaven" (Talmud, *Aboth* 2:12).

The unconditional meaningfulness of life, the third basic tenet of logotherapy, has its obvious counterpart in the exhortation within Judaism to express one's faith in God and in the meaningfulness of life "Even though He takes your Soul" (Talmud, *Berakoth* 54a), a statement which is echoed in Frankl's affirmation that life possesses an unconditional meaning in any circumstance, even in suffering and in death.

But the connection between logotherapy and Judaism is more than a similarity of words or sharing of ideas. It is the basic thrust of logotherapy which is so attractive to the Judaic world view. Specifically, two notions are vital in this context: self-transcendence towards a world which has meaning and unconditional meaningfulness. Both of these concepts relate to the main contribution of psychology to mental health, integration, the forging of mental unity out of discordant impulses and aspirations. Theologically, integration is to see the world as one integrated whole.

Monotheism, which is intrinsic to Judaism, insists on seeing the one God as the architect of the entire universe, the Creator of the world, a world which is integrated so that light and darkness are part of the whole day, birth and death are part of life, joy and suffering are integral aspects of human existence. Paganism stood for the compartmentalization of life into gods of the day and of the night, gods of life and of death, gods of rain and of drought. The Judaic imperative to recite a blessing over good tidings and bad, to pray by day and by night, to celebrate and to mourn, indicates the theological integration of monotheism.

The notion of self-transcendence towards values is a key element in integration. There are an increasing number of clinicians today who espouse some form of aspiration to goals and values. In most instances this is seen as an effective tool for realizing a desired state of mental health. However, for Frankl, self-transcendence is not merely a mental health exercise, it is the essential human dynamic. Whereas most other clinical approaches see the notion of goals and values as essential for the ideal of self-actualization, logotherapy uniquely proposes self-transcendence as the ideal which should be embraced. Then, as a matter of course, albeit tangentially, self-actualization will come about on its own. By orienting around goals, by becoming part of the world of values and ideals, the individual becomes integrated into that world; it is essential to the human process.

Logotherapy offers a unique approach to values by asserting that, when actualized properly, they bring in their train the fulfillment that human beings find elusive if they point at it directly. From a Judaic perspective this is an important observation. It says, quite simply, that in observing the transcending Jewish religious observances and in following the highly ethical and moral sensitivities which Judaism proposes, we find the fulfillment we seek. In other words, a life properly lived is its own reward.

Self-transcendence is not a tangential aspect of a broad clinical approach since it is seen here as *the* essential human dynamic. In this self-transcending approach toward integration, logotherapy shares a remarkable harmony with integration seen in the monotheism of Judaism.

A second area in which logotherapy is an integrating agent is in the treatment of suffering. We all face suffering in life. In a congregational setting, within which I have served for the past fifteen years, I have observed that religious commitment is not a guarantee that one will be able to surmount suffering. Very often individual faith is conditional, an implicit relationship with God which says "You scratch me and I'll scratch you." If things go well with me, I will continue to pledge my allegiance, but if God starts up then what have I gained from my faith? The shaky faith based on this type of investment mentality is one which crumbles at unfolding tragedy. There is no meaningful direction in life. There is no solid foundation of faith, there is no integration of both the good and bad into the totality of life.

Logotherapy insists on confronting suffering directly, based on an affirmative stance to life. Life has unconditional meaning, even in suffering and death. In spite of all, we are urged to say "Yes" to life, neither running away from suffering nor seeking it. Suffering can be used in a meaningful way and translated into positive experiences. After all, suffering is a basic component of life.

An integrated life anticipates highs and lows, periods of joy and of melancholy, periods of fulfillment and of challenge. It is an illusion to think that life can be a string of joyful experiences. The individual bent on the experience of joy will be unable to find meaning in suffering. Such a person has turned life into affirming and negating components, in a manner somewhat akin to paganism and a far cry from integration.

Maintaining a positive stance to unavoidable suffering involves maintaining a positive philosophical view to the fact of suffering in general. For this, logotherapy suggests the possibility that suffering is intended to guard the individual from apathy. In Frankl's words, "As long as we suffer we remain psychically alive. In fact, we mature in suffering, grow because of it—it makes us richer and stronger."

Within the theological dimension, Jewish thought suggests the following attitude to suffering: "One should be grateful to God when overcome by suffering. Why? Because suffering draws the person closer to God" (*Tanchuma,* Tetze 3).

The logotherapeutic dynamic and the Rabbinic approach are essentially the same. The major difference is that within logotherapy the philosophical justification for suffering is because it maintains an alertness and aliveness to life's meaning, while within the Talmud the sufferer is urged towards a closer relationship with God which, once forged, leads the individual to greater commitment and religious fulfillment. In Judaism the God of joy and the God of suffering are the same. Within logotherapy the realities of joy and of suffering are basic components of a human life lived to the full.

Logotherapy's concern for suffering is motivated by its commitment to the unconditional meaningfulness of life. This uncompromising affirmative stance to life takes suffering into account and ensures that the reality of suffering, once confronted, does not allow a shrinking away from commitment to life. In an integrated life, a responsive and affirmative attitude to suffering is necessary.

Logotherapy, because of its unshakable conviction in the unconditional meaningfulness of life, approaches situations aggressively, in the firm belief that there is meaning in all of them. An empty life is not an option.

The philosophy and therapy which logotherapy offers was like a glove waiting to be fitted onto my hand. It offered me the scientific foundation with which to approach the metaclinical Rabbinical situation in full confidence that logotherapy, and, in my instance, Logo-Torah-py, would, in the long run, be immensely helpful. Its unshakable commitment to life became part and parcel of my Rabbinical dictionary. Let us examine its relevance to everyday feelings and questions.

Guilt is the ubiquitous anathema of modern society. What is wrong with guilt? Only if we perceive ourselves as guilty can we talk in terms of responsibility and improvement. If I didn't feel responsible, guilt would be impossible. To feel guilty is to affirm responsibleness and affirm the possibility of erasing the guilt through future action.

I once counseled a middle-aged person who was feeling guilty after the death of his father, who died in his sleep at home and was not discovered for a few days. The son's work schedule was so hectic that he neglected calling his father for a few weeks. "If only I had called, I maybe could have sensed he was ill, and sent over a doctor."

Instead of trying to alleviate his guilt, I agreed with him that he was guilty, for as a son he had a responsibility to his father. This startled him. Knowing that his mother was still alive, though living in another city as she had been divorced a few years earlier, I then proceeded to suggest reorienting the "guilt from" to the "guilt towards."

Why not use the *guilt energy* from the experience with the father as a reminder to be more attentive to the condition of the mother? This logotherapy-inspired insight went a long way toward redirecting the son's melancholy into a positive expression.

Perfection is another problem which can be ugly. The obsessed neurotic wants perfection but, realizing that it cannot be attained in the world at large, localizes it into one area, be it the floor of the house, the top of a desk, or the contours of the face. But imperfection is a legitimate reality. If persons were perfect, they would all be the same and no one would be unique. An angelic world leaves no room for human achievement. To strive toward perfection, but to realize the impossibility of attaining it, is the golden mean. "It is not incumbent upon you to complete the task, but you are not free to desist from it," says the Talmud in a statement about imperfection which anticipates the logotherapeutic stance.

Only human beings commit suicide. Animals may die through their own actions, but only the human being can will death and bring it to pass. Is this a negative feature of human reality? No, says logotherapy. Since the individual can at any time terminate life, the "decision to remain alive" is a way of saying "yes" to life.

Why do we get bored? Again, an ostensibly negative feature of human existence is turned on its head by logotherapy. Yes, there is boredom, but it is only because we feel the agony of boredom that we become motivated to fill the void with something useful and purposeful.

The ultimate philosophical question is "Why does evil exist?" The response of logotherapy is that it exists because without the possibility for evil, there would be no good. It is only because one can choose evil that choosing the good is a meaningful act. Frankl, a survivor of four concentration camps, has asserted that he prefers a world in which even a Hitler is possible to a world in which we are all robots programmed to sainthood. Perfection, remember, destroys uniqueness and human action.

All this seems to be more philosophical than psychological, but problems can be rooted in a distorted philosophy. The logotherapist employs Talmudic-type reasoning in the evolution of its philosophy, and Talmudic dialectic in the clinical setting. It is, in fact, a philosophy cum therapy which gently shakes the individual out of philosophical doldrums and opens up a new world of thought and orientation.

The upside-down thumb primarily redirects the individual's attitude toward surrounding reality, enabling the individual to come to grips with it better or to transcend it. Therapeutically, the upside-down thumb is most evident in the technique of paradoxical intention, an approach which has been assumed by many other therapies under different guises and titles.

How do you get an impotent individual to become potent again? Well, it depends on the nature of the impotence. Physiological impotence demands physiological responses, but an impotence which is rooted in the mental rather than physical sphere is another matter. In simple terms, the impotence can be cured by getting the person's mind off potency. A logotherapist would use a dereflective or paradoxical approach to get the person's mind off performance or even forbid the performance, thus taking off the pressure and allowing nature to take its course. Then, what should happen naturally, naturally happens.

Straight thinking would tell us that if you want something, you should will it and it will happen. But you do not fulfill yourself by running forever after self-fulfillment. There is an elusive quality in the search. Logotherapy recommends the upside-down thumb approach: "Fulfill yourself by forgetting yourself." "One who prays for another is answered first" says the Talmud. One who is concerned for the other is more likely to be fulfilled.

How do you handle the nervous performer who is about to get up and deliver an address to a critical audience? The performer is nervous and afraid of shaking, of hesitation. "Don't be nervous," you might say; but the logotherapist says, "Be nervous, and not only that, shake as much as you can, knock your knees together on the podium at a rate which would beat the current Guinness record for knee-knocking. Show them how nervous you can be." The upside-down thumb strikes again.

Paradoxical intention is merely an extension to the clinical realm of the paradoxicality employed by Frankl in the philosophical realm. Reality is not what it appears to be. Problems are really solutions, negative features are really positive impetus, the end is really the beginning.

Paradoxical intention takes the problem, be it sexual failure, coronary fixation, nervousness, or insomnia, and transmutes it into the solution. It counterweighs a faulty assumption with an equally potent new assumption, thus creating a balance which allows nature to express itself naturally.

Most important, in all these manifestations of the upside-down thumb, is that by using the upside-down thumb very often one can straighten out a crooked situation in a very uncomplicated manner without it appearing as a therapeutic endeavor. Rather it is seen as a natural approach to life, one which re-orients a philosophy and redirects a focus. It is easy, it is simple, and in most instances quite effective. It does not involve the grandiosity of putting individuals through a counselling situation or a clinical experience, and does not inflict upon individuals the sense that maybe they are sick; instead, that they are quite healthy and have the capacity and the will to control the direction they go. It sounds facile, but it has worked so often that any initial skepticism I had about its being too simplistic has been totally erased by experience.

The journey that began at the University of Ottawa has not ended. It has barely begun. Logotherapy has put into perspective the idea that psychology does not deal from a position of sickness, but from the position of health. It does not wallow in the depths of human misery, but focuses on the potentials to which all human beings can aspire. I have been opened to new vistas, been able to make the entire world a focus of concern.

In logotherapy, a sound Judaic approach to life can be translated into the twentieth century idiom. It is a meeting ground for Biblical values and mental health, a place where psychological wisdom and religious insight can meet, shake hands and walk together.

A LOVE STORY

Jacqulyn S. Clements

I'VE BEEN A PSYCHOTHERAPIST for twenty years, and I embarked on this adventure without God. At least I thought I did. In retrospect, it seems peculiar that I didn't know God was there.

I didn't grow up really poor. I always had food, shelter, clothes, toys for Christmas, and nickels to take to school for special travelling shows that performed in gymnasiums in those days. But by today's standards, it wasn't exactly materially plush. The place was Plainfield, Indiana, population 1,917. We lived in a rented duplex with old furniture, my father drove a third-hand car, and we had a coal-oil stove and small ice box. Appendectomies and tonsillectomies called for trips to an Indianapolis finance company for what was called a character loan. On such occasions my mother would dress my big sister and me in our best clothes, and we'd sit in the waiting room trying to look appealing as part of the propaganda. But none of this bothered me in the least. I couldn't have felt more secure if I had been a Rockefeller child.

My parents were optimists with great faith in life. I didn't realize there were any Joneses to keep up with, since I heard no complaints or comparisons in my home. I caught it by osmosis, the atmosphere of appreciation and all we had seemed grand to me. I was never told how hard they worked or what they'd done for me. In fact, my parents had the amazing capacity to forget all effort and like young

---

Jacqulyn Clements, Ph.D. has been Senior Psychologist at the DeKalb County Mental Health Clinic and is presently in full-time private practice in Virginia Beach, Virginia.

children, experience good things as blessings raining on them. My father was Peter Pan and my mother was Wendy.

During my years of personal therapy, I dutifully noted parental flaws and hang-ups, both real and imaginary. I even managed to seethe a bit. But I trust the feelings I remember more. The colors were so vivid and life glittered so much, it's still only my head that says I didn't grow up in a palace. And when my father didn't have the price of admission to some attractive event, he would sometimes just tip his hat to the ticket taker, walk in, and they'd all laugh. No, that's not cheating; it's called grace.

The first song I ever learned was "Jesus Loves Me," and it was easy to believe. My parents were real Christians although not fundamentalists in a negative, distorted sense (like long faces and no-no mania). Their childhood background was Evangelical and Reformed; she fell in love with him at seven when he gave her the little cotton chicken off of his Easter basket. As adults, they joined a Disciples of Christ church, and that's where the family went every Sunday.

At thirteen, while the congregation sang "Jesus Is Calling," I walked down the aisle for salvation and subsequent baptism. God had always seemed like my best friend, so this was not a dramatic conversion. I was awed, though, with the thought that I would receive the Holy Spirit at this time. I wasn't sure what the Holy Spirit was like, but the name certainly sounded exotic. When I'd seen my first nuns at age six when they passed by on a city street, and said, "That's what I want to be when I grow up!" my adult companions, figuring I was attracted by the nuns' garb, laughed. Actually it was their twinkling eyes that drew me. I was also fascinated by pictures of Sally Rand and thought perhaps I'd like to be a fan dancer.

My parents didn't engage in much God-talk at home, and we didn't have a family altar. We did pray "Our Father, from whom cometh every good and perfect gift, we thank you" at meals and at night I did "Now I lay me down to sleep." This latter prayer has been under attack in recent years as a potential psychological nightmare because of the line "If I should die before I wake, I pray the Lord my soul to take." I found it no such thing. It gave me a warm, protected feeling as I fell asleep at night. It was a reminder that the real me was spirit. It reinforced my individuality and lessened dependence on parents. Even now, in times of stress, I like to fold my hands in bed and say once again, "Now I lay me down to sleep . . ."

I went to summer church camp as a teen-ager and rededicated my life, with tears, to the strains of "Follow, I Will Follow Thee." Outside observers, who sometimes judge such activities as morbid or traumatic, don't know what they're talking about. It was glorious. So was the night I attended a Youth for Christ rally in Indianapolis and caught my first vision of taking the Gospel to the whole world. "All Hail the Power of Jesus' Name," and I was ready to go when called. I also enjoyed singing "Living for Jesus" by myself at home as a private dedication. "I own no other Master, my heart shall be Thy throne; my life I give, henceforth to live, O Christ, for Thee alone."

I only recall one troubling (at the time) aspect of my youth as a Christian. When I was sixteen, I dreamed about Jesus one night, the only dream I've ever had about Him. If somebody told me I was going to dream about Jesus, I would have been pleased; my mental picture was of a gentle man holding a lamb or suffering the little children to come unto Him. In my dream I walked down a path, turned a corner (although it looked like a desert), and suddenly ahead was a solitary tree and a robed male figure standing beside it. I knew it was Jesus. Our eyes met. Instantly I awakened from the dream with a feeling of terror. There was no impression in the dream that He would hurt me. My fright was power shock. When I looked into His eyes, I experienced something akin to a million volts of electricity. I think I also was scared because the dream had some quality of super-reality about it. It wasn't until many years later that I realized I'd encountered the resurrected Christ in that dream, not simply the man from Galilee.

From this background (with the exception of Sally Rand), it might sound like I would rush off to Bob Jones University to prepare for a mission field in Africa. Actually I went to Indiana University, got married during graduation week, and went on to get a Ph.D. in clinical psychology. My attraction to psychology stemmed from an interest in the original meaning of *psyche* as soul rather than from a desire to help people. Who or what were human beings? What forces really shaped our destiny and how? But "soul" and even "mind" were dirty words during this era of psychology. By the time I finished graduate school, I was agnostic.

As I recall, my questions about Christianity (to the extent I even gave it thought anymore) weren't about miracles. Surely the God who created life itself and all those galaxies could pull off a simple virgin birth. I was puzzled by justice and the judgment. We moved to Atlanta after college years and I missed church (as a community of people) enough so that I joined a super-liberal church. We were for love, brotherhood, and good things; but it was essentially a humanist stance.

I was enthusiastic for several years with my agnostic position, and I felt I'd really been enlightened. My parents were not alarmed. Dad told Mom it was just a phase I was going through. When I heard about this, I thought, "Poor Daddy, so naive." To me it was like once you don't believe in Santa Claus, you can't believe again even if you wanted to. I was faithful to my new beliefs, witnessed to friends, and helped recruit several people for the super-liberal church. I couldn't understand how anyone with much intelligence or education could still be attending those orthodox churches. Surely they didn't really believe that stuff anymore.

Professionally I worked at a child guidance clinic during these early years in Atlanta while my husband (also a psychologist) taught at Emory University. Eventually we went into private practice. I had my personal therapy and also did a considerable amount of workshopping and further training.

Although trained and experienced in various therapy approaches, I never did adopt one particular style. I've always emphasized the positive. I don't attack or dwell on defenses; I'd rather see them melt as the person doesn't need them anymore. I'm more interested in not eliciting defenses and distortions than in having them demonstrated on me. I see people in new ways, often before there is a shred of evidence. This comes easy for me and, if it didn't, it probably wouldn't work out the same. I try to see beyond to a deeper than conscious level.

At one point I almost got tripped up as a therapist by "knowing too much." The more I learned, the more complicated therapy looked. I heard several horror tales from other therapists. I met some people in their fourteenth year of therapy who looked like they hadn't started yet. I wasn't doing very well in my personal therapy either. Then I made a leap of faith. Somehow I set aside those pessimistic thoughts about therapy in general and about particular clients. Perhaps I remembered that we see through a glass darkly and that all things are possible with God. But this knowledge wasn't at a conscious level yet.

Meanwhile my enthusiasm with the super-liberal church began to wane. I remember one night at a pitch-in dinner there when, once again, I didn't get any meat. If you weren't in the front part of the serving line, there just wasn't any left. I'd also noted several people (not poor) contribute only small bowls of salad although there were four or five in their family. I hungrily recalled those mountains of fried chicken and juicy ham slices at my childhood church pitch-ins. My sorry super-liberal church dinner was a small thing, yet it set me wondering. Was that love we touted only a head trip or spur to political action? How much love was there really one for another? Why were so many of the brethren downright stingy?

I also found Easter in a liberal church quite disappointing. What could you say if you didn't really believe Jesus was resurrected? One year we discussed the cheapest way to bury people. Another year a guest speaker somewhat snidely ridiculed a book reporting supernatural phenomena. One Easter I rebelled and went to a Baptist church. By then I thought when you died, that was it, and the soul was simply the bottom of the shoe to me. Nonetheless, I began to cry when some people went down the aisle at the end of the service to get saved. Saved from what? I no longer knew, but I was happy for them.

My disillusionment with liberal religion didn't promote faith in anything else, though. I just started sleeping later on Sundays instead of attending the services. The reason I still participated at all was because of the loving pastor and a few close friends there. While I realize now that there were always spiritual aspects in my work as a therapist, this did not prevent an increasing spiritual dehydration in my own life during the agnostic years. I didn't think of it like that at the time. The erosion was so gradual and subtle, I didn't realize it was a problem until something better started to happen.

In August 1970 I went to the Association of Humanistic Psychology convention in Miami. Before it started, I went on the chartered boat cruise to the Bahamas. That boat trip seems part of the awakening somehow; maybe it was the ocean and the clear view of the stars. Early in the convention I was in a small group and we were to close our eyes. We were told that at a signal from the leader, some truth about ourselves would be revealed to us. We weren't to think or try, just see what comes. Then after opening our eyes, we'd tell our "truth" to each member of our small group. The words that popped into my mind at his signal were "I am very powerful and I will never die." Good grief, I thought, and rather wished I'd come up with an Oedipal confession instead of such a preposterous sounding ditty. Being honest, though, I announced it around the circle. Nobody laughed.

The next day, I walked unseeingly by the convention book table and then whirled around suddenly and went back. I instantly bought Ira Progoff's *The Symbolic and the Real.* A silent voice had told me to purchase it. Although not explicitly Christian, this book had a spiritual impact on me. I began right then to record my dreams, and three weeks later I terminated my personal therapy as a long overdue step.

The first dream I recorded involved deep water with big, beautiful fish (a Christian symbol) in it. I was a little frightened of the fish although the overall effect of the dream was positive. After encountering the fish, I explored a new campus with excitement. But it was night and I could only see partly. Subsequent dreams seemed to be encouraging me to end my therapy. I'd known this was a good idea, but I guess it took God through a dream notebook to get me out of there.

I gradually began to sample fare from today's spiritual cafeteria. I read books about clairvoyants and parapsychology. I looked into Zen and Eastern approaches. I delved into mystery religions. I learned how to see auras. I got fascinated with astrology and eagerly awaited the date when Pluto would transmit my ascendant, figuring I might get reborn. (Actually I got up that morning with diarrhea.) Fortunately I was more of an arm-chair speculator with many of these things than practitioner; I've since become aware of the hazards (physical, mental, emotional, spiritual) in some of these paths. Somehow I knew not to dabble at all with sorcery, séances, or "guides" (a modern term for familiar spirits).

On January 1, 1972, I felt I was to leave Atlanta—just take off! This made no particular sense. I loved Atlanta and had many friends there. We had a thriving practice in the prettiest offices we'd ever had. We lived in a beautiful place with pool, tennis, golf course, and even a small lake with ducks who waddled up to my back door at times for a snack. This "go" impression was so strong, though, that had my husband not been in agreement, I think I would have gone alone. Fortunately, he had long harbored a fantasy of taking a year off for travel; so ten months later we stored everything and took off for we knew not where. We spent some time in Florida, took a Carribbean ship cruise, went to Europe for several months, and ended up in Virginia Beach where we decided to resettle. I didn't realize when we first came to Virginia Beach that it is a hotbed of Christianity as well as other spiritual disciplines. I didn't know that the north beach section I chose to live in was at the point where the Jamestown settlers had stepped off a boat in 1607, erected a cross, and dedicated the land to God.

The month before we left on our sojourn, Kathryn Kuhlman came to Atlanta. My heart had always believed in miracle healings. I did not attend as a cynic. Nonetheless, I was very impressed with my first direct observation of them. The most memorable aspect of this event, though, was experiencing the Holy Spirit. I felt a Presence even while waiting in the rain with a sack lunch to get into the building. Later, to my surprise, I was aware of where the healings were taking place shortly before there was a stir in the audience or Kuhlman called them out. Although there was a consistent overall Presence, increased "voltage" at certain times and places in the auditorium gave an impression that the Holy Spirit was moving around geographically. At one point, I suddenly felt something like fire (although it didn't hurt) within me. She then stopped in the middle of a sentence, pointed toward our small section, and exclaimed, "Oh, my! You people take anything you need, right now." I'm not certain what I received physically, but I surely got a spiritual whammie.

While in Europe we visited many old churches and cathedrals. A number of these are nearly deserted now because Christianity has almost faded out in France and England. But the vibrations were still in the empty buildings. In Rome we were escorted to a small side room in a Catholic church where some bones of saints were kept. Although I'd never had strong anti-Catholic sentiments, this type of thing always sounded gross to me. I wasn't at all sure I wanted to go into the "bone room," but I went. The moment I entered, the Holy Spirit was so strong I leaned against a wall for support. Also, the Christian art we viewed in Europe, especially from the Renaissance era, impressed me.

I wasn't consciously aware during my agnostic years that a gradual loss of meaning and cohesion had occurred even in relation to cultural things. As I began to believe, literature, art, music, and other creations came together again. I often think of this now in relation to our humanist public education. What does much in our culture and past mean to many youth today? I wonder how anyone can even vaguely understand Western civilization without comprehending at least the rudiments of Judeo-Christian thinking and beliefs. I suspect there is a significant emptiness of meaning in most of my younger clients.

As I took my spiritual journey, the Bible as truth and the reality of Jesus became overwhelmingly clear to me fairly soon. I didn't return to a more orthodox Christian position all at once, though. I'd gathered other things along the way and still had a few blocks. I tried to reconcile some theories based on reincarnation with Christianity for awhile. It never worked. For centuries people have speculated about the metaphysical possibilities for such an occurrence as physical rebirth, but this has no relevance for the spiritual path revealed in the Bible. "Working out karma" does not jibe with salvation through Jesus. Looking back I wonder how I ever imagined people could untangle a web of many supposed lives when they can't even do it with one. All systems I studied, except Christianity, were variations of earning favor, not grace. Many required extensive study, maybe years of effort, even above-average intelligence. Subconsciously, I sensed all along that none of these were the best path. I finally realized that ultimately, in terms of destiny (rather than just enjoyment, self-improvement, or heightened faculties), there is only one way. Yes, I know, that phrase can sound dogmatic.

It occurred to me several years ago that while "seeking for truth" is in vogue, to claim you have found some is a mistake in many circles. To "search for God" is okay, but don't act like you found Him. I noticed that there is often an underlying attitude that this quest is just a game, that we invented God, and any story about Him is equally true. Religious freedom (a precious civil right) does not mean that there aren't spiritual truths and hard-core realities. Moses either went up on Mt. Sinai and got those Ten Commandments from a living God, or he didn't. Jesus is either the Almighty Messiah of Israel and Savior of the world, or He isn't. As modern people we have learned to compromise, but there isn't really any half-way God who ever half-way did anything. Is Christianity narrow-minded? Suppose truth itself is narrow, maybe an infinitesimal dot?

At some point in this journey, I received the baptism in the Holy Spirit. This is what the early Christians had, starting at Pentecost. Christianity didn't spread like wild-fire through parts of the Gentile world because it was a good story or they were looking for a Jewish hero. It was experiential, with signs and wonders. Although the world calls it a "religion," the core of authentic Christian faith is a personal relationship with Jesus.

My old concern, over not understanding many aspects of a judgment, was finally resolved in prayer one day. I realized that the judgment was God's problem, not mine. What a relief! My assignment is to love. And I now trust God to do the rest.

In July, 1978 I walked down the aisle of a Disciples of Christ church in Virginia Beach. I don't remember what they were singing. God just said go, and I went.

I am persuaded that all aspects of a therapist are necessarily part of the relationship with a client. This includes values, beliefs, faiths, life-styles, and their intermingling. I am now a Christian and this permeates my work as a therapist and my theoretical orientation as well as the rest of my life.

I realize now that even before I became a total Bible believer again, the solidity of Judeo-Christian ethics had been confirmed for me. Some aspects had stuck with me from childhood and never departed; others returned after painful learning experiences or further observations of life. A difference now, I suppose, is that there is no longer any inner wavering. Believing in the absolute values of the Bible does not lessen my capacity to work well with people who lie, cheat, fornicate, and all the rest. Although my clients usually know what my personal beliefs are, this does not hinder their experiencing my acceptance of them, whatever they've been up to.

Moralizing is as destructive in therapy as it is in other interpersonal relations, but it has no necessary connection to one sort of beliefs. Some of the most cringing, or at least boring, moralizing I've ever heard has been from so-called free thinkers. To me, moralizing is really an attitude, a voice tone. If someone insists on defining moralizing as simply verbalizing right or wrong, good-bad or whatever, then I surely am a moralizer. Whether this latter type of activity is a positive or negative in therapy depends not only on how it's done but also on the validity and truth of the value system itself.

Although I now hold Bible-based values regarding sex, I've never harassed clients about sexual episodes. I do share some views in this area, though, when it feels right. With sexually active young teen-agers, I typically comment (just once usually) that I don't think it's good for them. Emotionally speaking, it's too much too soon. They nearly always understand and agree, although they don't swear off that night. If I mention that pre-marital sex is not God's ideal, I always add that Jesus was very loving to whores and saved his sharp words for the self-righteous hypocrites. They love to hear how sins of the spirit are more serious than weaknesses of the flesh and that sexual gossipers and sourpusses are offensive to God.

I am an activist with clients in regard to lying. I don't mean if they lie to me. I usually accept, without comment, all kinds of malarkey. But, when clients admit in therapy that they lie to people I'm glad to remind them, at the right time, that lying is a terrible habit. It's not good for them. Lying destroys their self-respect; it gnaws at their soul. In the case of children or teen-agers who can't (or won't) obey their parents in certain respects, I suggest they at least keep their mouth shut or take the punishment. Of course I empathize with how or why they started lying before I advise them to cease as soon as possible. I feel very comfortable doing this. It's as if a client had cancer and I knew a cure, I'd enthusiastically pass on the information.

I've found that discouraging lying has had some excellent therapeutic results, especially with the young. Allan is a good illustration of this.

Allan was a fifteen-year-old boy from a middle-class home, referred by the court while on probation for seven felonies of burglary. He also was close to failing at school and rebellious at home. Psychological testing suggested Allan had superior intellectual potential but deficits in verbal skills. I explained this to him and encouraged him not only to verbalize feelings but also to talk to more people about things in general, to practice putting ideas into words. During the first therapy session I asked him how he happened to take up burglary. I don't remember what he said. We never discussed it again. About a month later, I gave him my don't-lie pep talk.

Allan was fortunate in getting a very loving and excellent literature teacher at school when a new semester started. The most dramatic changes started, though, the day his father asked him if he'd done something and Allan simply stated, "Yes." He liked the way he felt afterwards and began to get honest in other ways.

Therapy terminated in eleven months. Allan had no further trouble with the law. He had new friends, and A's and B's on his report card. His parents were enjoying him. His probation officer wished for more kids like him, and his lawyer was so impressed he hired Allan for a summer job. This is, of course, the kind of inspirational outcome I wish I could frame and hang in the waiting room.

Although I relate to people, I hope, in a unified or integrated sense, I conceptualize persons as being body, soul *(psyche),* and spirit. As a psychotherapist, my main focus is still on *psyche,* but I am now more concerned with the whole person. Of course I don't conduct evangelistic services during therapy. I do pray for all of my clients, usually in private, but occasionally (with permission) in their presence. Since I started praying, clients seem to get better much quicker as well as get more "breaks" in life. I'm also glad to include spiritual teaching, at whatever level is appropriate to the person, if requested by the client or led by the Holy Spirit to do so. Like many therapists, I'd grasped the validity of some basic spiritual laws like forgiving and gratitude years ago, although I guess I thought of them simply as facts of life. Other spiritual laws, or hints for healthful living, have become much clearer to me as a result of Bible study. So many things now make exquisite sense to me; it all fits together for the first time. After all the brilliant new ideas (including mine) I've seen flop in my lifetime, it is nice to finally find Someone who knows what He's talking about.

Cathy's case is one where significant work was done in all three spheres of body, soul, and spirit.

She was seventeen and had superior intelligence but was often irritable, neurotically discontent, and anxious. She had come home drunk several times, was an almost daily pot smoker, and had at least experimented with other drugs. It was Cathy's idea to get therapy, somewhat unusual in this age range. She was seeking help for her anxiety and unhappiness, not her drug taking.

We spent some time tracing several resentment patterns back to their origins. To her surprise, she decided she was full of old grudges and a spoiled brat to boot. She took my knock-off-lying advice to heart and did that. Once when she backslid and told a whopper, she asked her parents not to let her have the car for six weeks as a punishment. After five months of therapy she came to her session very excited about a new revelation: she must have been crazy to take those drugs. She subsequently found that she was too attached emotionally to give up pot and only half-successfully reconstructed her old rationalizations about it. I encouraged her to continue trying to minimize its use but pointed out that she likely needed to get something better inside her first (probably at a spiritual level) so she wouldn't need (want) it anymore. She understood but still felt discouraged.

Cathy then told me she'd felt something was wrong with her back for years. I referred her to a good osteopath. She faithfully went for treatments every week which surprised her mother because Cathy had always hated going to doctors.

About this time, I went to a Camp Farthest Out (a Christian retreat). In my prayer group, I requested prayer for Cathy. (I didn't give a name; God knew who "teen-age girl" meant.) I sat in a chair in proxy for Cathy and the group laid hands on me. During this praying, I had a sense of almost certainty regarding a healing for Cathy. I also had a prophetic impression that God was going to use her in a ministry to other teen-agers. When I got home, I found out Cathy had impulsively attended a meeting of a Christian youth group and had had a good time. She later went to a party with her old friends and stayed straight. She was feeling great. Although I told Cathy that people had prayed for her at the retreat (she was glad), I did not share the healing or prophecy impressions with her.

A month later Cathy forgot an appointment, cancelled the next one, and then for the first time showed up for her session stoned. She looked like a rain-soaked alley cat. Cathy talked easily, though, and rattled on and on. Near the end of the session, I commented that the voice sounded like hers but somehow it didn't seem like her talking; it was more like a phonograph record. She said, "That's how it feels to me. I'm not connected to it. It's scary." This "phonograph record" impression wasn't like the dull monotone of a head-tripper; it had a more eerie, brain-washed quality.

Cathy came to the next session straight and, without prompting, described some fairly intense feelings of depersonalization she'd had in the past even when not stoned. She said it was terrifying. She came to her next session and said she was not scared anymore. Later in the hour she described a new experience with the family dog. She'd never been mean to him, but he'd just been sort of a thing to her although they'd had him several years. She'd resented it if her parents occasionally had her walk him. During the past week, it was like she suddenly awakened and saw him for the first time. She'd been voluntarily walking him every night since then even if she was tired. "He's a nice dog and he likes to get outside like that." Therapy terminated after two more sessions because Cathy was spending the summer with an aunt who lived in another state. She said she would return for therapy in the fall if she needed it but optimistically predicted that she wouldn't. She did not return in the fall.

A few months later I heard from the mother that Cathy was completely off drugs, seemed happy, and was doing well at home and school. She was even working as a volunteer aide at a half-way house for disturbed teen-agers. The people in charge said Cathy showed an extraordinary talent for helping troubled kids.

Besides personal hunger, another thing prompting my spiritual search was a subtle uneasiness about the world of psychotherapy, not only the world in general. Many beautiful things had happened in the therapy world (good encounter groups, more honest and deeper communication, clients and therapists seen as persons), but other trends concerned me deeply. For example, I began to wonder if neurotic symptoms weren't sometimes being "cured" by the person flipping into a stance of social alienation. While therapists have toyed with the so-called superego for many years, this loosening was going far beyond the level of "It's okay not to iron your sheets." In at least some therapy circles many guilt feelings or moral concerns were looked down on. This attitude, combined with increasingly loose value advocacy, could help promote this thing I call a flip.

While this switch to more alienating modes apparently alleviated some neurotic symptoms and was usually accompanied by an initial burst of energy, ultimately it resulted in loss. I think neurotic anxiety was replaced by a slowly growing, amorphous, gut-level anxiety. Eventually more and more stimulation was required to keep the elation going or to prevent a depression and nothingness from taking over. Instead of achieving growth and liberation, it looked to me like people were jumping from the briar patch into some quicksand. But however alarmed I was about dismissal of guilt, I realized guilt feelings could be a destructive force and I had no new notions on the subject.

This area didn't clear up until I got back to the Bible. I'd forgotten that Satan is the Accuser. I now believe that Satan is an actual spiritual being (the Archangel Lucifer), but whether he is conceived thus or seen simply as a symbol for destructive forces, he is the real accuser. While violation of life's laws can bring consequences and God did say "repent" fairly often, He never commanded anyone to run around feeling guilty. Self-hatred is never listed as a virtue. God does not torment people!

Recalling that Satan is the Accuser produced one of those "clicks" where impressions I'd gained or things I'd done as a therapist suddenly slid into Bible teaching with a perfect fit. It is a significant aspect of a Bible-based theoretical orientation and if I were to address a Christian audience, I might well speak on this topic. Asking myself, though, if my deeper comprehension of God and guilt has changed my basic therapy style, I think the answer is mostly no.

I always have believed in the validity of guilt *per se* despite the displacements and distortions often involved in what people term "guilt feelings." I never have hesitated to agree that behavior is bad if I really think so, like saying, "Yeah, that really was a rotten thing to do." I've even on rare occasions used that most-forbidden phrase, "Why, shame on you!" to clients; it can be a high compliment to a better self if you say it right. These are not, by the way, the sort of comments I'd recommend to other therapists as a technique if they don't feel intuitively and peacefully right. If even a tiny part of you wants the people to suffer from guilt feelings or you're trying to change them, forget it. Agonizing guilt feelings are not one of my hang-ups and I never had urges to change anybody except my husband and my therapist. I never even had much of a yen to help people. Rather than relinquishing my Sally Rand fantasies for Florence Nightingale, I just switched to Lana Turner and Rita Hayworth.

Although I've never thought of myself as a guilt-oriented therapist, I remember once years ago deciding I was probably more of a "self-respect" style therapist than "love" oriented. This didn't mean I didn't desire to be a loving person or that I didn't believe in the healing power of agape love. I think this notion was a response to the limitations of most people's love capacity and the neurotic elements often involved in a search for love. Although infants, apparently, need love to survive and love (God) really does make the world go around, people frequently seek affection (reassurance) when their deficit is self-respect. Early in my career as a therapist, I had several child clients who were in an orphanage. They showed a lot of affect hunger besides anxiety and miscellaneous other symptoms. I had no urge at all to pet them or give them extra cookies. "My God," I thought, "quit selling your soul for a few crumbs of love or attention from the world; you can make it all right!" I treated them like self-respecting people even though they weren't yet. These children did very well in therapy and elicited more favorable responses from people afterwards. I've seen several women clients right after their husbands have left them. One of the first pieces of advice I give them is to clean the house and closets, dress well, and cook nice meals for themselves. I encourage them to cry and grieve, but not to slob. This isn't to fool anybody. It's because there is strength in self-respect and they need an extra portion at this time.

While I believe in giving encouragement to people, I've always felt that self-respect must be valid and autonomous. While treating people respectfully is important and even loving, it does not give them self-respect; it does, of course, foster self-respecting behavior by lowering anxiety and defenses. Confidence may stem from talent and recognition, but self-respect is more related to integrity, discipline, and the choices we make in life. The relationship of self-respect to guilt is that sin lessens self-respect. People can seem ego-enhanced over minor things, but there is a deeper barometer inside. I'm not saying human nature alone is good. Without God, we've all had it. But I do believe there is a deep and universal yearning for God in people, and God is holy.

Because most people are dominated by the *psyche,* they tend to emotionalize things. *Sin* means missing the mark and *repentance* means to turn, a switch in direction, a change of mind. That's why feeling bad or being agonizingly sorry usually amounts to little. As a Christian, of course, I see the ultimate and crucial solution to guilt as being salvation through Jesus. A frequent response to the born-again experience, even with people who had no consciously strong feelings of guilt before, is a sensation that a weight has lifted. But that is not the point; with or without feelings or sensations, their standing before God and their relationship to guilt has been altered. As a therapist, I'm not dealing at this level. I'm not Jesus. I can't save anybody.

In line with my faith in the Bible, I now see the *psyche* in a different way. I believe God made all of man and woman (body, soul, and spirit) and saw that it was good. What went wrong? When they were disobedient, the spiritual connecton and fellowship with God died. Eventually, of course, the physical bodies died too. But the error of Adam and Eve and its consequences were perpetuated in the human race. We all fell at Eden. In God's perfect plan, spirit was to be the "boss," directing and dominant over the soul, psyche. It, in turn, was to be a sub-foreman over body. This human spirit, in fellowship with and submissive to God, meant people could live in holiness, peace, joy, and also eternally. With a separation from God and a dead or dormant spirit, the psyche took over completely and "ego" began to develop.

Parading one's insecurities by way of bragging or boasting is fairly universally recognized as bad news in the mental health field. But ego in another sense is usually viewed as good. As the organizer of self, sufficient "ego strength" is seen as crucial to mental health or sanity. This is likely a part truth. Given dead spirit, there has to be some integrator if we are to function above a mere physical, animal level. Yet, in some ways this ego is an illusion, a false identity, and a usurper of the throne meant for Spirit. The new creation involves a restoration of the intended spirit-soul-body relationship. This results in a new kind of people, qualitatively different, of which Jesus is the first-born.

I find the Bible has a much more positive and workable approach to mental health than all the psychology books I've read. Many of the principles work well even for non-believers although the potential is vastly higher, of course, for Christians. Christian mental health includes peace and joy and does not require good parents, a great and stable society, or other favorable circumstances in life. A Christian is highly responsive to other persons in active, not reactive ways. Ideally there is total dependence on God and no grasping, emotional dependence on other people. Neurotic ties are short-circuited because they're part of a false system. There is no yesterday to the born-again believer walking in the Spirit; all decks are cleared, each moment is new, the eternal is now.

My faith in the Bible also gives me information on what's going on in the world. If I didn't know the latter days as described in the Bible, I'm not sure I would see much hope anymore. I really believe that fairly soon (after the holocaust?) Jesus will walk through that East Gate into Jerusalem and rule the world from the throne of David—just like God said He would.

Over the past fifteen years, almost without exception, my young clients have expressed their feeling that catastrophe is coming to the world. They don't expect to get a chance to grow up or reach middle age. They doubt if planet Earth will be here much longer. I now tell them I believe Earth will still be here and human life go on, that a new age is coming. I agree, though, with their sense of terrible and chaotic things which will happen before then. My agreement in this latter area does not appear to increase their anxiety. On the contrary, it confirms their sanity and seems to bring some relief.

Carol, age 13, hated school, was often truant, argued and had violent moods at home. She'd run away shortly before coming for therapy and been beaten up by a motorcycle gang. At nine, her mother had put her and four siblings in a children's home for several months while she sought work in a distant city. Carol recalled she had cried continuously after this separation. Then one day she decided she would never cry again and she never had—not for her mother or anything else. Carol realized by now that not crying wasn't good for her; she had tried to cry in recent years but couldn't anymore. This girl apparently had a reputation for being "tough" and said most of the teachers at school were scared of her. Despite her traumatic and unstable background, Carol still had a real zest for life which was very refreshing, at least to me.

After several months of therapy, Carol commented that the reason she hated school wasn't really that the teachers or work were so bad. She resented having to spend all that time in an old stuffy building. "I like to walk in the woods and see flowers and trees. I want to see the beautiful, natural things while they're still here. It may be too late after I graduate. People are destroying the earth; something terrible is coming." I said I could see what she meant, and I really could. I commented that I believed the Earth would make it and peace come but hard times, getting even worse, would happen first.

She spoke of enjoying just sitting quietly on a log in the sunshine. I asked if she liked to talk to God. She looked a little surprised and then laughed. She said, "Yeah, I really do. I talk to Him a lot in the woods when I'm alone." After sitting silently awhile she said, "I don't love me, but I think maybe God does." Three or four tears rolled down her cheeks. A few moments later she leaped out of her seat, clapped her hands like she'd won a jackpot, and shouted, "Hey, look, I did it—I cried!"

Therapy was terminated shortly after this for financial and other reasons. I don't think Carol has turned into an honor student or won any citizen awards yet. I have heard that she gets along with her mother very well now, voluntarily helps her in many ways, and is the most loving and responsible member of the family.

I'm not sure I'd even want to be a therapist these days if I didn't have God with me as an extraordinary consultant as well as healer. Occasionally I drop the whole thing on the Lord.

One day a teen-age client asked if I'd promise not to tell his parents if he told me something. I said I couldn't guarantee it since I don't offer minors complete confidentiality. They know from the beginning that if they tell me something very serious, like they're shooting heroin or robbing banks, their only choice will then be whether to tell their parents themselves or for me to do it. He decided to tell me. His little sister, quite young, was going to get a secret abortion. Local doctors had arranged it in a neighboring city, the cover-up story was all worked out, and the parents didn't know a thing about it. I thought, "I wish he hadn't told me that one."

There were valid medical concerns in this case and my guess was that the parents would probably agree with the girl's decision to get an abortion. But the notion of one so young going through it secretly as well as the conspiracy aspects gave me an uneasy feeling. I wasn't concerned that telling the parents would interrupt or disturb my client's relationship with me. But my being the one to tell them didn't feel right. And I certainly wasn't going to request that the client blab on her. I decided it was unsolvable so I'd cast it on the Lord instead of stewing over it any longer. I told Him that I was not going to do anything, and if He thought it best for these parents to know, then He'd have to take care of it. It was His problem now.

A couple of weeks later my client reported that when his sister and her boyfriend arrived at the hospital admission desk, the woman in charge acted funny and with no explanation said the doctors had changed their minds and wouldn't do it. She did, however, helpfully call another nearby hospital who said they would do it that day. Arriving at the admission desk at the second hospital, they found it was a higher charge and they'd already scraped up all the money they could. They returned home, walked into the living room, and little Sis said, "Mom and Dad, there's something I want to tell you. . . ."

This may sound strange but when my client told me about this outcome, I didn't recall my prayer at first. It wasn't until I was driving home that evening that I remembered casting it on the Lord. I laughed right out loud and muttered, "Hey, Jesus, that was really neat!"

My recovered faith helps me channel more of God's love to clients. I want to be guided by Him. My "ears to hear" aren't great yet, but they're improving.

The healthier I am, the better therapist I'll be. I feel more centered now. I am more centered. "Thou art the Christ, the son of the living God," and on this Rock I'll stand. This time forever.

A BASIC GOODNESS

William U. Snyder

I WAS BROUGHT UP in a strictly religious family. My father, and later my brother, were Lutheran ministers. I had considered that profession myself, and went to a denominational college noted for the large number of ministers it prepared. Actually, I chose that college because of its pleasant ambience and its handsome scholarships for ministers' sons. In college I soon realized that my deep skepticism about dogma would prevent my ever being ordained; I was the college rebel who fought the compulsory daily chapel requirements successfully for a whole semester, and never went to church while there.

Why was I a rebel? I've often speculated as to why my older and younger brothers accepted our parents' indoctrination so enthusiastically and became conservative, while I was a liberal from a very early time. At eight, I would not pray because it seemed pointless. I couldn't hear anyone reply, and I wasn't sure anyone was listening. At 16, I made my grandmother cry because I refused to go to communion. I suspect I felt rejected by my father; he was the "Mr. Religion" in our family. So my rebelling against authority and religion was probably "getting back" at him, at first. Eventually it became a life style and determined my therapeutic style.

Portions of this chapter have appeared before in an article entitled "The Agnostic Psychotherapist" which appeared in *Voices: Journal of the American Academy of Psychotherapists,* Vol. 16, No. 1, Spring 1980, Issue 59, pp. 28–30.

William U. Snyder, Ph.D. was for 17 years Director of Clinical Training at Pennsylvania State University. He is presently Distinguished Professor of Psychology at Ohio University, Athens, Ohio.

When I faced the question of what to do professionally, I preferred medicine and teaching. The former sounded, in view of my older brother's experience, full of boring courses like chemistry and anatomy, and teaching sounded like a financial disaster. But I did encounter something I became engrossed in—psychology. I read my brother's textbooks from his psychology courses and was deeply interested, so I quickly gravitated to that area. I took every psychology course the college offered and felt convinced that I wanted to teach it. I didn't know about clinical practice at the time, but I knew I liked the idea of helping people; it was the one thing about the ministry that I knew I would enjoy.

My college psychology professor helped me obtain a graduate assistantship in the psychology program at Duke, a school which we chose because it had "about the only Christian psychology department in America." It was headed by William McDougall, probably the last remaining advocate of "hormic psychology," a humanistic, teleological psychology. Duke was disappointing, however. Many of the department members seemed to be interested primarily in the learning process of the rat. But when I was introduced to clinical psychology, I knew I had arrived in the "chosen land."

Three months after I started work on my Ph.D. at Ohio State, a young and exciting professor arrived in the department—Carl Rogers. The course of my graduate education and my career were then clearly set; I became an enthusiastic disciple.

The man himself was captivating, but his ideas were even more so. That a psychologist had every right to help people by way of therapy was a message I was yearning to hear. And that this enterprise could be such a warm, meaningful relationship was a heady insight. I never lost my initial enthusiasm for it, nor for Rogers.

But I had been steeped in learning theory, and earlier had even picked up a smattering of psychoanalysis. These influences also stayed with me, producing an unashamed and consciously constructive eclecticism.

I went through 30 years of agnosticism and hard-nosed logical positivism. At 60, my wife and I started wintering in Sarasota, Florida, while still teaching at Ohio University in the fall and spring. Looking for companionship, we found the Unitarian church filled with like-minded people, including several psychologists and a psychiatrist. So we became enthusiastic, agnostic Unitarians. There is an interaction between my agnostic Unitarianism and the strong concern I feel about people. I've felt no need for a personal God because I see life's purpose as being thoroughly fulfilled in contributing to the fulfillment of the lives of other people. But if a person is agnostic, why should he need Unitarianism, or any other church? Well, really, as a religion, I don't need it. But as a situation for relating to pleasant like-minded people, I find it desirable and I identify with the social causes which the church espouses as well.

Once a colleague from another department, observing our agnosticism, asked me if psychology was our religion. I admitted that was probably true. Actually it would be more accurate to say that it is psychotherapy. I'm not concerned with other aspects of psychology, and have focused on psychotherapy almost exclusively for over 30 years.

Yet, my religious background imbued me with three precepts which have informed my therapeutic efforts throughout my career: a strong ethical sensitivity, a powerful impetus to serve, and a deep aversion to any exploitation of other persons. The service and non-exploitative needs brought about my devotion to practicing and teaching psychotherapy and also a dislike of charging fees for my services. It was unthinkable for me or my brothers to go into any occupation other than a service profession. "People, not money, are what life is all about," was a guiding principle of our family. Even the legal profession would have been unacceptable to my parents, because they saw lawyers as self-serving; business was totally unacceptable. I always believed that our worth is measured by how much we do for the well-being of others.

My ethical sensitivity explains a particular bias I hold; I am unsympathetic to gambling. I had one client who spent many of his days at the racetrack, with a consequent deleterious effect on his studies. He claimed that he didn't lose much money and actually made a little over the long run, so that this pastime wasn't harmful. After he repeated this point many times, I asked him to estimate his average earnings for a day at the track. He said $25.00. I pointed out that I could make twice that amount in a half-day of consulting work, and was helping people rather than taking money away from them. That was when he called me an incipient puritan!

I have strongly warned my students not to become sexually involved with their clients, and I even discourage their touching them except for a handshake. It is not the sexual involvement that I dislike, but the exploitation of an unwilling partner.

I usually limit my therapy practice to graduate students in clinical psychology. I feel it is contributing to my primary commitment of training clinical psychologists and so do not charge the students for this therapy. As a salaried professor, I can afford to serve clients without charge, rather than function in an entrepreneurial manner necessary for most practicing therapists.

The concern about possible exploitation of the other person probably led to my ready acceptance of client-centered principles. It was a way of letting clients make their own choices, and not pushing my positions onto them. Also, I think my strong rebellion against authority caused me to be oriented staunchly toward a noncontrolling sort of therapeutic relationship. I dislike any attempts to control me, and I feel it is wrong for me to try to control my clients. The therapist might suggest possible solutions to conflicts, but only the client should make the choice. But, I think that a healthy skepticism frequently leads to an eclecticism of beliefs and approaches, and this really characterizes my own approach to psychotherapy.

Is it possible for the agnostic therapist to counsel religious people? Yes, although not as much, perhaps, with religious as with other personal problems. I have found it a bit difficult to work with intensely fundamentalistic, fanatical types. My ability to empathize falls a bit short with very dogmatic, doctrinaire persons who know what "God will do." Several cases illustrate the problem I have.

Mrs. T. and her husband were young ordained ministers, graduate students in a helping profession and contemplating divorce because of an unsatisfactory marriage. Mr. T. complained that his wife was frigid and hostile, and Mrs. T. said she couldn't love her husband any more because his spiritual devotion had seemed to dissipate. "He is more interested in psychology than in the ministry." Mr. T. was obtaining therapy from another therapist. Mrs. T. came at her husband's request, but denied having any psychological problems; she consistently maintained that all the problems were her husband's. Somewhat inconsistently, she said that she had always been able to "take her problems to the Lord," and that prayer was the answer to all problems. Mrs. T. proved to be very rigid and moralistic in most of her attitudes, and criticized her husband for drinking beer as well as for studying psychology. She considered his therapy a disloyal act, and accused him of undermining their marriage by telling his therapist "bad" things about her.

For two sessions I tried to see if I could find a crack of any sort in her self-defensive armor, but failed to find any. Even if her husband left her, she said she would trust the Lord to help her to find the right answer to the situation, and such an act on her husband's part would be evidence to her of his lack of religious faith, and of bad faith toward her. She questioned whether I could help her since she didn't feel that psychology "had the right answers," and besides she believed me to be "a lapsed Christian." At the end of two sessions I said that we seemed not to speak the same language and since she couldn't see any problems with which I could help her, I thought we should discontinue. She agreed and said she hadn't intended to return any more. This couple later were divorced, and the husband became a successful psychologist and remarried.

One of my early cases, Mrs. C., was a sixty-two-year-old professor's wife who was suffering from a severe depression, and was somewhat suicidal. She had had an unhappy childhood because her mother died when she was six years old and her father was a remote, withdrawn college professor. He had little time for his children, but seemed to prefer his sons. All her life Mrs. C. had spells of depression, characterized by crying and withdrawing from people. Her husband was like her father although more accepting, but very passive and somewhat depressed himself.

One son was in a penitentiary because of a frequently repeated sexual offense—he asked little girls to expose themselves. Mrs. C. found this situation humiliating. She also was unhappy because her other son had become a psychologist, and her daughter had married a Jew, another disgrace. She considered herself a failure since she saw all of her children as failures. She was a devout church member, and had gone to her minister for consolation and counseling, but he had told her, "There has been sin involved. Ask the Lord to forgive the sinners." This so enraged Mrs. C. that she gave up her lifelong habit of attending church. She hated to go out of the house and when the family was not present, she would spend hours screaming in despair.

I saw her for two years, using a supportive, reassuring psychotherapy. I didn't attempt to contradict her erroneous premises, but tried repeatedly to reflect her feelings of despair. Nothing, however, seemed to help lift her depression. Mrs. C. often threatened suicide, and I made her promise that she would telephone me before attempting it. She never called and she never tried suicide. Often she asked me, however, to name any good reason why she shouldn't take that step. When I'd say that most people eventually got over depressions and found life quite worthwhile, she would reply that most people weren't the terrible failure she had been.

I did not attempt to argue any religious reasons for avoiding suicide, since she appeared to have renounced religion, and both of us would have known that such a gesture would have been hypocritical on my part. Mrs. C. warned me not to tell anyone, including the university psychiatrist, that she was contemplating suicide, and always said that if I told anyone she surely would commit the act. I felt very strongly that I had to show my complete trust in her by never revealing her confidence to anyone, but worried a lot about the responsibility I felt trying to prevent the suicide placed on me. I tried to get her to go into group therapy, in addition to the individual therapy, and also to seek religious counseling and to go back to church. She absolutely refused to do any of these. She pointed out that neither her children nor I went to church as far as she knew.

At the end of two years we agreed that perhaps her depression had resulted from a lack of mother love, and that since we had not been successful in lifting it, possibly a female therapist who might be a sort of mother substitute would be more effective. For a year she went to the woman therapist I recommended, but improved only slightly. This therapist persuaded Mrs. C. to go with her to her church, and the client seemed to find the church attendance more helpful than any of the therapy had been. At the end of a year, Mrs. C.'s husband retired and the couple moved away.

However, it has not been difficult to work with clients who have a different religious background from my own. About half my clients have been Jewish, reflecting our graduate student population. Also, about a quarter of my clients have been Catholics or lapsed Catholics. Almost all of them know about my agnosticism since it comes up in my classes when religion is mentioned in the context of its effect on a therapeutic relationship. Students react to me as if I were a devout white Anglo-Saxon Protestant. I have decided that that must be the image I project.

Being perceived as a "believing" WASP has a significant bearing on the therapy relationships with my clients. If it impairs the relationship, we work on it in therapy. Invariably they transfer any feelings about religious or racial discrimination onto me, and we have to discuss the problem. I always reflect their feelings extensively, and then point out the many similarities and commonalities we have that should make us feel close to each other. Music, psychology, intellectual interests, literature, liberal politics, and, strangely enough, even religion, we have in common. Many, although Jewish or Catholic in background, are agnostic or atheistic themselves; when I am aware of this I use it to indicate a similarity.

With Catholic clients who object to my religious background, I point out that all of my ancestors were Catholics. My Great Grandmother Ulrich became a Protestant because the priest refused to marry her to her Protestant fiancé. I also point out that in St. Ulrich's parish in Augsburg, Germany, half of the many Ulrichs are Protestants and half are Catholics, and the Lutheran church is literally nestled under the buttresses of the cathedral. With Jews I frequently point out that Christ was a Jew.

How I handle the religion question with Jewish clients is illustrated in the case of Mr. Y, who had deep-seated feelings of inferiority, combined with sexual impotence in his marriage. He had strong homosexual impulses which he subsequently directed toward me. He frequently discussed his homosexual compulsions and related them to various things, including his father's beating him severely when he was a child. He equated submitting to a strong sexual figure with being loved, but then, much later, said that no one could love him because he was "just a lousy Jew," which made him worthless. He said that there was no way of escaping this because of his circumcision, and contended that all Jews were dirty. Although no logic could convince him otherwise, I pointed out how deeply convinced I was that we were equals and I discussed our similarities. He said that the only way to challenge the idea of his "hereditary" worthlessness would be to destroy God and the world. I interpreted this as a wish to destroy his father.

In the earlier phases of his therapy he said that he hated his parents' religion, and that he and his wife were opposed to all Jewish customs. Late in therapy he started to feel proud of his Jewish heritage. Some years later when they had a son, they had him circumcised and decided to observe some of the traditional Jewish rituals and ceremonies in their home. He told me that he would not have been able to discuss his disaffection with Judaism had he not been aware of my similar "problem."

Looking back over forty years of practice, I see three groups which I might have handled more appropriately in a direct manner. With the chronically or clinically depressed, I clung too tenaciously to my Rogerian training and "faith," instead of turning to interventions such as electroshock therapy combined with psychotherapy or to a more behavioral approach of forced activities for the client. I now see "getting busy" as a means of emerging from a chronic depression.

The second group with which I should have functioned differently is that of the character disorders. I was too patient and trusting, although aware of being manipulated. I believed in the self-actualizing drive and had too much faith in the client. I now believe that we could utilize some ongoing negative or even punitive devices in cases where self-control is deficient.

The third group that I have had difficulty with are the schizoid and mildly schizophrenic clients. I couldn't build a strong relationship with them but tried to build something, without making much progress. Early in my career I treated a young student who couldn't face going out into a career, even though he was well trained with a master's degree in engineering. During the second year of treatment, he sank further and further into despair and hopelessness. He previously had shock therapy, was treated by a psychologist, had two hospitalizations and extensive outpatient treatment with several psychiatrists. But he never was able to make much progress. He did marry, finally, and hold some fairly low-level jobs not at all commensurate with his level of training. At one point he told his second therapist that he couldn't imagine why I had stuck with him so long when it was all so hopeless. Well, I liked him tremendously and was always "cheering for him," hoping that he would realize his true potential. Also, I was challenged by the difficulty of his case and believed that my therapy methods would work with any patient if enough effort were applied. I soon learned better.

I now wonder if the reason I have had less success with character disorders, deeply depressed persons, and schizoid persons, is because it is so very difficult to establish a convincing and truly effective relationship with them.

Clients change in their perceptions of me, in this order, as (1) a distant, godlike figure, (2) an intensely admired father, (3) a rejecting parent (because he thought I was suggesting termination of therapy), and (4) a good friend and colleague. At the end of the therapy I sometimes ask clients how they perceived me, and they invariably report some sort of metamorphosis.

An extreme example of adoring devotion is illustrated by a client who had threatened suicide after going on a drunken binge which included reckless driving. He entered the interview crying, and very shortly went into an orgy of remorse, during which he said, "You are my only friend, the only one who has faith in me and can see through my unlovely self to the real person beneath." By showing understanding and acceptance, I had helped him come to a beginning acceptance of himself. Then he threw himself on the floor and started kissing my shoes, sobbing out his profound gratitude. I reached down and patted his shoulder comfortingly, saying repeatedly, "It's O.K., Don," the way a mother would attempt to comfort a small child who had been hurt.

Many clients say they perceive me as a friend or buddy. Mr. Quinn kept asking me to go on hunting trips with him; on one occasion he told me that he had only to see me in the hall, and everything would seem to work out better for him. One time, while telling me about some "bad" things he'd done as an adolescent and in college, he suddenly said, "I just had the thought, 'Do you still love me, Mother?' " Often he said that his main problem was that of finding someone upon whom he could be dependent, and he compared me to a loving father or older brother to whom he could go for advice. His own father had been stern and remote.

A surprisingly large number of clients have expressed strong sexual feelings toward me. Since the majority were males, reflecting the ratio of male to female graduate students, this proportion seems quite high. I don't think that a high proportion of graduate students in psychology have strong homosexual inclinations; there is a selective factor present—the students who come for therapy tend to be the ones with more problems, and these are often sexual ones. I usually perceive these sexual overtures as expressions of the wish to become more closely associated with me, and I interpret the situation to them in those terms. They are a natural outcome of the therapy relationship and a form of positive transference. Virtually all of these young men have been successfully married, although sometimes the successful marriage is not the first one, and it may follow the therapy.

About a quarter of my clients express various degrees of regret about leaving therapy. Usually, however, their attitudes are realistic, and are a temporary reluctance to terminate a warm and pleasant relationship.

My own positive feelings toward clients most often take the form of paternal fondness for them, feeling quite protective and supportive. I have wondered whether I feel this more than the average therapist does. Since I don't have any sons or daughters, it seems to me possible that my clients often become surrogate children. But I don't see anything unhealthy about this; in fact, I believe that the ability to feel strong affection for the clients is an important therapeutic skill.

Occasionally I have affectionate fantasies or dreams about a client. These generally take the form of images in which I am protecting them or looking out for their interests. Sometimes, however, they are dreams about companionship. About Mr. Quinn, who wanted me to go hunting with him, I actually dreamed that we went hiking or camping on the Appalachian Trail. In the case of another client, I dreamed that I pulled him out of the path of an approaching automobile, and that after he had a fight with his wife, my wife and I offered him temporary shelter in our living room for the night.

I have never told my clients about my fantasies or dreams about them, since I have felt that this could undermine their confidence in my objectivity, and it might stir up too much response on their part. However, I often have told them about my paternal or fraternal feelings toward them, and this has been a frequent source of fruitful discussion of our relationship. Almost invariably after telling the clients about these feelings, they respond very positively. In a research project in which I measured their and my own positive and negative affect by a questionnaire after each interview, I discovered that the clients' affect became very positive after I revealed these positive feelings.

A good example was Mr. Gilbert, who had had a very lonely childhood because his father had deserted the family when he was young. Mr. Gilbert became an isolated, withdrawn person. Being inducted into the army was a very traumatic experience for him. He had a number of homosexual liaisons, eventually became psychotic, was hospitalized, given shock therapy, and discharged with a diagnosis of schizophrenic in remission. (We hadn't known any of this when we accepted him into the graduate program.) He was a difficult client who often skipped interviews, many times went for long periods without talking, and had a hard time expressing himself. In a psychotherapy practicum, he was assigned to use my office at one time. This made him very uneasy. He revealed that he was reluctant to sit in my chair, as if "attempting to replace the father." I encouraged him to feel comfortable about using my office and the chair. In the discussion I said that I perceived him as a favorite son. He found this incredible, but finally agreed that just as he knew he felt a lot of empathy for his own clients, he could believe that I might feel that way toward him.

The relationship is important to me because many people are deeply in need of a trusting and loving person on whom they can feel dependent. And I have positive feelings for people I see. It is genuine, not created or feigned. Usually this experience of love is new for the patients and it causes a re-evaluation of their self-worth. To have somebody show a high and genuine regard for you is very exciting and fulfilling. Many people experience this in other ways in their lives, but those who have not often show tremendous growth when it occurs in therapy. Just providing a loving relationship may not be enough, however; this love means most when it is combined with insight and mature judgment about the possible ways to alter the disturbing situation.

I enjoy my work. Basically, I am a cheerful, optimistic, trusting person who believes, like my mentor, Carl Rogers, in the basic goodness of most people. (My high school yearbook described me as "a man of cheerful yesterdays and confident tomorrows!")

I believe that life should be oriented toward helping others. As I have grown older, I feel even more strongly that what matters in life is human relationships, rather than financial gain or personal power. I think that in becoming a therapist I was really perpetuating the ministerial tradition of the family. There's not much difference between pastoral counseling and routine psychotherapy, really. We are all doing the same thing—helping people think through their problems and arrive at a more fulfilling life style, in a setting where they know they are loved.

UNCOVERING THE REAL

William Kir-Stimon

I GREW UP with a phrase reinforced by the typical Orthodox first generation Jewish family structure. "They didn't mean it" was at the bottom of every ethical and moral question that ever existed. It took me some time before I came to the understanding that the New Testament exhortations of turning the other cheek and suffering little children were probably based on early injunctions by Jesus' canonical Jewish mother. This never-to-be-forgotten dictum could mean anything—"He never really meant to kick you," "She didn't mean to hurt your feelings," "They didn't really mean to take your lunch," or any one of a thousand other variants.

Stripped of the righteous but guilt-producing covert anger that was thus invoked, this really meant "They know not what they do" and you alone are responsible not only for what you think, believe and do but for those around you as well. Couple this with the varied interpretations of the Ten Commandments and you have an effective, crazy-producing paradigm that could only be resolved through the ministrations of a Freud or Talmudic scholar. Outside of one's personal responsibility, the only place to point a finger would be "those out there"—the Gentiles or Philistines, or God himself. Since no one knew any better than you, a member of the chosen few who were witness to God's word, it was up to you to educate the Philistines through example and forgive their sins. This left one with a wrath that could only be turned inward in an extremely ingenuous

---

William Kir-Stimon, Ph.D. is a clinical psychologist, formerly Director of Counseling Services and Research at the Rehabilitation Center of Chicago. He now practices psychotherapy in Flossmore, Illinois.

naiveté or a pervasive but sugar-coated depressive stance toward life. What a horrendous double bind.

As survivors and children of the Holocaust, we recognize the lack of any ultimate and final explanation for the meaning of good and evil in ourselves, in "them," and in God from whom all things seem to flow. The prophets and saints were angry toward those of little faith and pleaded against God's wrath by prayer and good deeds. Yet Job's impotence, helplessness, and questions were never really answered.

Today I am still struck by the impossibility of thoroughly delineating what is conscious and unconscious or willful and unwilled, despite all the theories and experiments. What remains is the inexplicable single fact that six million Jews were cremated in the Nazi ovens with hardly a murmur from the rest of mankind. I cannot equate this with the horrors of Hiroshima, our international C.I.A. "interventions," the Turkish slaughter of Armenians, PLO or Khomeini terrorism, the violent burnings at Watts and Miami. The dimensions of Auschwitz, Buchenwald, Belsen and Theresienstadt have an utterly different reality that casts a Hollywood fantasy flare over the dictum, "They didn't really mean it!" I find myself more and more involved with questions of moral and ethical import, and nothing in my professional armaments gives me any weapons to deal with them.

This brings me to another aspect of the whole mélange of self/no self, being/non being, or the possible demise of one's identity before it gets under way. At what point in my personal and social development do I have the right to say, "Hold on now; whether you mean it or not is almost immaterial—I know what I feel and I want you to listen." I suppose it's at that point that adulthood begins, when I can uncover and acknowledge the "real me," a complete and total being with a more or less acceptable and somewhat unified ego. Up to this juncture, my life appears to be, if not to others at least to myself, somewhat disjointed and pieced together. I move from experience to experience, at the mercy of reacting to this one's behest or that, this situation or that, rather than from my own core.

The "I" thinks, feels, and moves according to rules and roles picked up from models of father, mother, grandparent, spouse or significant other. It functions first this way and then that, in ways dictated by one or another figure hidden deep somewhere in me as though I were constantly asking myself: Did he/she/it mean this or mean that? Should I do this or do that? I speak then, gesture, react as from a genetic base or one imprinted strong by early and repeated exposure. And the real "I" lodges dormant, as it were, awaiting release from all the dark dybbuks invading psyche and soma.

When the intensity of longing for freedom begins to erupt, especially in the course of a fruitful psychotherapeutic experience, the anxiety brought on by the conflicts between the "me" and "not me" can be overwhelming. And the "they didn't mean it/I didn't mean it" litany resounds like a concatenation of brass bands.

Is there a small moment—maybe an infinitesimal one—when I realize the consequences of what they/I have done (thought, felt) and then block it all out, conveniently forget, and place the whole mess in an unconscious pool of memories which I hope will be lost forever? Do all of us honest folk—churchgoers, country and family lovers, conscientious providers—really lie to ourselves and to "them"? Do we know what is going on? "See, my hands are perfectly clean; I had nothing to do with it." . . . "It's your therapist that is creating this problem, breaking up our marriage." . . . "It's your schooling, your friends, your books, your mother." . . . "They did it, they made me do it." . . . Why create such devastating diversions to hide what is so evident?

What comes to mind are the masks all the characters wear in Eugene O'Neill's play *The Great God Brown* and the soliloquies heard only by the speakers and not the listeners in his *Strange Interlude.* What comes to mind is the deviousness with which we cloak the latent meaning in our own dreams, the deep censoring that keeps us from remembering when we awaken. No wonder we seek a figure on stage to remind us of our responsibility for ourselves and an empty chair to help us see our literal absence! It seems as if there is indeed a game going on in which we play hide and seek with ourselves, a shell game of sorts looking for the full I in all the empty places. What gets lost, of course, in all this meandering search is the fact that I can find "me" only by experiencing "you."

The process of fusing the non-self with my emergent I, of committing myself to myself, is an explosive one and releases tremendous energy. What arises at this juncture is not a combination of the models I emulate or genes that came my way but an entirely new element, a self-in-self, many of whose needs and qualities are still largely unknown.

In no way, however, is there any possibility of undoing the fusion and returning to my separate component parts. In the vitality of the real, I must be totally accepted, realized, fulfilled—or totally negated and destroyed. At this point life simply is or isn't. And for my emergent self there can no longer be a middle ground, a settling for less than the full, replete I.

Even then there are days when "I remember mama" and I try to level out the intensity with which I perceive and respond to stimuli (whether internally or externally derived). I selectively misperceive, misjudge, misinterpret, and behaviorally react in such a fashion as to ensure that my traditionally—and by now ritualistically—"tried and true" reactions remain in force.

Dare I put aside the sweet self-righteous thrill of "They didn't really mean it"? And, of course, "I didn't mean it" either. Rather stamp down feeling before I become overwhelmed with nostalgia for myself, rather withdraw and protect my vital energies and vulnerabilities from being swamped, drained off, or even exposed. And there I teeter between "them" and "me."

This tendency toward re-establishing a balance is evident in the whole creative and re-creative process, its antecedents and consequences. For intensity needs both experience and boundary. And to each of us is meted out a portion of cosmic energy to invest as best we can.

This openness to my full potential as an individual and social being, whether it is ever actualized or not, leads inevitably to three basically frightening, terrifying, realizations. For one, it means acknowledging being forever alone, utterly and completely alone in the deepest corners of one's soul, even at the very moment of greatest "success" and personal freedom. It means, secondly, acknowledging the isolation (and need for contact) of every other being in the world, even those unaware of their separateness and the character of their lives. Thirdly, it means bringing me face-to-face with the absurdity and the beauty of a universe that seems to be completely at odds with our own life span and cognitive style, with our need for a conscious value system in a void filled with poetry and murder.

Underneath these realizations is always the finite inevitability of Time in which we are so inextricably imbedded, of happenstance ever ready to jolt us out of equanimity, of the fact that we have never been and shall never be in complete control of our destinies. All this, despite our tremendous achievements, the artistic, scientific, and religious monuments to our ever-questing soul. All this, despite the social and economic revolutions we envision coming out of seeming love and care for our fellow man. What a dilemma!

There are many reasons, then, for tricking myself out of uncovering the real I. Chief among them is the fear of anxiety created by taking a truly existential stance. In this respect "They/I didn't really mean it" or "He/she/they/we didn't know any better" has been a culturally, socially, religiously acceptable disclaimer of ultimate responsibility for myself. If Eichmann, Hess, and Borman can get away with it by simply "following orders" and refuse to deal with their own negative necrophilic characters, how much easier not to acknowledge the government's devious mentality, the Latin American murders, and the tortures and intrigues that are a part of the whole international scene. To accept the horrendous guilts engendered by our genocidal, homicidal, and fratricidal behavior is indeed too much for the human soul to bear.

Even on Yom Kippur, the Day of Atonement, one can ask only for absolution from sins against God. Forgiveness of crimes against others can only be achieved by a personal re-involvement, accepting one's own role, confronting the enemy, meeting and resolving the ancient dybbuks still lurking in the dark between them and me.

"They/I didn't really mean it." Indeed?

Much easier to hold onto the myth of my own perfection, my total omniscience—and ignorance. Accept the temporal limitations of my existence? That's too much. To accept the majesty of creation and the absurdity of my tiny being? Again, too much. Better, the withdrawal, the settling, the burial of myself before I can recognize its personal freedoms and boundaries, viable options, will and intent. Ah, all the crimes I have committed against myself, the suicidal repression of the I, the failure to give witness to the sacredness of life, my life! Better, not to know and feel and do. Again the concatenations: "Do they really mean it? . . . Do I?" Back to the Torah.

Perhaps it is there, in that glorious compendium of Book and Tradition, that I will find the answer. In the Torah lies the tempering of the Known with the Unknowable, the tempering of law and mercy, suffering and joy, violence and justice, the evil of indifference and the resolution of ultimate peace. With a folklore that suggests the Torah itself antedates even the time of Creation, this compilation and spiritual heritage of the prophets and anonymous scribes has been studied by centuries of my forbears. Persecuted and banned from existence, it has nevertheless survived as Word and Symbol beyond, beyond belief and the scrolls of the Ark, constantly resurrected from the ashes of destruction. Perhaps the moral justification of it all can be found there and in the perpetual oral and written reinterpretations of the Mosaic code. Our people have survived the world tactic of utter decimation because the focus of the Torah has always been on Truth as a way of life, not as an ultimate but as a dialogue between question and answer, Questioner and Answerer, a pre-Aristotelean, pre-Socratic dialogue that resulted in a covenant of faith between man and God, in what has been termed God's search for man.

Perhaps the answer is really in the questing. My professional responsibility (and religious obligation) is not to find the practical resolution for anyone else's problem but my own, nor to find acceptable excuses for their imperfections or mine, their guilts and fears or mine, but to acquire the learning and wisdom inherent in the very search for meaning. The essence of Torah is the emphasis on study and re-study, interpretation and re-interpretation, the looking into oneself and oneself-in-the-world, which in the end is its own reward.

Psychotherapy does not provide answers but is simply an aid in asking the appropriate questions and searching oneself for the answers that are untapped within. Therein, too, the moral imperative to express my being, not to impress the world but to release the urge of my own creativity. Now, let you be to search out your own meaning and focus on my own responsibility for uncovering the real I, the who and what that "I really mean."

FACTS, FANTASIES, FICTION AND FAITH

Mary Jo Meadow

SOMETHING INSIDE ME REBELS at denying realities other than the material one. I am not only a scientist, but also a poet, and am uneasy about total imbeddedness in the world that ordinary science defines. "When I behold the heavens . . ." and the internal spaces in myself and other people, scientific paradigms seem inadequate when they reduce all understanding to laws like those governing the forces and particles composing the heavens.

Other spheres, such as astrological charts and Tarot symbols, draw me into a world of vital creativity. "But, Mary Jo, surely you can't let anyone hear you say things like that," protests a friend, and sometimes I agree. Yet is there any therapist who has dared to enter this world who can still doubt its "reality"? Must those with more vision be locked into material reality by those with less vision? Is it not arrogant to deny this reality to those whose poetic nature recognizes and demands it? Yet how terrible to be unable to break magical connections or get away from an evil spell! How dreadful to be unable to return from this world! How sad to be unable to enter it!

Dreams, magic, myths, fairy tales, and occult symbols hold "truth" transcending anything they say directly or anything natural science can offer. In this reality, the acausal concurrent happening of events that belong together suggest different relationship patterns than those that deterministic science defines. What happens, belongs. What is, fits. Lawful in its own way, but with laws other

---

Mary Jo Meadow, Ph.D. is Associate Professor of Psychology at Mankato State University in Mankato, Minnesota where she is also Director of Clinical Training. She maintains a small practice in Mankato.

than those acknowledged in contemporary scientific paradigms.

Depth psychology is often faulted for its insistence that people are extremely complex and inexhaustible in exploration. Poets, however, appreciate the personal richness uncovered, the awesome spectacle of Psyche gradually being unveiled, the understanding of human foibles and limitations revealed, and the encounter with interior gods, demons, fairies, and spooks. Do such considerations not put the therapist outside of science? Perhaps so; perhaps therapy here becomes art.

Sometimes, however, even poetic understanding falters, and I must admit that I am a religious person—though not accepting the "party line" of any one religion. Awareness of the negative aspects of religious institutions makes it difficult to embrace any wholeheartedly, just as recognizing value in many traditions tempers my enthusiasm for confining myself to one. Increasingly heightened, however, is my awareness of all human beings—indeed all things—making up one larger organism striving to survive and develop. I cannot deny this vision of reality.

I see clients as part of a cosmic process much larger than the single individual. So what if they are "adjusted" to the objective world? So what if they appreciate their own intricate psychic convolutions? We lose sight of something much more important if the religious dimension is denied. Purely human qualities like joy, love, sorrow, humor, and ecstasy take on importance beyond mere "adjustment" or "self-understanding" when one lives as one cell in the cosmic whole. How can we doubt the reality of this world? We who have seen individuals confined to the isolated "hell" of refusing to be only a part, insisting on being the whole in oneself. We who have seen the "heaven" of those who harmoniously relate to the whole of a larger reality.

The worlds of religious and psychotic people are similar. Perhaps the major difference is that psychotics actually have experienced a reality about which religious people faithfully recite belief statements. Both claim the same intense importance for tasks demanded by a cosmos with a definite purpose and meaning. Both recognize the individual as one part of a larger whole, a part which must manifest its own unique strength and bear its own individual burdens. What a pity that institutional religion so often legalizes, codifies, concretizes, cans, and directs its message to the particular interests of a special group of people! How sad when religion is reduced to material world formulations and fails to conceptualize the unity of the cosmos, when religions insist upon the unique reality of only their own symbols! How unfortunate when individuals with inadequate adjustment and self-understanding create or accept horrifying and stringent religious understandings for themselves! How beautiful the unity and simplicity of such realities pared of personal emotional terror and the skewed interests of particular groups!

But there is more. Being also a mystic brings me yet another understanding of reality. Those fires that burn in the skies also burn in me; the waters that move with the ocean's tides move within me. That which constitutes the essence of your being also is my own core and meaning. And I—Mary Jo—am simultaneously that which "is" and that which "is not."

"All flesh is grass," says the Old Testament. "Maya"—illusion, or that which is in constant flux—say Indian writings. How real is something beyond—eternity, completeness, perfection, and the transcendence of paradox, ambiguity, contradiction, and opposition? Very real, say the mystics who experience it. Those who try to describe this reality are called saints, fools, or "crazies." A vision beyond description, beyond words, is known only by being experienced: goodness, truth, and beauty. But it is a world far removed from anything most people call real, a reality in which one cannot remain long on any one occasion, yet a vision one can constantly remember. It is a reality few ever touch and which most, in their ignorance, scorn.

Yet my clients must "adjust" to the material world. They live most of their lives there. To fail to consider this is unethical. Many clients may be unable to venture beyond the objective world, and the best they can hope for is adequate coping with it.

Many others are capable of more. Must they be confined to treatment solely related to the external world? Those clients who are able to explore beyond themselves, are enriched far beyond "adjustment" by so doing.

Dreams, myths, and fairy tales can open up a new reality to the able client. Dream or fantasy exploration can introduce one to "inner space" in ways which produce highly positive self-awareness. One becomes more than a mere machine among other machines. A sense of personhood—of one's uniqueness and even irreplaceability—can develop. This may or may not produce more external "adjustment." It is probably not the most adequate tool for adjustment, although being grounded in one's self may have striking benefits. Introducing a person to herself or himself, developing personhood, must be valued in its own right.

How far might one go in exploring or building personhood? I have seen astrological counselors provide clients with self-understandings which unleashed great capacity for managing difficult situations in highly competent ways. Objectively true or not, this understanding of self—one the client was willing and able to believe—not only provided personal meaning, but also added coping ability. Similarly, exploration or creation of experiences in the past has given some people a more stable sense of themselves and their own continuity as persons. Such interpretations of self acquire their truth much as many of our other opinions, including some scientific ones, do: in the acceptance of the person involved. They become part of that person's truth or reality.

But are we then becoming a new psychotherapeutic priesthood? Whether one wills it or not, therapy increasingly becomes the religion of many people. When clients, however, have a religion of their own, therapists should respect the faith that integrates a person into the cosmic totality. We should not disparage a faith that does not work against the client in some important way. We probably sin more by deterring people from appropriate religious values—attempting to focus their vision solely on the material or personal world—than in any other way.

Unfortunately our patients often have destructive religious perspectives of personal construction or distorted versions of time-honored faiths. We face religious perspectives encouraging excessive self-denigration, misplaced moral concerns, narrowed rather than expanded vision, legalistic mentality, absolutist thought, subtle superiorities and prejudices, pseudo-science, and misplaced generosity—stances working against wholeness. Some clients are able, with clergy or therapist, to examine inadequate religious perspectives. Theoretically, such work should be the realm of religious leaders. Practically, many of them have abdicated to purely psychological understandings, or cling to inadequate perspectives themselves, and are unfit for the task. Historically, the healer and religious leader were one and the same. Often we must either deal with religious issues or deny their importance by refusing to do so.

The therapist who has not seriously explored such concerns personally will not be able to offer much of value, and referral is in order. If we only take something away from the client without replacing it with something more suitable, we are in the sad position of the therapist in the play *Equus* who took away his psychotic patient's horse-god, but could only offer the youth in its place his own bleak and colorless material reality. The boy would become adjusted, hold a job, probably marry—but would forever more lack passionate involvement in anything, anchored to the immediate present to which he had "adjusted" himself.

What of those clients who do not see themselves as separate entities? How do we distinguish mysticism from psychosis? A well-adjusted person with good self-understanding who can view oneself in a cosmic social sense and yet has "mystical" vision, clearly differs from a "mystic" who functions poorly on these other accounts. Common thinking tends not to make such necessary distinctions, and labels in blanket fashion all such vision as schizophrenia. Some therapists who respect schizophrenic thought go to the opposite extreme, sanctifying all such divergent thinking.

Almost always, a life must acquire the ability to be "in," if not "of," the objective world if it is to have any fruitfulness or value. In affirming this, we must be careful what we deny! Schizophrenic productions may contain important messages. Delusions and hallucinations may indicate things missing or distorted in the person that have implications for one's total being, not just for adjustment to the immediate environment. They may open an individual to awarenesses which remain out of reach for most persons. Genuine mystics function well in life. They can maintain close interpersonal relationships, become less egocentric and self-concerned, and joyfully participate in their lives. Such people may be misunderstood in ways which lead them to a therapist. Recognizing such people is important to me so that I can refer them to teachers who can help them in their quest for fuller consciousness.

My multi-leveled view of reality has implications for particular beliefs.

I believe in the darkness of vision. The farther we move from the apparent and manifest—the objective material world—the darker the vision becomes. We agree, without knowing with certainty that our experiences coincide with others', on the nature of the objective world. The subjective world—the inner personal experience of any given person—is at root uncommunicable.

Experience of religious reality is even darker; Christianity recognizes this by saying that we "see through a glass darkly." A feeling of relatedness to the entire cosmos, the appealing beauty of an organismic view of total reality, and the instruction received in a particular religious tradition all produce a pull toward endorsing a religious world view. The securities such vision promises—that ultimately all will turn out right; that "God's in heaven, all's right with the world;" that the meek, the pure, the poor, and the sorrowing will have every tear wiped away—add to its appeal for most people. The demands of such vision—that one refuse to disrupt the harmony of its functioning, that one value others as oneself, that one follow the moral imperatives flowing from the vision—feel right and fitting to the sensitive inquirer. At times we may feel overpowered by our experience of this reality, yet we recall that others have been overpowered by the experience of realities with conflicting claims. If we hold to the common denominator in all such visions—the organismic unity of the whole—we do so realizing with William James that we choose to believe or disbelieve as our own passional nature dictates.

We do not like darkness and its connotations. Darkness stands for not knowing, being confused and unable to understand. It means error or ignorance such as sin, an error of conduct, or not knowing how to interpret what is happening around us. It thus stands for being in danger, helpless, defenseless—for being lost, lonely, and longing for closeness and security. One can learn to love the death that darkness can be as the end of excessive preoccupation with oneself and petty concerns. In the terrible aloneness, devastating self-knowledge, and awareness of personal evil and impotence found in darkness comes the light of truth, the peace that surpasses understanding, and intimacy with Ultimate Reality.

I believe in moral ambiguity. The many views of "appropriate" behavior offered by different sciences, religions, and philosophies vie with one another. The moral code learned in childhood continues to exert emotional pulls long after it has been critically evaluated, and some new values adopted and old ones discarded. The ability to change is due to an interaction of later socialization with our own endowment; not all people can critically review their moral options.

Many people seem preoccupied with trivial moral issues. Concern with one religion's dietary proscriptions seems anachronistic in a hungry world. Tithing to a small wealthy church seems grossly shortsighted when others lack shelter and medicine. Concern about sexual "immorality" seems ludicrous when rapes, murder, and warfare are the ordinary course of life. Beside those of such apparently limited vision are others who choose solely for pleasure, power, or other personal satisfaction. Imposing a morality on them would feel more fitting were we surer that we are not so acting ourselves. How often might our choices be based primarily on desire to avoid guilt or approve of ourselves, a righteous satisfaction in doing the "right" thing, or—even more mortifying!—hope of some more tangible payoff. For every time we become aware of such motives, how much more often might we be deceiving ourselves?

Who is to judge the moral philosophy of another person or legislate another's morality? Surely any person with a coherent position, whether personally derived or a traditional one adopted, is entitled to it. How dare anyone think of imposing personal moral positions on other people? Awareness of moral ambiguity fosters humility, tolerance, and compassion.

I believe in seeking truth by many different approaches: observation, experimentation, and deduction as well as introspection, dream interpretation, and such "occult" materials as astrological records and Tarot cards; also by religious teachings, traditional wisdom, and the opinions of others as well as analogy, metaphor, and interpretation of symbols. We limit ourselves, reduce ourselves, if we insist always on being logical, scientific, and anchored to observable reality that can be consensually validated. Fairy tales and folklore educate us as well as a computer printout. Religous scriptures, poetry, literature, and the writings of mystics teach us things we cannot find in any other way. Meditation on the Tarot, an astrological natal chart, a Zen koan, a Taoist saying, or a hexagram of the *I Ching* brings awareness of heretofore unrealized truths. Dancing, religious ritual, keeping a personal journal, or sitting in the dark silence of interior prayer may open precious new understandings.

I believe in both the reality and the resolution of paradox and contradiction. For example, although they are obviously in some way opposites, I fail to see any ultimate difference between self-affirmation and self-denial. I must deny myself to be that part of the larger whole that I am; yet only in so doing am I maximally affirmed. In affirming being the part, I am necessarily "denied" for the sake of the larger whole; I cannot be the center of the universe (or the universe itself) while I am being only a part. If I try to affirm myself outside of being the part, such phoniness denies myself at some deeper level. Such erroneous attempts at self-affirmation lead to—or *are,* in essence—a real denying of oneself. A phony self-denial (mock humility, or obeying a deity construct in exchange for the promise of personal immortality or some kind of heaven) is at rock bottom a false self-affirmation, an attempt to dictate rather than accept one's place.

Either way, the apparent contradiction or paradox is transcended; self-affirmation and self-denial each contains within itself the other, and either act calls the other into existence. Phony self-affirmation produces a destructive self-denial, just as phony self-denial proves to be a "mock" (or "mocking") self-affirmation. Although I am speaking here of the need to lose one's life in order to find it, the principle holds true for many paradoxes.

I believe we are most complete and most human as we more fully inhabit all of the realities earlier described. None should be disparaged for the sake of any other. We imprison ourselves if we refuse to inhabit any realm; we are impoverished if we cannot enter some realm. I believe in adjusting myself to my environment: establishing caring and supportive relationships, doing good work in my job, seeking professional advancement, playing with gusto, and experiencing external reality widely.

I believe in studying myself: listening to my dreams, getting acquainted with my interior gods and demons, exploring the meanings I see in occult symbols, and understanding my own motives and aspirations. I believe in accepting religious meaning: studying the ancient wisdoms, pondering philosophical issues, discerning (or creating) my own meaning and place in the total scheme of things, and trying to conduct myself in ways compatible with evolving religious understandings. I believe in seeking spiritual reality: in silent meditation, in openness to truth in any guise, in joyful participation in the "isness" of things, and in embracing goodness, truth, and beauty where I find it.

Finally, I believe in the idiosyncratic nature of what is optimum for each person. The varying degrees of, or particular style of, one person's adjustment, self-knowledge, religious viewpoints, and spiritual vision will necessarily be different from those of every other person. To the extent we accept and value differences, we allow our clients and ourselves our own unique personalities.

To some extent, our clients adopt our views of adjustment, health, well-being, and wholeness. They also pick up our opinions, beliefs, and values—including how we value participation in different realities.

I value facilitating the maximum movement possible for any client. The more I enrich my client's perspectives, the better I have served. At times my work as a therapist shades into the work of a priest or guru. Whether we like it or not—and I do not object—our clients often look to us as bearers of hope, salvation, and guidelines for appropriate living. Probably more therapists are concerned with sins of "commission"—fearing to impose their own values on clients—than of "omission"—offering clients only the limited view of psychological health as the ability to work, relate to others, and have lusty orgasms. Yet widening someone's vision need not impose any particular value content on it. More options are simply given.

As a corollary, I value using whatever works for a given client. My bias is against drugs except for disorders with clear evidence of genetic or other biological etiology. However, for some clients, medication (which I always hope will be temporary) seems called for. I believe a certain minimal adjustment to the external world must precede fruitful exploration of other realities. But I will begin where it is possible to begin, be it with a natal astrology chart, dreams, or a religious framework. I am willing to take seriously and with respect what a client has learned in experimentation with psychedelic drugs, in a fundamentalist religious sect, from the occult traditions, or in any other generally "unacceptable" fashion.

I value self-determination. Although I have my own ideas about what I want, I must be sensitive to the client's wishes and abilities as I offer something more than she or he currently sees. I also must determine what is appropriate to offer any client. I may, in honor, try to "package" attractively what I judge good for my client, but must avoid proselytizing. That is a thin line to walk! If a client says "no," I must take "no" as my answer, and recognize that I probably offered other than what the client could value or presented my offer in an unacceptable way.

Some people may be capable only of adjustment, and I do them best service in maximizing this, using the most appropriate scientifically-justified techniques to accomplish it. The excessively introspective may need luring back to the external world. However, if they resist this, they must be allowed to specialize their lives as they wish. Some clients with an inadequate religion will be unable to examine it. Our ability to help them will be limited by this, a painful acknowledgment which demands a profound respect for their rights. Just as we, our clients have a right to choose a personally destructive religiousness or no religiousness at all.

Therapists also have self-determination rights, including the right not to work with the goals of some clients. For those people insensitive to the environment outside of what immediately impinges upon them, we can avoid using techniques inappropriately with them—avoid teaching assertiveness to the insensitive, communication skills to those who will use them to defraud others, "winning" to the selfish. We need not get into mindless application of particular techniques simply because they effectively accomplish certain outcomes. If such clients are not interested in our understanding of appropriate goals we can refer them. We similarly can refuse to encourage the excessive self-absorption of a highly narcissistic client. We need not remain a party to inappropriate self-focus even if that is the goal of the client. We can choose our clients.

I value accepting defeat. Sometimes people simply will not see things as I do. They will not accept the "reality" of which I am sure. How recalcitrant of them to want to understand things according to their own faith! Imagine the audacity of a client whose guilt you probe up one side and down another who decides to cure it with absolution from the clergy! Or one who decides that the understandings of his Tarot reader made much more sense and worked better.

When I start thinking that my vision is necessarily the best or that I can comprehend and work for my client better than anyone else could, it is time to realize that arrogance is winning out over appropriate humility and that the truth is being subordinated to my need to be right, competent, or brilliant. My clients have a right to choose other than the management of them that my faith undergirds. Other people working with different visions and values produce their own positive outcomes. Accepting defeat is fostered by realizing how limited the perspective of any one person is, how hemmed in it is by temperament, intelligence, education, early learning experiences, desires, hopes, wishes, ambitions, emotions, and mere chance.

My faith is not mine alone. Besides my professional training, my strong and deep interest in the arts and in occult traditions has informed it. I read widely in both Eastern and Western religions. I have studied the works of mystics from many traditions, and have practiced meditation and interior prayer with guidance from several traditions. I am indebted to all these sources for my faith.

My faith is intellectually and emotionally satisfying to me. It "fits" the person I am now, and offers me direction for moving in the ways I choose to move. My work as a therapist and in my total life flows from it. However, I retain my right to revise it, abandon it, or renounce it in the future. I share it freely. I listen to what others have found so that it may enrich my understanding. I seek deep, honest, and faithful companionship with others inclined to such a pilgrimage.

My faith has demonstrated its usefulness, and I consider it reasonable. I can claim no ultimate truth or value for it other than that which my own experience accords it. If there be some Truth, if some Absolute claims us as part of its own, if I have in any way penetrated beyond the confines of my own productions perhaps my faith, with yours, converges upon that Ultimate Reality. Someday I may even know this is so.

KNOWING AND BELIEVING

Dugald S. Arbuckle

THE DICTIONARY MAKES CLEAR the difference between "to know" (to recognize as a fact on the basis of information possessed) and "to believe" (to have faith or confidence, to accept as true). This difference, however, is blurred in today's technological world, and there would appear to be as much knowing in religion as there is in science. To know has become more important than to believe, and many devoutly religious people appear to confuse what they believe with what they know.

Long ago, the Greeks saw human beings as reasoning individuals. With the advent of Christianity, faith became the requisite human characteristic, and reason, if it clashed with faith, very often became a sin. It was a blind faith. What the good book said was so, and the scientists of the day who dared to present evidence which contradicted the Bible did so at their own peril. Although we have known for a long time that Galileo was right in his pronouncements about the sun and the earth, and the Catholic Church was wrong, it is only today that the church, in its typical ponderous fashion, is reconsidering its position.

Modern Western science was a revolt against this blind faith which ignored and refuted knowledge, but when science turned from the examination of objects to the examination of people, people became objective things. Medicine continued the scientific trend by viewing

---

Dugald S. Arbuckle, Ph.D. is now retired from his Professorship at Boston University. A Fellow of the American Psychological Association, Dr. Arbuckle was elected to the Presidency of the American Academy of Psychotherapists. He maintains a private practice in Boston, Massachusetts.

the person as a patient with a disease (with the major attention on the disease, not the person), and psychologists added to the dehumanization by considering humans to be patients with problems.

And so, we have become conditioned to distrust going beyond what we "know," and use unnecessary external measures to explain what we do. That is likely the major reason why we have doctors, therapists, medicine men, Gods, and other "beyond me" means of doing things for us. Members of helping professions usually help us remove blocks to our growth and movement that have been established by us. It is our faith in the healer that provides us with the necessary motivation which in turn enables us to get well. Professional helpers are testimony to the astonishing degree we are conditioned to believe that we cannot do alone what we actually can do.

Most religions condition the faithful to believe that magical powers reside in some supreme supernatural being, and this belief is sometimes reinforced by the occurrence of "miracles." Often there is no doubt that what happens is indeed a miracle, and God is given credit for doing something about the individual's human condition. Christian Scientists, for example, put their faith in God rather than in medical doctors, and their healing record stands up very well against the standard medical treatment for many of our medical ills. However, if people believed in themselves as much as they believed in the power of God, the same positive results would have taken place. The only difference would be that the individuals would be more accurate in crediting who brought about a miracle. This would likely increase their own self-esteem, since it is nice to believe that God may help me, but even nicer to know that I can help me.

As a child, I had absolute faith in the wisdom of my mother. For almost any ailment or bruise she had a standard remedy. It was, "Have a glass of water, Dugald, go to bed and have a good sleep, and you will be fine in the morning." Almost invariably I was, and my mother's treatment was just as effective as, as well as economically and psychologically more sound than, the treatment by medical aids that stock the average medicine cabinet today. True, I was putting faith in the infallibility of my mother rather than in my self, but I was a bit closer to me than I would have been by putting my faith in God or in pills.

But so often it is ourselves that we find the hardest to trust, and one of the sad, though understandable, themes that runs through the literature on prejudice is the "I cannot be free until they let me be free. . . ." The fact of external prejudice is very real, but if my feelings of self worth are dependent on the smiles of others, then I will never find that for which I search. If I am fortunate, I may find that for which I search within me.

Self abasement is evident in much of the "liberation" literature on sex and race which accepts the concept of the inability of individuals to do anything about their human condition without institutional approval. A Black person or a woman, however, does not become someone by a change in legal restrictions, nor by the gracious smile of a white person or the approval of a male. It is the pride of individuals in their ability to stand on their own feet, and their inner satisfaction that create changes in people and in institutions. It is people who create and destroy institutions, and one reason prejudice remains so rooted today is because we continue to fantasize that if and when someone removes restrictions we will automatically achieve a state of individual freedom. But freedom will never come to those who wait for it to be granted, nor will it come to those who feel that all that is required is the destruction of the immediate oppressor. In many countries today, Black oppressors have taken the place of their white predecessors, and in some occupations and political positions in the United States, female oppression has replaced male oppression.

The stress is always on the external, on the outside, rather than on the inside. The phrase "Young, beautiful and Black" is an understandable attempt to help a young Black person to have pride in self. But the young person will eventually be old, just as the old person was once young, and we are born black or white. Individually, we have nothing to do with that. We can, however, be beautiful, not because we are black or white, young or old, but because we have made ourselves into beautiful human beings. I am the one who makes me beautiful.

For many young people in the last two decades, drugs have become the means of achieving a high, a way to get into a world beyond the everyday consciousness, to move into a stoned land where life is different, to trip beyond our current conscious restrictions. But they do not really remove themselves from one world and go into another. They use the rationale of the drug to open a door in their own house, but this they always have had the potential to do. Innumerable studies show that even experienced marijuana smokers get much the same effect when they smoke placebo as long as they firmly believe that they are smoking good marijuana.

Probably the greatest disservice of behaviorists is to reinforce the feeling of individual helplessness, to make easier the acceptance of a philosophy of self irresponsibility. In B.F. Skinner's world, all of our woes and joys are dependent on others, never on ourselves. His society is the ultimate serfdom; happiness, like everything else, comes from the outside, from "them." We allow ourselves to be determined by others, and it happens only because we allow it to happen.

Faith, however, whether it be faith in God, or faith in one's intellect, or faith in one's total self, is still faith. But if my faith is in my ability to go beyond the limitations set by others, or even by my own intellect, then I am indeed closer to being a responsible human being.

We have now come full cycle. Modern scientific thought generally holds to the concept that knowing and reality are synonymous. This means that if something can't happen on the basis of our knowledge, then it can't have happened even if there is overpowering evidence that it did happen. All too frequently, instead of a healthy skepticism toward the "impossible," we have a totally dogmatic disbelief. The dogmatism of religion has been replaced by the dogmatism of science.

Thus, we have an astonishing, blind faith in technology. As we struggle with the energy crisis, the pro-nuclear people have absolute confidence that science will find a way to make nuclear energy safe as well as cheap, and the anti-nuclear people have an equally fervent faith that technology will provide us with all the energy we will need from the sun and the wind and the water. Both talk as if they know, rather than as if they believe, This reflects an uneasiness with not knowing. After all, if I know something, then I cannot be wrong, but if I believe something, then I might be wrong.

Cardinal Newman once stated that the truly religious person was one who could live certainly with uncertainty, Most of his fellow Christians were, and are, not quite so stout of heart. Many want to know, not just believe, that they will get to heaven, and they prefer to know, in some detail, just what they have to do to get there! The "I know" religious denominations are increasing their membership much faster than the "I believe" denominations, and science maintains its hold on us because we continue to fantasize that science *is* knowledge.

Many psychotherapists accept the notion that the science of things and matter and diseases can, without much significant modification, become the science of people and their behavior. Historically, the scientific treatment of a damaged engine or a damaged human organ became the model to be followed in the scientific treatment of an aspect of human behavior such as an exaggerated suspicion of others. This exaggerated suspicion became a neurosis called paranoia, which in turn became a disease to be diagnosed and treated like any other physical disease.

Traditional science is, in one sense, a contradiction of itself. It states that what cannot be empirically tested cannot be considered to be real or factual. On the other hand, we cannot prove something to be real and factual if we do not have the appropriate means of measurement. Thus, what cannot be measured cannot be accepted within the realm of reality, and must, therefore, be "unscientific."

Much of what I see as the appropriate subject matter of psychotherapy cannot fall within the realm of traditional science because it does not fit into the framework of "observe, test, prove and remain detached." Thus, human emotions and much of human behavior must be accepted as non-scientific. In scientific terms, an opinion, a belief, an experience could not be classified as knowledge, or at least would be highly suspect. A human experience is subjective and often unmeasurable.

The human mind can be studied and investigated. Thus, psychology can be considered to be scientific as long as it is limited to the study of the human mind. While this may not present an exact dichotomy of mind and body, it would seem as if the mind is the body. From a "scientific" point of view, it would appear that the unconscious is the conscious of which we are unaware, and it cannot be considered to be scientific material until we become aware of it!

The supernatural, the paranormal, cannot be considered to be within the realm of science because they are not scientifically "real." Traditionally, science accepts the concept of reality rather than realities. A reality, in turn, is something or some event or some happening which can be explained. What is beyond our known senses cannot be a part of science because we cannot see it, hear it, smell it, touch it. Therefore, a person known as a psychic healer might cause an observable change in the physical condition of an individual by placing hands on the body, but this event is not scientific because it is not understood. Even when photography shows that "something" is emanating from the healer's fingers, it is still suspect because we do not understand it.

We deal with people and their behavior and the environment they create. A psychological theory is an educated choice by a human being of a certain rationale for the behavior of certain kinds of people in a particular environment at a particular time. I assume that if Sigmund Freud had been born at a different time in a different environment, his fertile brain would have produced a very different theory about a human condition known as hysteria.

It does not mean very much for a psychotherapist to be described in terms of psychological theory. Many psychotherapists try to deny the existence of themselves in their behavior as therapists, and appear to believe that they actually can, and should, operate by some rigid code based on the theory they have adopted. Dr. X, however, who calls herself a Freudian, could not possibly hold to the same therapeutic behaviors as Sigmund Freud, any more than Dr. Y, who calls himself a Rogerian, could hold to the same therapeutic behaviors as Carl Rogers for the simple reason that they are different human beings. Psychotherapeutic orientation of an individual can be determined to a much greater extent by the beliefs and feelings of the individual about people and their behavior, and to a still greater extent by the actual behavior of the individual. My behavior, after all, is the mirror of my belief, and I have known several "Behaviorists" who are much more human than some "Humanists" I know.

Many therapists share with the devoutly religious the need to know, and they magically transform what is obviously a belief or an assumption or a guess or an interpretation into a solid bit of knowledge. The devout Seventh Day Adventist *knows* what will happen to his soul after he dies, and the devout analyst talks with equal certainty about what the id does and does not do. But there is no direct evidence regarding the existence of a soul, nor is there any evidence of something called an id. The concept of the soul, like the concept of the id, is a human creation, subject to the frailty of all human conceptions.

Many modern-day therapists practice much more on the basis of faith than knowledge. Yet they, too, confuse knowing with believing, rather than accepting their lack of knowledge and being comfortable, but careful, with their belief, especially when they are dealing with the health and well-being of others. Many body therapists could be more humble, and it is frightening to hear some of these therapists talk with the fervor of a religious convert about what they know about the body, although an examination of their background gives no indication of any intensive study of the human body. They know that a certain kind of pain in certain part of the back is related to problems with one's father, and they know that various parts of the body are related to different personality disorders, and they know that by pressing different parts of the foot one can make connections with practically any part of the body, and they know that energy emanates from one's hands and does good things for the body, and they know exactly what happens when one sticks an acupuncture needle in a certain part of the body.

Actually, of course, they believe all these things, and if they were more humble about their knowledge (or lack of it), and more proud about their faith and their belief, they probably would be more effective. It is as dangerous to have total faith in one who confuses knowledge about the human anatomy with beliefs about it as to have faith in one who cannot distinguish between the practical dogma of a religion (the Pope on contraception), and the faith and the spirituality of religion.

A medical doctor I know has studied the human body for forty years and is very wary about telling anyone what he actually knows about the body. His problem is that of accepting his lack of knowledge and being over-cautious about making bold guesses as to what might or could be. He is exactly the opposite of the phrenologist or astrologer who totally ignores knowledge and blithely tells one's life story, past and present, on the basis of the bumps on one's head or the configurations in the heavens. Many will believe because they want, desperately, to know. Believing, for them, is not enough.

Not long ago I had a "treatment" in a "healing church" by a casual young healer whose training consisted of a week-end workshop in the treatment he was giving me. He spent a few minutes "feeling" around me for negative and positive energies, waved away various negative energies, made several guesses about my life on the basis of these energies (all of which were totally incorrect), and chatted briefly with colleagues who passed back and forth as I was getting my treatment. He periodically made several mysterious motions in front of me, behind me and above me, then indicated that the treatment was finished and asked beamingly, "Now, how do you feel?" I felt turned off, I had no faith in him, and thereby no faith in what he was doing. The main result was the generation of some irritation which might, I suppose, be described as a form of energy!

On the other hand, I once had a "healer," a man I trusted and respected and believed in, put his hand on a painful knee, and we both concentrated on the "something" that was coming from his body through his hand to my knee. I could feel it, and he could feel it, and there was a change in the pain. We both knew that something positive had happened. We did not know how it happened, only that it had happened. And that, of course, is the crucial point. If I have a firm belief that another man can somehow transfer to me some of his healing power, and if that other man shares that firm belief, then there is a good chance that something will happen. This something, of course, can be negative as well as positive. I remember as a child seeing a very superstitious woman turn white as a sheet, then faint dead away, when the local witch put a curse on her.

Clients are usually hungry for answers. They want to know, and too frequently a client who wants solid answers can very easily seduce a therapist who cannot be satisfied with believing, but must also know. A recent, and, I am sure, not unusual conversation with a depressed client illustrates this need to know:

Client: What do you think—can I ever really get out of this?

Me: Yes—I believe you can . . .

Client: But I always seem to slip back—how can you stop me?

Me: I sure can't stop you—but I'd like to be able to help you to be better to you. . . .

Client: So you really think I can make it?

Me: I believe you can make it . . .

Client: So you think I will make it?

Me: I feel damned sure you can make it, Henry, but you've got to decide whether you will make it or not.

The major contribution of the newer body therapies is that they tend to view the body in a holistic sense. They reject the dichotomous either/or, and they accept the reality of mind and matter, thinking and feeling, knowing and believing. All parts of us are irrefutably related, and I cannot deal with one aspect of me without affecting another part. It is absurd to accept the idea that a damaged knee might have some impact on some other part of the body, yet stoutly refuse to accept the fact that any emotion is a part of my physical and spiritual being as much as it is a part of my emotional being.

While science in the West is just beginning to accept the concept of a holistic human being, it has long been accepted in the East. We have known that it is possible to gain voluntary control over internal body functions, but it was from the East that we first heard reports of individuals being able to affect their heartbeat, salivation and body temperature, being able to survive with little oxygen, being able to prevent the production of a blister from a burn or the flow of blood from a cut, being able to walk on red-hot coals without damage to the feet. What one believed affected what happened to one's body.

Biofeedback is a good example of a modern technique used in therapy in which technology has made clear the connection between what we know and what we believe. It gives evidence that I can control my body, and it deepens one's belief that I have some involvement in determining what happens to my body as well as determining the meaning of what happens to my body. In a similar way, one can develop cognitive control over bodily processes through yoga, zen, meditation and hypnosis.

Transcendental Meditation is another movement where technology has provided evidence that what one believed had happened because of meditation actually did happen. Meditation affects blood pressure, lactate levels in the blood, oxygen consumption, and the degree of stabilization of the nervous system. On the other hand, one has to believe in the power of the supposedly secret "mantra." After all, there is no evidence that a word chosen from the Hindu holy books will have any more effect on me than a word from Webster's dictionary!

All of these procedures give evidence that I can train myself to modify and control internal physiological processes. This does not mean that I will do it. There is still a need for a faith to sustain me, to encourage me, and to provide the will to do what I believe I can do.

But, any human experience is a good deal more than knowing about. In a knowledgeable and diagnostic sense, many psychotherapists are quite capable in their relationships with a client. They may, however, be quite ineffective in a meaningful human relationship because they are incapable of feeling with the client, going where the client goes beyond the realm of the intellect. Some therapists are comfortable when talking about problems, but are decidedly uncomfortable if any attempt is make to get them involved in a feeling sense with a human being who has a human problem. Obviously, more often than not, the therapist cannot have had the particular experience which produces a particular feeling. No male therapist will ever experience giving birth to a child, and while some of us have had the experience of believing we were going to die, we can only believe that one can die. Too frequently, unfortunately, the training of therapists stresses intellectual prowess, and ignores experiential capacities. But, patients often know more from their direct experiences than do doctors from their minds.

We can experience the inner subjective world, but we can never specifically know it. To accept it, we must go beyond the narrow restrictions of the mind, and run the risk of believing without necessarily knowing. But, psychotherapy viewed as a science stresses what we know about human beings and human behavior. Too often then, the client becomes objectified into something to be examined and clinically understood rather than a human person to be experienced, believed, and accepted.

An expanded, more highly developed state of consciousness takes us beyond the need for an either/or world, a world which is a creation of those individuals who have been unable to develop and actualize themselves beyond the point of needing external and false security. In the either/or world I am strong because someone else is weak; I am capable because I know someone who is less capable; I am beautiful because there are other people who are not beautiful. All of this, of course, represents the needs of humans who are not yet capable of accepting the inner reality of their own strength, their own capabilities, their own beauty. They cannot see the goodness and virtue in themselves, but must depend on the assumed lack of it in someone else to buttress their feelings about themselves.

Psychotherapy has encouraged this either/or illusion with its division of the population into "normal" or "abnormal," "sane" or "crazy," "sick" or "well." Too much professional time is spent in a useless diagnostic merry-go-round putting people into pigeonholes. Medical and psychological diagnostic categories are more often than not cultural inventions to describe people who, in one way or another, do not fit the cultural norms. The categories are quite limited as well as invalid. Must people who come in for help be put in a category? It is as if in physical medicine we had discovered twelve diseases and from now on everyone who is described as sick must be put in one of the twelve categories.

A perfect example of this irrational categorization is reported in a 1972 issue of *Science* (#179) based on research by D. Rosenham, a professor of psychology and law. He, three other psychologists, a pediatrician, a psychiatrist, a painter and a housewife, all quite "sane," had themselves committed to mental institutions. Once committed they described their life histories as they actually were, and behaved as they did in their normal life. However, the only people who perceived the pseudo-patients as normal were other patients. The staff continued to insist that they were schizophrenic or manic-depressive. It took 52 days to get out of the hospital. Three pseudo-patients walked out and the other five were discharged with the diagnosis "schizophrenia with remission."

There is an unconscious and non-intellectual form of what might be called insight. It is more subjective, and defies analysis. The more therapists are willing to accept the reality of this "unknown," the more likely it is that change will occur. A typical example of this sort of experience occurred with me a short time ago. The week before, a client had had a very emotional session, with much anger and grief directed toward a woman who had left her, even though my client felt that she had loved her, cared for her, and invested a lot of herself in her. When the client came in the next week she said to me, "Wow—was that heavy last week. But you know, I felt that something very, very important had happened—I don't know what it was. I felt lighter. I was different inside." Neither of us was concerned with what had happened, and we certainly didn't know what had happened, but we could both accept the fact that something very good did happen.

At a higher level of consciousness, life can be accepted as a constantly changing panorama, with no place for the either/or. It is motion, and when change ceases, so does life. Such a view of life accepts the reality of ambivalence, and the fact that there are many answers to one question, many ways to do the "right" thing. It is only when we can accept the reality of the differences in life that we can include others in our life. We have no need to exclude them, and we can truly say, "Come in—as you are—be with us. I am the measure of me, and you are no threat to me."

In summation, then, I think that:

1. Faith is real and valid. The "fact" about believing is that I believe, not what I believe. The fact that a client of mine believes that he can do something, and the fact that I also believe that he can do the something, regardless of what the evidence says, is as powerful an impetus to movement and change in human beings as exists. I am not an effective therapist if I do not have a deep and abiding faith that somehow, in some way, the human beings who sit with me can find the road to a happy and effective life. I do not know they can do this, but I believe that they can, and I am willing to invest much of myself because of that belief. If I believe that I can determine the meaning of my life and my death, even though you may have the power to determine whether or not I live or die, then the sort of life I live will be much different than it would be if I believed that you determined whether I lived or died and gave meaning to every

aspect of my life and death. With the former belief, I am forever free. With the latter, I am little better than a human slave.

2. I don't have to know what is happening to my clients and to myself to accept the reality that something is happening. Allowing myself to experience what is happening is much more important than doggedly trying to determine why it is happening. "Why are you doing that?" has its place, but it is often overdone, and it undercuts the experiencing. It is hard for me to intellectually answer the question "Why do you climb cliffs and mountains?" and imagine the degree of consternation if after a passionate "I love you," one was faced with "Why?"

3. If we accept and believe in the concept of the holistic human being, then we do not accept or believe in the human fragmentation of the dichotomy of either/or. Knowledge is real, but faith is equally real. It is faith that gives meaning to knowledge. I know my clients have the ability to live a life that is happy and fulfilling, but I must believe in them if I am to help them in their struggle. "I know that the struggle is difficult and painful, but I have faith that each of us can become the person we wish to become." Surely, without this deep and abiding feeling about oneself and about the other person, the therapist is little more than a futile shadow. I remember being with a depressed client week after week, month after month, until he finally began to move and grow. Later on, he said to me, "You know, in all those awful months, I was always aware that you were the only one who really believed in me."

In today's wondrous and terrifying technological world, we are satiated with knowledge, including knowledge about you and about me. But the gap between what I know about me and what I can do about me appears to be increasing. I need a faith in me to put this knowledge together, so that it can make more sense, so that I can use it for my betterment and for the betterment of others, rather than for our total destruction.

HIDDEN CONNECTIONS

Seymour Rubenfeld

WHAT COULD I POSSIBLY write about faith? I am a Jew so at odds with his God that I could count on one hand the number of times I entered a synagogue in adult life. I, a fugitive from the Talmud since my adolescent rebellion when I refused to go to a Yeshiva because I wanted to chase girls instead, who thinks that almost all Hebrew "prayers" read as repetitious flatteries to some heartless mideastern potentate? I was so scourged by the Holocaust I could not bear to have my children taught how to mouth that sacrificial, fixated babble; and yet, and yet—fiercely proud of us remnants of a two-thousand-year-old crucible, and ready to pay and yes, damn it! pray for the survival of Israel. With so many contradictions, rather than a pronouncement on faith I need a scorecard.

What can I add but another humanistic amen, another soliloquy on commonplace mysteries? Writing this I just, literally, flew over Manhattan: all that myriad human ant power thrusting rose-red towers into a pure winter sundown. What am I, to write anything on faith?

Yet, as a friend told me, all religious feeling is relatedness. The more relatedness, the more meaning, because meaning is, after all, the relation among things. That conversation opened a gate in my mind and let me go. Memories, experiences sewn together. I do have some articles of faith as a basis for my work.

I believe in the meaningful quest for the relation among things. I believe in the hidden connections among the events of the world.

Seymour Rubenfeld, Ph.D. was Chair of the Group Therapy Training Program, Washington School of Psychiatry, Washington, D.C. and is a clinical psychologist who practices, consults and teaches in McLean, Virginia.

We all are creatures of curiosity, made to grasp the ordered and chaotic beauty of the world. To grasp it with our senses and minds, to disclose it and marvel at the pregnant muteness of a stone, or a tree, or at the ovarian earth as it presses out its red egg at dawn. Finally, we are called to acquaint ourselves with the familiar mystery of another self.

The work I do is analytical and synthetical. My activity reflects and fulfills our nature, the patient's and mine. I marvel at the paradox that metals and all the heavier elements in our bodies were created somewhere in the universe billions of years ago. Our lives, by comparison, are like the split-second lifetraces of subatomic particles on a physicist's photographic plate. Yet it may be that we are the only spheres of our own illumination, the human feelings that flow between us the only immortal current in the inchoate wild dance of particles and waves at the dark heart of the form and order conjured inside those spheres. What is Mont Ste. Victoire without Cézanne? Is it? His later paintings of it ceaselessly press the question. Therapy enlarges a person's sentience in order to give the world back his own answer to existence, by creating a meaning through one's love, work, and play.

We serve this destiny like Sisyphus pushing the boulder up the mountainside only to be ordered to repeat the action throughout eternity. At worst, we will all be wasted, lost. Nevertheless, we are privileged to play a game fit for gods. In this game we endlessly relate all the things of the world, outer and inner, to all other things. And like Sisyphus, we are destined never to see the end of our efforts.

How we view the nature of existence has a great bearing on what we therapists think we are dealing with and what we do about it. A colleague says it this way, "If I trust the instincts of another; if I help that other to trust his or her own instincts, those instincts will lead to another and better kind of relating on the patient's part." Are these instincts basically wild and destructive? If so, people must be helped to govern them in an enlightened way, and we approach treatment with a surgical singlemindedness, with the cool of a lion tamer and the detachment of an anthropologist in the bush. At least that is the myth of orthodox psychoanalysis. What we need then is the unswerving steadfastness and the dispassionate yet passionate zeal of a priest at an exorcism.

I believe, though, that a patient withholds his most secret self from someone who withholds relatedness. He or she is not strong and bad, but rather feels weak and fearful at heart. Cool objectivity does itself out of its goal to see most deeply. I believe a person instinctively recognizes a situation like the original deprivation that led to shame, guilt and insecurity and will not take that extra step of trust and dependence necessary for healing unless that objectivity is leavened by my real feelings of concern.

My faith leads me to orient treatment in a way that classical psychoanalytic technique distrusts as "mushy," "soft," or "love." But I have faith that our basic instincts reach out to relate. We seek another whole person. The satisfaction the mother takes in giving, the baby gives in taking. From the first we need to experience satisfactions that give peace, joy, pleasure, pride. I either create an empathetic therapy that grows because of its mutuality or my efforts are going to be distorted by the lack of it; I admit no other possibility.

I am, therefore, persuaded that a therapist who reflects back those needs of a patient to feel understood and accepted encourages independence and actualization. "Support," "empathy," "relationship," are not a matter of "technique" but intrinsic aspects of recognizing and responding to the fundamental reality of the other. My notion of therapy sees no need to perform anatomical dissection on "infantile needs" and "ego operations," nor is it reduced to laboratory analysis on the byproducts of the master configuration of the self gone awry. I believe in a therapy that induces growth by recognizing the hangups and fixations of a patient as reflections of much larger losses and damage.

I once stood looking at a boulder in a classic Japanese rock garden above the Silver Pavilion in Kyoto. This beautiful, eloquent rock was chosen and placed there, just so, by the artist 400 years ago. I had an indescribable experience of the rock and I having a similar being, and of the artist intending me to comprehend the unity of the rock and me. I was so certain of the artist's intention, I felt the back of my head as if it were open and he were looking out through my eyes. So I was and was not I. I was he, and the rock, and any human sensibility inhabiting my eyeballs and physiology. Time collapsed. Its beginning and ending dissolved into a unity of Zen relatedness. Once later I had a timeless, peaceful sense of infinity and eternity woven into a moment of clarity while looking over the bridge of my love's nose in a still white room on a cool sunny morning. I discovered she was having much the same experience. Our closeness seemed deathless, far beyond our personal dissolution. It was a transcendent co-meditation near enough to eternity to exalt me.

I spoke earlier of a Sisyphean attitude toward therapy. Nevertheless when therapy works, I have the sense of being in the presence of someone whose humanity is a complete response to the world's infinite extendedness and the ultimate origins, like a flower containing and unifying everything and having no need of further justification through actions or accomplishments. There I find a quiet joy, a transcendent solace for the Job in me who keeps asking, "Why? Why?"

Everything is in us, and can be between two of us.